BURNED

The True Story of the Sheila Bryan Murder Case

by
Jana Cone

PublishAmerica
Baltimore

First printing

ISBN: 1-59286-513-5
PUBLISHED BY PUBLISHAMERICA, LLLP
www.publishamerica.com
Baltimore

Printed in the United States of America

This book is dedicated to the family and friends of Gail Sullivan,
and to all those who have suffered the worst our legal system has to offer,
yet, somehow, survived.

For Billy
with all
my best wishes
James

ACKNOWLEDGMENTS

"I have gathered a posie of other men's flowers, and nothing but the thread that binds them is mine own."
- John Bartlett

First, I would like to thank Donald Davis, with the Colquitt County Sheriff's Office, and John Heinen, with the Georgia Bureau of Investigation. Without their help, and willingness to answer an untold number of questions, this book would not have been possible. It was a complete act of faith that they trusted me to tell this story.

Many people worked with me to make this book possible. Charles Stines, Chief Assistant District Attorney of the South Georgia Judicial Circuit in Bainbridge, GBI Medical Examiner Anthony Clark, Colquitt County Coroner Rodney Bryan, Georgia State Patrol Trooper Chris Gay, Omega Chief of Police Walter Young, and many others in law enforcement shared their time and knowledge with me. I am deeply grateful.

A very special thanks goes to arson investigator Ralph Newell, his office manager – and daughter – Lisa Baker, his wife, Patty, and his very able investigator Larry Helton, who were all so gracious and hospitable during my day-long visit to their office. Arson investigator Ronnie Dobbins with the State Fire Marshal's Office deserves special thanks as well. I am also thankful to Mike Flippo, Fire Chief of Tift County, and his able staff of firefighters. I am particularly indebted to Paul Boyd and Rita MaGahee.

Another special thanks goes to Tifton attorney Joe Kunes, who was kind enough to lead me through many of the complicated legal issues in the case. His legal insights cast light on many dark places.

In the court clerk's offices in Tift, Colquitt and Thomas counties, there are many people to thank. In Tift County, Kay Marchant and Gwen Pate made the unbearable bearable. For their endless patience and guidance through all the record books, I sincerely thank them. Jane Gregory and Carolyn Braswell in Colquitt County helped me immeasurably with the transcripts.

In Thomas County, David Hutchings and his staff went above and beyond the call of duty to help me accomplish my tasks there.

At the *Moultrie Observer*, Dwain Walden and Alan Mauldin are not to be forgotten. And a special thanks to Lou Ziegler, with Thomson South Georgia Newspapers, who hired me to write about this story.

To Sheila Bryan's family members, Danny and Kay Weeks, Donald Weeks, and Kevin Sumner, and others, I thank them. Kevin's wit sustained me on many cloudy days and Donald's sincerity and dedication was always a lesson to me. To Ernest Weeks, the patriarch of Sheila's family, I tip my hat.

To Sheila's attorney, William E. (Bill) Moore, Jr., a special thanks for his insight into the defense case. And to prosecutor, Brad Shealy, the same for his insight into the prosecution's case. To Jill Bright, wife and able assistant of Sheila's attorney, Converse Bright, who was always the bright spot during long days at trial, thanks for your kindness.

To all the people who were willing to talk to me under cover of pseudonyms, your insights have helped tremendously to shape this book.

I am forever grateful to Ann Rule, the best true-crime writer among us, both for her encouragement and willingness to point me in the right directions. Thanks, Ann. Your replies to my e-mail are appreciated.

Caroline Benefield did an excellent job with the maps, and I thank her. H.B. Marcus did an excellent job with the web site (JanaCone.com), and I thank him.

To all the staff at the Tift County Commission on Children and Youth, I will always remember your willingness to pitch in when I was away from my desk at my "day job."

Without the encouragement and support of my dear friend and colleague, Lillie McEntyre, I would have thrown in the towel. Her willingness to jump into this adventure with me – and do the first "read" – will never be forgotten.

For all the "spit and polish" and fine tuning, I thank my editor and new friend Linda DeVore. Without her critical eye, I feel sure I would have dangled some participles.

To my sister, Lucrecia Davis, I say, "Thanks, sis, for the idea for the web page and all of your encouraging words." To my mother, Margaret Davis, I apologize for all the time we lost together while I worked on this book.

To my literary agents, Ron and Mary Lee Laitsch of Authentic Creations, thanks for all the hard work.

Last, but certainly not least, I thank my ever-patient husband, Norman Cone, for putting up with this "obsession" for so long.

AUTHOR'S NOTE

This is a factual account of the Sheila Bryan murder case, the true story of a south Georgia housewife who stood trial for the murder of her mother.

To make this book as accurate as possible, the author has carefully reconstructed the events in this case from investigative files, police records, official court transcripts, and the memories of many of the participants in this story. It is never possible to reconstruct reality, but the author has made every attempt to record the events as they happened, as accurately as possible.

As is probably the case with any work of non-fiction, the author has found it necessary on occasion to recreate dialogue and events, based on reports, recollections, and other sources. In a few instances, material is presented slightly out of chronological order to make the story more readable.

The larger issues of truth and justice in this case will be for the reader to decide. To determine those issues, the reader will have, for the first time, the benefit of all of the known, and much of the before-now unknown, facts of the story. Truth and justice do not necessarily emerge in today's courtrooms. Rules of evidence and legal maneuvering dictate what juries will hear, as well as what the public will hear via the press.

The author believes that in *BURNED*, the story of the murder case of Sheila Bryan is as true and complete as it will ever be told.

In a few instances, pseudonyms have been used in order to protect privacy and spare embarrassment. The first reference to a fictitious name is marked by an asterisk and is italicized.

Who ran to help me when I fell,
And would some pretty story tell,
Or kiss the place to make it well?
My mother.
My mother.

Jane Taylor
1783 – 1824

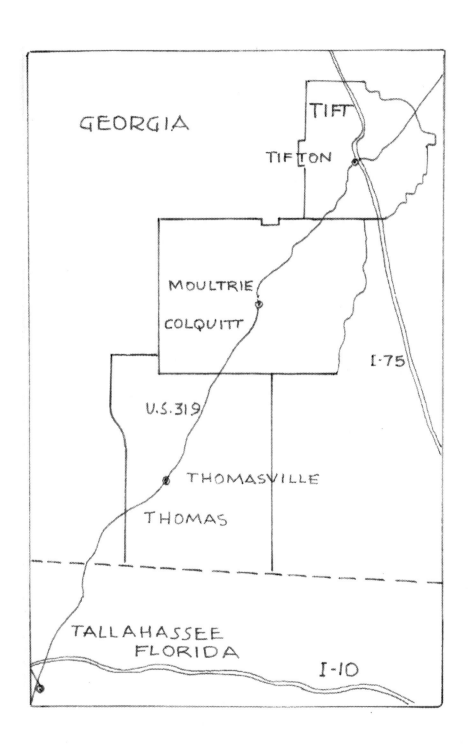

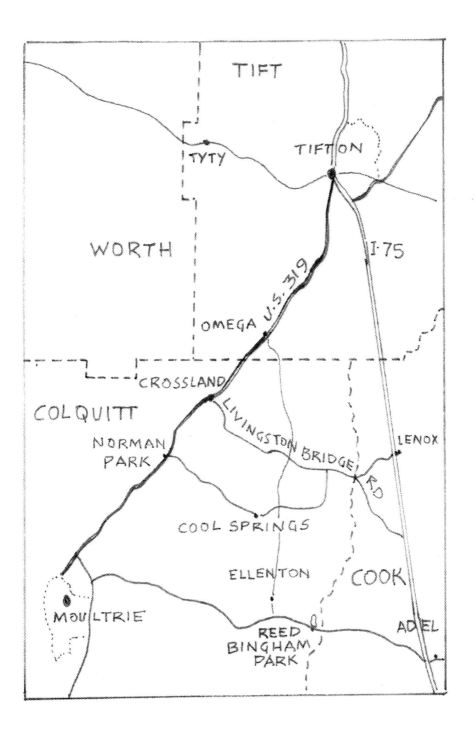

PROLOGUE

In August of 1996, the small town of Omega, Georgia, was the home of Tift County resident Sheila Bryan, whose family occupied one of the forty homes in the town's only subdivision.

On a Sunday morning that summer, Sheila Bryan would take a ride on Livingston Bridge Road with her mother and rearrange her world – and most of this south Georgia world as well. Before it was over, Tift, Colquitt, and Thomas counties would be involved, along with the Georgia Bureau of Investigation (GBI), the Colquitt County Sheriff's Office (CCSO), and the State Fire Marshal's Office. The small town of Omega would be divided, brother against brother and sister against sister. Legal costs would be staggering and court fights would drag on far longer than anyone could have ever guessed. Friendships would break and careers would be tossed. A national television crew would move in and try to get a fix on the locals and the Bryan family, putting everyone under the klieg lights for up-close-and-personal scrutiny. Some would predict that Omega Baptist Church, the spiritual and social hub of this community, was going to split in two. Only one thing about the case was known for certain: Something terrible happened out on Livingston Bridge Road, but hardly anyone could agree on exactly how or why Sheila's mother, Freda Weeks, died.

A sense of place might help those unfamiliar with south Georgia to enter into the mindset of those involved in this story.

Motorists heading north out of the Florida panhandle, having enjoyed its boating, fishing, and beaches, hook up to Interstate 10, which cuts across the panhandle from Jacksonville on the east coast and continues westward to the Alabama state line and beyond. About midway across the panhandle, Interstate 10 runs through Tallahassee, where many motorists make the turn north on Highway 319 and travel across the Florida state line and into Georgia, headed to Interstate 75, which will funnel them up and out of the Peach State.

Florida bids its guests farewell with a liquor store at the state line – the last chance to grab a cold one before heading into south Georgia's dry counties and the heart of the Bible belt. Leaving the moss-draped live oaks behind, travelers will pass through Thomas, Colquitt and Tift Counties for some ninety miles before getting on Interstate 75 in Tifton to make their way back to their northern homes. Locals sometimes refer to this as the "30-30-30 route": thirty miles from Tallahassee to Thomasville, thirty miles from Thomasville to Moultrie, and thirty miles from Moultrie to Tifton.

Once out of the bumper-to-bumper congestion in Tallahassee, the drive north on Highway 319 to Tifton is a scenic, pleasant trip. With only a few exceptions for construction, the highway is four-laned, and traffic moves along quietly and smoothly. A far cry from the monotony of the interstate, the drive through these southwest Georgia counties is resplendent with historic plantations, antebellum homes, pecan groves, peach orchards, and centuries-old magnolia trees.

All of the southern half of the state of Georgia is included in a geologic zone known as the coastal plain: a transitional land mass between water and dry land. The area is typified by low, gently rolling hills and plains with meandering rivers. Heavy, red clay soil is predominant in this region, and while it is difficult to farm, it can be highly productive when carefully tended. Droughts are frequent, but with the addition of irrigation systems in the mid-1980s, farmers have been able to maintain their row crops (peanuts, cotton, corn, soybeans, and tobacco) as well as their horticultural crops (peaches, watermelons, and pecans).

This is the Old South. Residents of Georgia frequently speak of "the two Georgias" – Atlanta and the rest of the state. While Atlanta, which clearly did rise again to become the New South, is only two hundred miles from Tifton, it is light years away from the lifestyle practiced on the coastal plain. Things move slower here, even the traffic, what there is of it. Road rage is unknown in this part of the world, and social courtesies are the norm. Cars passing on a country road are expected to acknowledge one another with a nod of the head or the wave of a hand.

Georgia counties have county seats – the largest town in the county and the place where legal and government business is conducted. Thomasville, known as the "City of Roses," is the county seat of Thomas county. Roses are plentiful here, turning roadside parkways into verdant gardens of color and fragrance. The roses are tended by the town's ten garden clubs and have been highlighted at the annual Rose Festival since 1922.

Highway 319 runs through Victorian downtown Thomasville, with its brick streets and charming antique shops. More than fifty grand, historic homes line the streets. Bed and breakfast inns abound, along with seventy plantations. A few of the plantations, such as Pebble Hill, are museums and open to the public for tours, but the vast majority have been converted to private hunting preserves, where Northerners still come to hunt quail and deer and take part in dove shoots.

Highway 319 traffic leaving Thomasville and entering Moultrie, the county seat of Colquitt County, is routed around the downtown area on Highway 133, a bypass road. It is here, along with the schools, shopping centers, car dealerships, and mobile home sales centers, that the CCSO is located on the east side of the road. The local law center and the county jail are in good company with the Georgia Bureau of Investigation's forensic crime lab next door.

If Thomasville is proud of its roses, Moultrie, which is nationally known as the "City of Beautiful Homes," feels the same about its azaleas. The azaleas bloom in the spring and adorn the countryside with magnificent, intense color. Colquitt County is proud, too, of its Moose Moss Aquatics Center, a world-class diving facility that hosts competitions from around the country and the world. Moultrie, which hosts the Sunbelt Agricultural Exposition, draws over 200,000 visitors annually to the largest outdoor farm show in North America.

Living is easy here, where the median household income is $22,307, and the average cost of a brick home is only $51,600. The climate is mild, ranging from a January average of 55 degrees to an average of 82 degrees in July. As the populations of Thomas, Colquitt and Tift counties have swelled to around 40,000, the county seats typically have only about 15,000 living in the city, while the rest of the counties' occupants reside in the outlying areas in smaller towns and on farms. Thomas and Colquitt counties have a land area of some 500 square miles, but Tift county is about half that size, with the same population density.

Tift is considered the more cosmopolitan of the three counties, and Tifton is Tift's county seat. With I-75 hugging the west side of Tifton, bringing the snowbirds traveling to warmer climates or tourists headed for DisneyWorld or Florida's gold coast, fast food eateries and strip malls abound.

Billboards along the interstate boast that Tifton is one of "The Top 100 Best Small Towns In America." Most residents of Tifton are aware of the honor, but are unaware that the title came from Norman Crampton's book by the same name or that Crampton rated Tifton #54 of the 100. Nor are they aware that the criteria for this honor included a combination of factors: medical facilities, low cost of living, sustained growth, diversity, and a low crime rate.

Crime is certainly not unheard of in southwest Georgia, but it is low compared to metropolitan areas like Atlanta. In 1996, the year of this story, the GBI would report six murders in Tift County, five murders in Colquitt County and four murders in Thomas County, while Atlanta's Fulton County would report twenty-three murders for the year. The same holds true across the board for reported crimes such as rape, robbery, assault, burglary, larceny, and vehicle theft.

Arson is a crime prevalent in this area, many people believing a match can solve a lot of problems. There were so many unsolved arson cases in Tift County in the late 90s – over twenty major cases – that state and local fire officials put up a billboard with an arson hot line number, offering a $10,000 reward for information leading to a conviction.

Overall, however, it is a safe place to live, and Tifton's Chamber of Commerce happily includes crime statistics in its newcomers' packet, along with a small package of Georgia roasted peanuts.

Tifton is proud to be the home of the largest magnolia tree in Georgia and the second largest in the United States. Additionally, Tifton lays claim to being the "agri-research hub of the universe," home to the Coastal Plain Experiment Station where the turf grass industry was founded. It was also at this research facility that many new varieties of peanuts were established, building this industry into Georgia's largest cash crop, now rivaling "king cotton."

Omega is the southernmost town in Tift County, and it is the first Tift County town passing motorists on Highway 319 encounter on the last leg of their drive north to the interstate. It is often described by residents as "a one stoplight town," which is literally true. Folks around Omega like to say that Kelltown, a small community some five miles north, was once named Alpha. There is no validity to the story, but as people say around here, "They tell it to be the truth." It is generally believed that the name Omega was chosen for the city because it was located at the end of a railroad spur line from Tifton.

Omega, which was originally a lumber town called Surry, was founded in 1889 with a population of fifteen. By 1996, the population had grown to eight-hundred-ninety-four residents, and the city had three churches, an elementary school, a recreational park, and a forty-home subdivision. Omega claims the title "Plant Center of the World," and ships vegetable plants all over the United States and Canada. Since Omega is primarily a farming community, it has two cotton gins, a peanut warehouse, sweet potato packing companies, a fertilizer plant, and greenhouses.

Livingston Bridge Road, which lies in Colquitt County, is one of hundreds of connector roads criss-crossing the rural Georgia landscape. Its only purpose is to connect one main road to another. Livingston Bridge Road connects the Ellenton-Omega Road to Highway 319. Clearly blessed with a practical name, the Ellenton-Omega Road is as much a descriptor of where it goes as it is a name – it begins on Highway 319 in Omega and runs east out of town, soon turning southeast and continuing on some twelve miles to the small farming community known as Ellenton. Less than one mile out of Omega, Ellenton-Omega Road crosses from Tift County into Colquitt County. Halfway to Ellenton, Livingston Bridge Road joins the Ellenton-Omega Road and curves around back to Highway 319, to another small community named Crosland. The entire length of Livingston Bridge Road is only five and one-half miles.

Some would call Livingston Bridge Road "the middle of nowhere," but they would be the uninformed. People from miles around are familiar with Livingston Bridge Road and travel it on a regular basis. In August 1996, most of the people from outside Colquitt County coming to Livingston Bridge Road from surrounding counties like Cook, Tift, Worth, Irwin, Turner, and Berrien did not necessarily know the road by its name; they knew it as the road to Jernigan's.

Jernigan's restaurant sits far back in an open field on Livingston Bridge Road, halfway between Ellenton-Omega Road and Highway 319. When Henry Jernigan built the restaurant in 1985, he was living out his own version of *Field of Dreams*, testing the theory "build it and they will come." Build it he did, making the restaurant rustic and befitting of its rural surroundings. Screen porches and picnic tables surround the inside dining room on two sides. The ceiling and walls are rough-hewn cypress and ceiling fans hang from the open rafters. It has a comfortable, homey feel people like, and the menu of all-you-can-eat fried catfish, cheese grits, and coleslaw is worth the leisurely country drive. The price is as agreeable as the food, and many times on Thursday nights, there is an added attraction – gospel singers.

So, the people come from miles around to eat at this restaurant in "the middle of nowhere." By the carloads they come, bringing the entire family with them, eating catfish and singing along to the good old country gospel music. The crowds are so great, the lines to get inside so long, that Jernigan's only needs to be open three nights a week: Thursday, Friday and Saturday.

When Sheila Bryan took her Sunday morning ride with her mother on August 18, 1996, she was not headed to Jernigan's. But as fate would have it, that ride would come to an abrupt end just a stone's throw from the entrance to the restaurant at the east end of the bridge over Ty Ty Creek.

Part One:
Investigation

"The difference between fiction and reality?
Fiction has to make sense."
- Tom Clancy

CHAPTER ONE

Sunday, August 18, 1996

The rattlesnake was the first sign of trouble, and perhaps a portent of things to come.

Whap! Whap! Whap!

Danny Weeks swung the stick as hard as he could, striking the snake with blow after blow. Danny's wife, Kay, sat watching from the car. She hated this. She wished now she had never said anything at all about the snake. She was driving their white Chrysler LeBaron, and if she had just thought about it, she could have driven over the snake and kept going. Danny had been sitting in the back seat with their four-year-old daughter, Ellie, because Kay's mother was sitting in the front with her. By the time Danny saw the snake, if he had seen the snake, they would have already been past it. But no, she had pointed it out, and that was all it took.

Kay supposed this was a man thing. Danny just couldn't abide seeing a snake without killing it. She didn't like snakes any more than Danny did, but there were times when she would rather go by the "live and let live" rule. And this was one of those times.

Everyone was hungry and it was already past noon. She just wanted to get on to the restaurant in Enigma. Danny had eaten at the small restaurant before and had really liked it. The restaurant was several miles from their home on Charlie Hamm Road in Norman Park and, because this was Sunday, it was going to be crowded by the time they got there.

Whap! Whap! Whap!

Danny was in his good Sunday-go-to-meeting clothes, and now he was out there on the dirt road taking whacks at the snake. Kay didn't think it made any sense at all. But she knew there was no need to argue with Danny about it. After eight years of marriage, she knew what to argue about and what not to bother with. Once she had said the word "snake," it was a done deal.

The air conditioner in the car whirred away as Kay watched Danny bludgeon the snake. It was so hot and the sun was so bright, sweat poured off Danny as he took swing after swing at the snake. *Come on, Danny, the snake's dead enough*, she thought. She watched as Danny threw the snake in the bushes beside the road. *Finally*, she thought, *now we can go.*

"I gotta go back and change my shirt," Danny said, getting back into the car. Kay backed the car up until they were in front of their house. They had hardly gotten out of the driveway when she saw the snake, so she didn't have far to go.

"Hurry up," she said, as Danny jumped out of the car again. "We're running late."

As an associate professor of English and speech at Abraham Baldwin College in Tifton, Kay was used to keeping schedules. After seventeen years of teaching, paying attention to the time was second nature to her. For Danny it was different. As a drop foreman for Black Industries in Moultrie, Danny spent his days putting down phone lines, and while he kept track of the number of hours he worked, he didn't pay much attention to the time of day.

They were different in other ways, too. Kay was used to dressing up for work, so she was comfortable in her Sunday clothes, which were the same clothes she wore on a daily basis. Danny was most comfortable in his jeans and work boots, and he only dressed up on Sunday when they went to church and out to dinner, as they did most Sundays.

She was comfortable in the Chrysler and Danny was comfortable in his pickup truck. Since they thought of the Chrysler as her car, she usually drove whenever they went off with the family in the Chrysler.

When Danny came out of the house, Kay was glad this little detour was over. She put the Chrysler in drive and headed back down the road, past where they had seen the snake, and on out the dirt road to where it met the paved road.

She turned left onto Livingston Bridge Road, finally headed for the little town of Enigma and the restaurant on Highway 82. She had not gone very far when she passed the entrance to Jernigan's and saw a woman standing in the middle of the road just at the bridge. The woman started waving her arms and running down the road towards the car.

"What on earth?" Kay said aloud. "There's somebody on the bridge – a woman is on the bridge."

"Well, stop the car," Danny said, leaning forward over the seat. Kay slowed the car as she continued to drive towards the woman and the woman continued to run towards the car.

Just as she got to the bridge, Kay stopped the car. The woman was screaming but Kay couldn't understand what she was saying. Kay let her window down and pulled forward, meeting the woman.

"The car wrecked! Mama's trapped in the car! The car's on fire!" the woman was screaming.

Danny was out of the car in an instant. "Kay, go call the fire department!" he yelled. "Go to Dutch Hall's house, he's the closest. Hurry!"

Before Kay could say one word, Danny had taken off running down the road with the woman. Kay turned the car around and headed back down Livingston Bridge Road, the way she had just come.

Hurry! Hurry! Hurry! was all she could think. She had to get to a phone. It was less than a half a mile to Dutch Hall's house but it seemed to take forever. *Faster! I have to get there faster!* She saw Dutch Hall's house on the left. She didn't know the man, but Danny did. *Please be home*, she prayed, as she swung the car into the driveway.

Suddenly there were dogs all around the car, barking. *Oh, no!* she thought. *Now what am I going to do?* Afraid of the dogs, and gripped with panic, Kay blew the horn, long and hard. *Please come out, please hurry!* Kay blew the horn again and again and again. *Please come out of that house! Please! Please! Please!*

Finally, a man came out the door and walked towards the car. Kay jumped out of the car as soon as she saw the man. "There's been a car wreck and the car's on fire and there's a woman trapped in the car!" The words flew out of Kay's mouth. "Call the fire department! Please! Hurry!" The man went running back into the house.

Kay stood by the car, waiting and trying not to think about the woman trapped in the car. She hadn't seen the car, only the woman running down the road, screaming.

What was that man doing? Why didn't the man come out and tell her the fire department was on the way? Where was he? The seconds seemed like hours. With a woman trapped in a burning car, every second counted. Kay knew that instinctively. She didn't know what to do.

She wanted to scream. The panic swelled up in her throat. She didn't want to frighten her mother or her daughter any more than they already had been. Her mother was an invalid and had to use a wheelchair, and her daughter was just a small child. She had to keep control. Somehow she had to keep control.

Kay started talking out loud. "What should I do? I don't know what to do." She had just turned to her mother and asked, "Do you think we ought to go back to our house and call from there?" when the man reappeared. He walked towards her with a phone book in his hand. Kay's heart sank.

"How do I call? Who do I call?" the man was asking.

Kay knew she was losing it then. It was hard to keep her thoughts unscrambled. She grabbed the phone book from the man and turned to the front page of the book. Her hand was shaking violently, her panic now physical.

Find the number, find the number, find the number, she repeated over and over like a mantra in her mind. The words and numbers swam in front of her eyes. Lots of names and numbers. Sheriff. Police. Different fire departments. Her mind a blur, Kay could not decide what number was the right number, the fastest number. She could not figure out which of the fire department numbers was the closest one. Seconds ticked away.

"Try this one!" she said, pointing to the number for the sheriff's office and shoving the telephone book back at the man. The man turned around and started back toward the house. He had only walked a few steps when he turned around and said, "Well, maybe you better come call. I can't see these numbers."

Kay wanted to scream again. All of this time wasted. Seconds ticking away.

Hurry! Hurry! Hurry!

Kay followed the man into the house. There were several other people there, sitting around the table, obviously eating their Sunday dinner. The man pointed to the telephone.

Kay grabbed the phone and dialed the first number on the list. It was the Colquitt County Sheriff's Office. Kay was thankful a woman answered the phone right away.

"There's a car on fire! There's a wreck! There's a woman trapped in the car! Call the fire department! Quick!" Again the words flew from Kay's mouth. The woman wanted a location. "Livingston Bridge Road. At the bridge by Jernigan's!" Kay screamed. Kay slammed the phone down, and as she raced out of the house, she yelled "Thanks!" over her shoulder to the people sitting there.

Kay got in the car and headed back to the bridge. Now all she could think about was Danny and that woman. Where were they? Were they all right?

What had happened to Danny?

As Kay approached the bridge she could see the smoke. Huge plumes of black smoke curled up into the bright blue afternoon sky. She still couldn't see the car. All she saw was the smoke, and her heart raced faster and faster as each plume of smoke curled and unfurled up into the air.

"Please, dear God, let them be okay," she prayed aloud as she pulled the car onto the southwest side of the road, down from the bridge. Where was Danny? Was he okay? She refused to let herself think about the woman in the car. *No, don't think about it*, she told herself. Somehow she had to calm herself down; she had to get control.

But all she could think about was the car exploding. What if the car exploded? What if Danny and that woman were by the car when it exploded? Danny was going to die. *No!* She couldn't think like that. But she was afraid to park too close to the bridge – too close to the explosion if that happened.

Kay parked on the side of the road, a good ways down from the bridge, and waited for what seemed like an eternity. *I don't want my husband to die,* she prayed silently to herself. *Please, dear God, let my husband be okay.*

Danny had not recognized the woman in the dark slacks and shirt. She just kept repeating, "Mama's in the car, mama's in the car," as he had jumped out of the car and run around to where she was standing.

"Where?" he had yelled, and she had pointed to the other end of the bridge.

That's when Danny saw the smoke. He didn't see the car, but he saw columns of black smoke unfurling into the air. He and the woman took off running as fast as they could across the bridge. When he got to the other side of the bridge, he saw the car.

The blue Mercury Cougar was down in a deep ditch just at the east end of the bridge. The car was engine-end down, with the back end of the car higher than the front. Smoke was pouring out of the inside of the car. It seemed to Danny that the smoke was coming out over the windshield of the car. He didn't see any flames, just the ugly, thick, black smoke.

Water! I need water! was all Danny could think. *Where can I get water?* He remembered the mobile home set back off the road on the right, just before the bridge, and turned and started running as fast as he could back over the bridge, the way he had come, toward the mobile home at the west end of the bridge.

As Danny got there, it appeared there was nobody at home. "Help! Anybody home? Help!" he yelled as he ran up the hill of the driveway. He spotted a bucket sitting in the yard and looked around for a water faucet.

Hurry! Hurry! Hurry! was all he could think.

Danny found the water faucet, and it seemed to take forever for the water to fill the bucket. He took off running as fast as he could with the heavy bucket of water, trying not to spill it as he ran back down the hill and across the bridge to the car. The woman was still standing on the bridge, right where she had been when he had left.

The car was fully engulfed in fire now. Where there had been only smoke, now there were red flames. Smoke was billowing out of the front of the car, from the windshield area and from under the hood. Danny saw the flames around the dashboard area.

The woman was standing on the road, crying and screaming as Danny reached her. Danny didn't stop to listen to what the woman was saying. The ditch was steep and he had to get down the ditch with the bucket of water and get closer to the car. When he got within five or six feet from the car, in one hefty swing, he threw the water from the bucket over the top of the car, hoping the water would get down in the part of the windshield where the smoke was rolling out.

"Get back! Get back!" the woman was screaming. Danny scrambled backwards up the ditch bank.

It was then the woman told Danny that the car was full of gas, that she had just filled the car with gas in Omega, and that the car might explode. Until then, Danny had not thought about the car exploding. He didn't know if the car was leaking gas. He could not tell, but he thought that the car exploding sounded like a real possibility. He backed up from the shoulder of the road to the pavement.

"Mama's in there. Mama's in there," the woman kept crying.

Danny didn't know what to do. How was he going to get the woman out of the car? He had not been able to see her. All he could see was the black smoke. He had to do something. As his thoughts raced, the woman gave him more information.

She was saying that the doors on the car locked automatically when they were shut, and that the key was in the car and she couldn't get the car doors open. Danny knew that the only way to get the woman out of the car was to find a way to bust the window out and unlock the car. His first thought was to look around for a tree limb or something to use to bust the car windows out, but the fire was too intense now.

Bright, cherry red flames were licking higher and higher. The heat was radiating off the Cougar and Danny could feel the heat all the way up the embankment. It was only a short time before the flames were coming out of all of the windows and the heat was pushing Danny back from where he stood on the road.

It was too late. He knew it was too late. His heart sank. He couldn't let himself think about the woman in the car. The woman standing next to him had started having dry heaves. He went over to her and put his hand on her back while she alternately tried to throw up and cry.

"Who's your mama?" he asked.

"Freda Weeks," she said.

It felt like an electric current had passed through his body. Danny knew Freda Weeks well, and it was then that he recognized this woman and realized she was his cousin. He hadn't seen her in a long time. It had been over two years since he had seen Freda Weeks and even longer since he had seen Sheila Weeks Bryan. Danny's father and Sheila's father were related, and Freda Weeks and his mother had been close friends, when his mother was alive. It made Danny sick to know the woman in the car was Freda Weeks.

Where was the fire department? Danny wondered. *Where was Kay? Why didn't anybody come?* Sheila was hysterical now, and there was little he could do. He was left to stand in the blazing sun with one woman burning in the car in the ditch and the other woman crying hysterically. He'd heard about women having nervous breakdowns and he thought Sheila might be having one. He had no idea what to do about that. Surely somebody would come soon. But nobody came.

The minutes seemed like hours.

Between sobs, Sheila told Danny that she and her mother had been out riding around, reminiscing, looking at places where they had lived and where they had friends living, and that they had been on their way to his house when she had run off the road and down into the ditch. Danny tried to comfort Sheila as best he could, but he didn't think there was anything he could say that was going to make things better.

Then Danny saw Kay pull the car up to the other side of the bridge. He told Sheila to walk down to the car with him. Danny had never been so glad to see Kay and Kay had never been so glad to see Danny, but they didn't speak of it.

Danny put Sheila into the back seat of the Chrysler with Ellie. He wanted her to be in the air conditioning and out of the afternoon sun. Mostly he wanted her to be with family and away from the car still burning in the ditch. As soon as Danny got to the car, he told Kay, "There's nothing I can do. We can't get near the car. It's too hot. It's too late."

A few minutes passed before anyone was able to say anything.

Danny broke the silence and told Kay that Sheila was his cousin. Kay didn't know Sheila, but she knew of Sheila. Danny had spoken to Kay of both Freda Weeks and Sheila in the past; they were part of his extended family. To Kay, this seemed to make the situation even worse, if that was possible.

Sheila was crying and shaking. Kay tried to think of words to comfort her, but it was hard to know what to say in a situation like this. Words had always been Kay Weeks' friend, but in this instance they failed her.

They sat in the car waiting, the silence filled with Sheila's sobs. Kay had never felt sorrier for anyone in her life. This was the worst situation she had ever known. What could be more horrible?

Dutch Hall pulled up right before the fire truck came, and Sheila got out of the car. As the fire truck came down Livingston Bridge Road, it pulled up past the bridge, right in front of where the car was down in the ditch. Danny walked over to Dutch Hall and told him to stay with Sheila and to keep her on the bridge, away from the car. Danny didn't think Sheila needed to be close to the car for a lot of reasons.

Kay waited in the car to see if Danny was going to come back to the car so she could take him home. Sunday dinner seemed a thousand light years away now. All she wanted to do was go home. This had been the worst day of their lives and she didn't care about eating or about anything.

Finally, Danny had come back to the car to tell her she could leave. He was going to stay and ride with Sheila to the hospital. Sheila had hurt her arm, and Danny was going to stay however long it took to see that Sheila was taken care of. Danny told Kay that he would call her from the hospital, and she could come and pick him up there.

Danny gave Ellie a pat on the head and told her everything was going to be all right now. Kay was glad to leave. She turned the car around and headed back to the house. It was less than two miles away, but so much had happened in that short distance. Somehow, she knew her life had changed forever in some inexplicable way.

Later that night, when they were alone, Danny told Kay she had been right. "I never should have stopped to kill that snake. If we hadn't stopped, and we had gotten to the bridge sooner, maybe I could have saved Freda Weeks."

It was going to be the first of many long nights.

CHAPTER TWO

Sunday, August 18, 1996

Twenty-five-year-old Jamie Hinson was spending Sunday afternoon with his parents at their house on Livingston Bridge Road. Jamie, his twenty-eight-year-old brother, Howard, and his father, Daniel, were all volunteer firemen with the Norman Park Volunteer Fire Department. Fighting fires was an interest they all shared and a commitment to their community they had all made.

Jamie was a welder with Van's Equipment Company in Moultrie and, like his older brother, Howard, a machinist with Parker Machine in Moultrie, he kept his pager with him at all times, ready to respond to a fire at a moment's notice.

It had been an uneventful Sunday morning, and after Sunday dinner, Jamie and his father were sitting around listening to their police scanner when they heard the CCSO had a vehicle fire reported on Livingston Bridge Road, with someone trapped in the car.

Not waiting for their pagers to go off, the two men sprang to their feet. The immediate problem they faced was that the fire truck was not with them at Daniel's house. The truck, which carried a thousand gallons of water, was parked at Howard's house, which was also on Livingston Bridge Road, about a quarter of a mile away. They knew that Howard was not at home and, although they knew Howard would get the page and respond, they knew they could get there quicker. But first they had to retrieve the fire truck.

They ran to Daniel's pickup truck and Daniel drove the two of them to Howard's house where the fire truck was parked. Jamie had just climbed into the fire truck when their pagers went off at 12:42 p.m., notifying them of the fire. Jamie would drive the fire truck and his father would follow in his pickup truck.

With siren blaring, Jamie and Daniel Hinson arrived at the accident scene just two minutes after the page had gone off. They saw the billowing, black smoke long before reaching the bridge and, as Jamie drove over the bridge, he looked to his left, down in the steep ditch, and saw the burning car. He stopped with the back of the truck even with the burning car. Daniel stopped his pickup truck directly behind the fire truck in the roadway.

The passenger area of the car was in full fire. All of the car's windows had been broken out from the intense heat, and fire was pouring out of every one of them. The man on the road was yelling that they needed to be careful, that the car was full of gas and might explode.

Jamie radioed in a code twenty-three, meaning he had arrived at the scene, and quickly grabbed the one-and-a-half-inch hose line from the truck and took it down to the car, while Daniel began working the pump. Standing on the driver's side of the burning car, Jamie began spraying water through the windows. Within two minutes, Jamie had the fire put out, but he knew that if there was a person in the car, there was no way anyone could have survived the raging fire. Once the fire was out and the smoke had cleared, Jamie saw the victim for the first time, and his worst suspicions were realized: The person in the car was dead and had been burned beyond recognition.

With the fire extinguished, Daniel Hinson got on the radio and made the notification that the fire was out and that there was a victim in the car. After the radio call, Daniel walked down the embankment to where his son was standing with the car. Jamie would have to stay with the car and continue to spray water on the hot spots that would flare up from time to time. One of the hot areas that continued to flare up was around the back speaker of the car. None of the weeds around the car had caught fire, and there had been no ground fire to contend with, only the fire inside.

While Jamie manned the hose, Daniel inspected the car and the victim. Walking around to the passenger side of the vehicle, Daniel saw that the gas tank filler door was open and that there was no gas cap to cover the open tank. He was familiar with vehicle fires, and this was unusual – and suspicious. A person might forget to close the gas filler door, but to leave off the gas cap and leave the filler door open was not something that was a normal occurrence. Daniel noted that the doors were closed on the car, as was the trunk.

It was about this time that Howard Hinson arrived at the scene. He had been on Chafin Road, just off Cool Springs Highway, when his pager had gone off, notifying him of the fire on Livingston Bridge Road. It had taken him about five minutes to arrive. Howard knew his father and brother would already be there with the fire truck. When Howard arrived, there was still no law enforcement personnel at the scene. He parked his car in front of the fire truck and walked down to the car where his father and brother were standing.

Walking to the front of the car, Howard proceeded to open the hood to check for any fire under it and to allow Jamie to spray the engine area, if necessary. He noted that the hood had been popped and was held only by the safety latch. Someone had opened the hood of the car, but why, and when?

Like his father and brother, Howard noted the open filler door and missing gas cap.

By this time, there were people arriving from every direction. Besides the Norman Park Volunteer Fire Department, the Ellenton Volunteer Fire Department and the Moultrie Fire Department also responded. In all, there would be fifteen volunteer firemen on the scene, along with the Colquitt County Firefighters Association Chief Gerald Psalmond, and Colquitt County Emergency Management Director Chris Wainwright. Law enforcement would also arrive, as would the county coroner, an emergency medical technician, and numerous civilian onlookers.

Gerald Psalmond, who was responsible for the firefighters and for writing the incident report, arrived only a few minutes after the Hinsons had extinguished the fire. As the fire coordinator for Colquitt County, Psalmond was responsible for overseeing the eleven volunteer fire departments in the county, as well as seeing that all of the volunteer firemen were well trained. Essentially the fire chief for Colquitt County, Psalmond had thirty years of firefighting experience under his belt.

Fair-skinned, freckle-faced, with copper red hair and a temper to match, Psalmond was a middle-aged man who could bear no fools when it came to investigating fires. Very little ever got past his beady little eyes.

He had received training in the cause and origin of fires while he was in the Air Force, and after moving from Virginia to Georgia, he had trained at the Arson Investigation School in Forsyth, Georgia. The curriculum in Forsyth had included vehicle fires as well as the use of accelerants in fires. Gerald Psalmond had investigated hundreds of vehicle fires, and there was little that he had not seen in the years he had been involved in fire investigation.

Psalmond arrived about 12:45 p.m. and noted the 1987 Mercury Cougar was sitting in a deep ditch, perpendicular to Livingston Bridge Road. He walked down to the car, where Jamie, Howard, and Daniel Hinson were standing, and inspected it. He first noted that there did not appear to be any collision damage to the outside of the car. All of the hubcaps were still on, and there was nothing in the way of paint scratches, although the car had traveled down a steep embankment.

Even though the windows of the car were broken out from the heat of the fire, Psalmond looked closely at the window tracks in the door and was able to determine that the passenger's side window had been completely closed at the time of the fire, while the driver's side window had been down about six inches.

Psalmond was well aware that with the open window providing an oxygen flow, the fire inside the car would have been sustained. On the other hand, if both windows had been closed, the fire, soon starved for oxygen, might have eventually extinguished itself. The car had an air-conditioner and Psalmond knew that on a hot day like this one, most people drove with the air on and both windows closed to maximize the cooler temperature inside the car. Like the lack of collision damage to the car, Psalmond found the open window suspicious.

Psalmond inspected the gas tank area of the car and noted the open filler door and missing gas cap. He instructed the arriving firemen at the scene to secure and search the area for the gas cap. Even after an extensive search, the firemen were unable to locate the gas cap, so Psalmond called off the search.

He knew that the gas cap had not been on the car at the time of the fire and could not possibly have just blown off in the fire, because the spring and washer from the gas cap were not inside the filler neck. The gas cap, made of plastic, would have melted onto the threads of the filler neck if it had been in place. But Psalmond saw no such melting, indicating to him that the gas cap was missing at the time the fire started.

Psalmond then began to inspect the inside of the vehicle. Strangely, it appeared that the greatest concentration of fire damage was located on the driver's side floorboard, in front of the front seat. That was worrisome. There was nothing in that area of the car that should have caused a fire. Besides, he knew that the floorboard was the coolest area of the car because heat rises. Beyond that, the floorboard had less material for a fire to consume.

Psalmond was well aware that there were three necessary ingredients for a fire: heat, fuel and oxygen. There should have been little heat on the floorboard, and it should have also been the area of smallest oxygen supply. The carpet on the floorboard would serve as fuel, but Psalmond knew that floorboard carpeting was treated and typically was slow to inflame. Unless an accelerant had been used, Psalmond could see no reason for the driver's side floorboard to have caught fire.

Psalmond noted that the fire had spread from the driver's side floorboard to the front seat and across to the passenger seat, then to the roof of the car, and then to the back seat area.

Psalmond inspected the fire victim, still seated in the passenger seat of the blue Mercury Cougar. There wasn't very much left of the victim actually, mostly the torso. He noted that the victim's seat was in a reclined position. All of the victim's clothing had been consumed in the fire.

Psalmond was in a quandary. This was arson if he had ever seen it. Normally, in a fire such as this one, he knew exactly what to do: call the state fire marshal and get an autopsy. It was his standard procedure, and he had followed it hundreds of times. But this day, he hesitated.

Things had gotten complicated for Psalmond because it was an election year and the sheriff was running for re-election. There was bad blood between his fire department and the sheriff's office. Accusations and hot words had been exchanged between the two departments, and Psalmond had decided that he would steer clear of anything the sheriff's office was involved in – at least until after the election. Maybe then there would be a new sheriff and a new relationship between the departments.

Psalmond knew the sheriff's office and many other agencies would be involved in this case. He decided he would let them handle it and follow their procedures – which were the same as his. There was no doubt in his mind that they would call in the state fire marshal and do an autopsy on the victim.

Psalmond stayed at the accident scene to help extricate the victim from the car. Once the car had been removed from the ditch, the firemen would have to use a Hurst tool, generally known as the Jaws of Life, to gain access to Freda Weeks' body. The Hurst tool is a hydraulic spreader that is inserted between the seam of the door and the body of the car. In a scissors-type action, when pressure is exerted, the car door opens.

When Psalmond left the scene, he had no idea that the Sheila Bryan case was like quicksand, and that there was no such thing as steering clear. And he certainly had no idea that years down the road he would be portrayed as some kind of "paid goon."

Psalmond drove away from Livingston Bridge Road not only with the certainty that his involvement was not needed, but also with thoughts about his observations of the gas tank area of the car that were very incriminating to Sheila Bryan. Those thoughts, which he had shared with his men at the scene, would not be shared with anyone else for many years.

But as he drove off, he chuckled. All the talk he had heard about the car exploding because of the full gas tank amused him. Psalmond knew that the car would have had a greater chance of exploding if the gas tank had not been full, because only the gas vapors burned.

"Silly people," he muttered as he drove out of sight in his fiery red truck.

Randy Stephens, a deputy with CCSO, was the first law enforcement officer to arrive at the accident scene, just after the Hinsons. Stephens' first observation was of a woman standing on the bridge; the woman was hysterical and trying to throw up. There was a man standing beside the woman, talking to her.

Several firemen were at the scene, involved with putting out the fire, which appeared to be almost extinguished when Stephens arrived; the car was no longer in flames but there was lots of smoke still coming out of the car. Stephens stayed on the road to direct traffic and give information to arriving personnel. Prior to other law enforcement arrivals, Stephens walked over to inspect the road where the vehicle had apparently left the roadway.

Stephens backtracked from where the burning car was located in the ditch and observed tire tracks on the shoulder of the road, traveling in a straight line, parallel with the road towards the bridge, which appeared to be the same path made by the vehicle in the ditch. Stephens could see a clear line of tire tracks, indicating the car had traveled along the flat surface of the shoulder of the road some distance before making a sharp right ninety-degree turn at the bridge guardrail, and traveling over the embankment and into the ditch. The tracks did not indicate the car had swerved or that there had been any attempt to get back onto the paved road.

Stephens had remained on the road the entire time he was at the accident scene. It was only when the car was eventually pulled out of the ditch and placed on the road that Stephens observed the fire victim. Stephens had thought it very odd that the seat position of the woman was laid back the way it was. Stephens did not know of many older people who rode in a car with the seat reclined. *Strange*, he thought.

Later in the afternoon, Stephens would be asked by the Georgia State Patrol trooper to transport the driver of the car, Sheila Bryan, to the hospital. Although the woman did not appear to Stephens to be injured, he did as he was asked and drove the woman, accompanied by her cousin, to Colquitt Regional Medical Center in Moultrie.

35

CHAPTER THREE

Sunday, August 18, 1996

The accident scene on Livingston Bridge Road was the responsibility of Georgia State Patrol (GSP) trooper Chris Gay, a careful, methodical, kind-hearted man.

Gay was assigned to the Thomasville Post of the GSP. The troopers assigned to the Thomasville post patrolled four counties: Thomas, Mitchell, Grady and Colquitt. The city police often handled accidents within the city limits, but accidents in the county were the responsibility of the GSP.

Trooper Gay had been assigned to patrol Colquitt and Thomas counties and was working the 8 a.m. to 4 p.m. shift when he was dispatched to the accident on Livingston Bridge Road at 12:38 p.m. At the time he received the dispatch, he was in Colquitt County, south of Moultrie. With blue lights flashing and siren sounding, he turned his blue and gray patrol car towards Livingston Bridge Road. Some distance away from the accident scene, it took Gay almost twenty minutes to reach Livingston Bridge Road, arriving at 12:56 p.m. As was the case in the majority of the accidents he handled, other law enforcement officers had preceded him to the scene.

CCSO deputy Randy Stephens met Gay at the patrol car when he pulled up to the bridge. Stephens briefed Gay on the accident and pointed out the driver of the vehicle, Sheila Bryan, who was standing on the shoulder of the road about thirty feet from the burned automobile, with a man whom Stephens identified as Sheila Bryan's cousin, Danny Weeks.

Sheila was crying and appeared to Gay to be extremely upset, and he did not think she should be standing so close to the car; he was afraid that she would see the burned remains of her mother. Gay walked over to Sheila and Danny, introduced himself, and walked them away from the car to the bridge area to wait for the ambulance.

Gay then talked to the firemen on the scene. He was told that the fire had started inside the car and that it had been an extremely hot fire that had gotten hot very fast; the firemen thought the fire was suspicious. They told Gay the gas tank filler lid was missing and the filler door was open. They also told Gay the passenger area of the car had been burned more severely than the rest of the vehicle.

Gay wanted to look the car over for himself. At age thirty-five, he had been with the Georgia State Patrol for two years and had seen hundreds of one-vehicle accidents. Before his employment with the GSP, he had worked as a police officer with the Valdosta Police Department for seven years, and prior to that he had been with the police department in the small town of Hahira for a year. The town of Hahira was so small that Chris Gay had actually *been* the police department.

By the time Gay got to the car, the fire had been put out and the firemen had raised the hood of the car to extinguish any fire in the engine compartment. Gay looked the car over thoroughly and was amazed. Other than the damage from the fire, there was no damage to the vehicle whatsoever. He couldn't figure it out. How could the car, which was a heavy car, run off the road and down the steep embankment without so much as a scratch? It was not what he had expected to see, so he decided he had better go back up on the road to where the accident started.

Before he began working on his accident report, trooper Gay noted that the ambulance had arrived, so he walked Sheila Bryan to the back of the ambulance, to be attended by the EMT. Gay did not notice any injury to Sheila, but he was concerned because she appeared pale, and he thought she might be dehydrated.

In order to complete his accident report, Gay had very specific information he needed to obtain. He measured the distance from the paved road to where the car was located: thirty-one feet. Then, walking along the shoulder of the road, he saw and photographed the path the car had taken along the shoulder before making the sharp right turn into the ditch.

The tall grass along the shoulder had been pushed down by the weight of the car, and Gay could clearly see the tracks where the car had traveled approximately sixty feet along the shoulder before turning down the embankment. The shoulder was wide and the car tracks were of all four wheels. In other words, the car had been completely off the roadway, traveling some sixty feet along the shoulder of the road before turning down into the ditch. There was no indication that the driver had tried to steer the car back onto the road. The path of the car had been so unusual that many years later,

Gay would still be able to picture the track of the car along the shoulder in his mind's eye.

On the road, Gay looked for skid marks and found none. In fact, all of the common things that he was used to finding in one-vehicle accidents were absent from this accident scene.

It was a hot, windless day and the road was dry as a bone. There had been no reason he could find for the car to run off the road. There had been no obstructions to the driver's line of vision, no defects in the road. The road, which was nineteen feet wide, was dry, straight, and level and afforded no reason for the driver to leave it. Nevertheless, Gay knew that people ran off the road for a lot of reasons that were not apparent from looking at the accident scene. He would have to talk to Sheila Bryan.

It was clear to GSP trooper Gay that Sheila was extremely upset, and he wished he didn't have to bother her. It had been his understanding that she had just watched her mother burn up in the car, and he was concerned about her state of mind. Putting responsibility over sentiment, he climbed in the back of the ambulance with Sheila and asked her if she wanted to talk with him then, or wait and talk later. She said she would talk to him then, and so trooper Gay said to Sheila Bryan, "Tell me what happened."

In broken sentences and between sobs, Sheila Bryan told trooper Gay that she and her mother had been driving down the road, and her mother had pointed out the bridge up ahead, and her mother had been talking about how the bridge had looked when she was a child. It was at that point, Sheila told Gay, that she had become distracted, and was looking at the other side of the bridge, and she had run onto the shoulder of the road and then into the ditch. Sheila told Gay that her mother had not been injured in any way and was okay when they got to the bottom of the ditch.

Sheila then told Gay that she had left the car, climbed up the ditch bank, and was walking back across the bridge to go get help to get her mother out of the car when she saw a car coming towards her. She said that when she was about halfway across the bridge, she had looked over her shoulder at her car and saw smoke coming from the car. She said she then flagged down the oncoming car and later discovered that it was her cousin, Danny Weeks. She said Danny Weeks had run to the house at the other side of the bridge and gotten water to pour on the car.

"How fast were you going when you ran off the road?" Gay asked.

"I was going real slow," she said.

Gay had his report form with him when he went to the back of the ambulance where Sheila was sitting. As he always did, he penciled in the information and would later give the penciled copy to the post secretary to type for him.

In order to complete his report form, Gay needed Sheila Bryan's driver's license and insurance card. She gave him her license and insurance card, and he wrote down the information. In the state of Georgia, a person's driver's license number is often the same as their social security number. Sheila Bryan's insurance company was Georgia Farm Bureau, and her policy number was ACV09889881305. Gay copied the information into the little boxes on his report form.

At the time Sheila handed over her driver's license and insurance card to trooper Gay, he had not thought anything about it. Later, others would think it strange that she had both her driver's license and insurance card with her. In fact, much later, she would deny that she had given trooper Gay either her license or insurance card that day. Nevertheless, the information appears on Chris Gay's accident report, which he filled out on August 18, 1996, at the accident scene, in the back of the ambulance with Sheila Bryan.

During the interview, Gay learned and put in his report that Sheila's mother's name was Freda Weeks, and that she was eighty-two years old and lived at the same address as Sheila. Sheila told Gay her mother lived in a mobile home located on her property.

With only one ambulance at the accident scene, the immediate problem Gay faced was deciding how to transport both the victim and the driver to the hospital. Gay decided he would have the ambulance transport Freda Weeks' remains to the morgue at Colquitt County Regional Medical Center in Moultrie and have CCSO deputy Stephens transport Sheila to the hospital.

By the time Gay completed his interview with Sheila and arranged for transportation, the wrecker had arrived and Gay had another decision to make. Because Sheila had said that her mother was perfectly fine prior to the fire, and because the cause of the fire was undetermined, and because Freda Weeks had died in the fire, Gay felt the accident needed further investigation. This meant he would need to impound the car; hold it at a locked lot for further investigation.

But first, Gay and the wrecker crew had to get the car out of the ditch, which should have been a simple thing, but, like so many things in this case would prove to be, it was not so simple.

The first call for a wrecker had gone to Ken Isaacs towing service, but their wrecker had been out of town, so the officers had contacted Biven's

Complete Automotive. David Hickey, the wrecker driver, responded to the accident scene with a roll-back-type wrecker. Once Hickey had the cable hooked to the back of the Mercury Cougar, and was attempting to pull the vehicle up the hill, the cable broke. Gay watched as the car rolled back down the embankment. The problem had been that the car tires did not roll, and the dirt had banked up behind the car while Hickey was pulling it toward the road. After his cable broke, Hickey contacted the next wrecker crew on the call list: Blanton's Auto Repair.

William Davis was the wrecker driver who responded from Blanton's, and he was able to get the car onto the road. Getting ready to pull the car, Davis noticed that the gearshift on the steering column was in Park. He reached in through the front windshield area and moved the gearshift to Neutral so that he could tow the Cougar. Eventually, Davis left the accident scene with the Cougar in tow, leaving the car at Blanton's impound yard, secured by a locked fence.

After the car had been impounded and both Freda Weeks and Sheila Bryan had left the accident scene, trooper Gay left for the hospital himself. He had one more part of his accident report to complete: alcohol and drug tests. He would have the hospital staff draw blood from Sheila Bryan for testing. On his accident report, he would write "pending" in the box marked "Results."

It was about quitting time when trooper Gay left the hospital. Returning to the post in Thomasville, Gay put the accident report in the hopper for the secretary to work on the next day.

On Monday, when Gay came on duty, he called the State Fire Marshal's Office in Albany to notify them of the accident and suspicious fire. As far as he was concerned, the ball was out of his court. He had passed it to the state fire marshal.

If the accident had been unusual, something even more unusual happened a few days later: Georgia State Patrol trooper Chris Gay received a thank you card from Sheila Bryan. He rarely received thank you cards, and it had been such an unusual event that trooper Gay saved the card and still had it with him many years later, even after he had transferred from the Thomasville GSP post to the Valdosta GSP post. In the card, Sheila had thanked him for his compassion and professionalism the day of the accident. She had signed it "the Sheila Bryan family."

"Now don't that just beat all," he said to himself.

CHAPTER FOUR

Sunday, August 18, 1996

Donald Davis had been looking forward to this all morning. Every Sunday without fail, Jeanne, his wife of twenty years, cooked a fine, country dinner. It was always a spread. This day it would be roast beef, creamed corn, field peas, butter beans, macaroni and cheese, a plate of fresh tomatoes and onions, and her homemade out-of-this-world cornbread.

There were a few things in life Davis looked forward to, and Jeanne's Sunday dinner was one of them. After dinner he hoped to indulge himself in a couple of his other favorite pastimes, puttering around the yard and watching race cars on TNN. By now, he and Jeanne had their Sunday afternoon routine down pat. After Sunday dinner, he would retire to the bedroom to watch the car races, and she would retire to their den and watch movies.

Davis had just sat down to the table with Jeanne and their fourteen-year-old daughter, Hope, and had filled his plate to overflowing, when the call came at 12:45 p.m. It was Sue Legette, dispatcher with the CCSO, telling him there was a 10-50 F on Livingston Bridge Road – an accident with a fatality. As a criminal investigator who had been with the CCSO for ten years, and as the on-call investigator for the weekend, he would reluctantly leave the table and head out the door. Jeanne was used to him getting up and leaving at a moment's notice; she would warm his plate when he got home.

Davis had never intended to work in the criminal justice field. His father had been a police officer in the small town of Berlin, Georgia, when Davis was growing up, and Davis had not been impressed with the occupation.

Davis was skilled with his hands and could turn out some beautiful woodworking. For many years, he had worked for a private contractor building homes. Eventually, he had gone to work for Destiny Mobile Homes, building cabinets for them. But in early 1991, Destiny didn't have enough work to keep him busy more than three or fours days a week. With a family to look after, he needed more money.

He and Jeanne had a friend, John Bass, who worked at the CCSO and, in a spurt of desperation, Davis had gone to Bass and told him, "I need to get a job." Bass checked with his boss, Sheriff Billy Howell, who responded, "Shoot, I reckon'!" and Davis started work that same evening at the county jail. Davis worked as the booking officer for about six months before being moved up to deputy, a position he held for the next three years. Then, in late 1993, he was transferred to investigations.

The job suited him, although it was stressful sometimes and had its highs and lows. Working the blood and guts of a homicide didn't bother him. Jeanne would tell him he had become cold hearted, and Davis sometimes wondered if she was right.

At age thirty-eight, Davis was a bear of a man. He stood six-foot-one and weighed three hundred pounds. If his size sometimes intimidated his suspects, well, so much the better. He liked getting in their face and letting them know if they were lying to him, he was gonna get 'em. "If I don't gitcha now, I'll gitcha later," he always told them. And he would. Persistence was his strong suit.

It was hot enough to fry an egg on the sidewalk when Davis left his house in his blue jeans and polo shirt with the CCSO insignia on it. Robby Pitts, another CCSO investigator, had loaned Davis his plain, black Thunderbird for the weekend because Davis' car was in the shop again. It was being repaired from another torn up transmission; Davis was easy on his woman, but he was hard on his car.

Davis didn't have far to go to get to the accident scene on Livingston Bridge Road. He lived in Ellenton, so the accident was only about five miles from his house. He was glad for that. Colquitt was a big county, and the fact that the accident was nearby meant he could get back to his plate sooner rather than later.

Davis had worked lots of accident scenes, many of them with fatalities. It was the department's policy that for any accident in which there was a fatality, the CCSO investigators would respond to the scene to take pictures, inspect the accident scene, talk to witnesses, victims, and the county coroner. But essentially, the accident investigation belonged to the Georgia State Patrol, and although he was required to be present and assist, the GSP was responsible for the case.

Davis pulled up on the bridge over Ty Ty Creek, just past the fire truck, and got out. By the time Davis arrived on the scene, some fifty people were already there, the main fire had been put out, and the Hinsons were just hitting the hot spots. Davis stopped and spoke with CCSO deputy Randy Stephens.

"Right off, it didn't sit right with me," Davis would say years later. "The first thing I noticed was the position of the car. It was sitting down in the ditch and it was perpendicular to the road. I've seen a lot of cars that have run off the road. They run off the road at an angle, and when you find them, they are sitting at an angle to the road. This car was perfectly perpendicular to the road. In order to get in that position, the driver had to have made a sharp right turn just at the bridge."

The second thing Davis noticed was that the gas tank filler door was open. He could see the open filler door from where he was standing on the road.

Once the fire was put out, Davis proceeded down the embankment to the smoldering car. He walked around it several times. He too noticed the gas cap was missing. He looked under the car and in it.

The body of Freda Weeks was in the passenger seat when he poked his head in the car. It was a God-awful sight for sure. He could not tell if this was a man or a woman. The torso and head were about all that was left. The flesh had been burned off her bones, and her legs and arms were basically skeletonized. But far worse than the sight was the smell.

Even after all his years in law enforcement, Davis would never be able to describe that smell. It made him want to wretch. It reminded him of what his uncle had said about the smell of death. His uncle had been in the service and had driven an ambulance that went around picking up dead bodies. His uncle had told him that it was impossible to get the smell out of the vehicle. It had seemed as though the smell penetrated the very metal of the ambulance, and no amount of cleaning or deodorizing would get rid of the odor.

Only able to tolerate the wretched smell for a short time, Davis went back to inspecting the outside of the Mercury Cougar.

Of most interest to Davis was the fact that there was no damage to the car. Other than the damage from the fire, there was no damage to the vehicle at all. *How odd*, he thought. He had expected to see some front-end damage, but there was none. He looked very closely at the ground in front of the car. There wasn't even an indentation in the dirt where the car had stopped. Nothing. Just nothing at all. *This is too strange*, he thought. It looked as though the car had been lifted by helicopter and gently set down in the ditch.

Davis concluded that for the car to be in the deep ditch, with the condition of the car as it was, the driver of the vehicle must have come down the embankment going about five miles per hour with her foot on the brake. But Davis kept his conclusions and thoughts to himself.

When he looked inside the car, he noticed the car had been left in Park. This told Davis that Sheila Bryan had just eased down the embankment and, when the car stopped, had put the car in Park. Most of the cars Davis had seen after they'd run off the roadway were still in Drive.

Davis also knew that if Sheila had gone down the steep embankment at an angle – instead of driving head-on as she had – the chances were very good that the car would have rolled over, and she would have been injured.

He talked with the firemen on the scene, who told him that when they had gotten there, the car had been totally involved with the fire. They had not been there long when Davis had arrived. Davis set about tending to the usual business of a traffic accident and got on the radio.

About 1:30 p.m., Davis went over to the ambulance where the driver of the car was sitting in the back. He wanted to interview Sheila about what had happened. Stephens had told him the victim in the car was Sheila Bryan's mother, Freda Weeks.

The next day, in the stilted style that investigators develop, Davis would write the incident report relating what Sheila Bryan told him while sitting in the back of the ambulance:

My mother, Freda Weeks, and I were riding around today looking at where she used to live and was raised. We were riding along talking, and I looked off. The next thing I knew, I had run off the road down in the ditch. When the car stopped, I tried to turn the motor off, but it wouldn't stop. I got out of the car and tried to raise the hood, so I could take the battery cable off, but I couldn't (raise the hood). Mama was sitting in the car. She was okay, so I climbed up the bank of the ditch. When I got to the top, I looked back at the car and it was smoking. I started down the road to get some help. When I got across the bridge, I stopped a car. It was my cousin, Danny Weeks. I told him that I had run off the road and needed some help. When we got back to the car, it was smoking real bad and was on fire. We tried to get mama out, but the car was on fire, and we couldn't. My mother was okay when I left her in the car. I don't know what happened.

During the interview, Sheila also told Davis that her mother was an Alzheimer's patient. She had not told Davis that she was locked out of the car.

Finished with the interview, which Davis thought raised more questions than it answered, he turned his attention to the Mercury Cougar that was just being pulled out of the ditch by the second wrecker to the scene. Freda Weeks was still inside the car when the wrecker placed the car back on the roadway. Davis noted that the firemen had to use the "Jaws of Life" to open the passenger side door and extricate Mrs. Weeks. The EMT and Coroner Rodney Bryan placed the body of Freda Weeks in a disaster bag and loaded her into the ambulance, to be carried to Colquitt Regional Medical Center.

After the ambulance left, Deputy Stephens transported Sheila Bryan to the same hospital in his patrol car. With the victims transported from the scene, Davis remained at the accident site with the wrecker drivers and other law enforcement officers to oversee the car's removal to Blanton's impound yard.

Davis kept thinking about his interview with Sheila Bryan. Something else in this picture didn't fit for him. This was a scorching hot day, ninety degrees hot, and Sheila Bryan was dressed in a dark-colored pair of jogging pants and a sweatshirt. The sleeves of the sweatshirt had been cut off about half way up the arm and the band had been cut off at the bottom of the sweatshirt. It didn't seem like the kind of outfit one would be wearing on such a hot day, and especially not if taking her mother out for a Sunday ride. It was a tacky outfit.

As he typically did after a vehicular fatality, Davis went to Colquitt Regional Medical Center, where he found coroner Rodney Bryan – no relation to Sheila – and Sheila Bryan sitting in a little family room off the emergency room. Davis observed and said little. Rodney Bryan was explaining to Sheila Bryan about how the body would be stored until it was moved to a funeral home. He asked her which of the funeral homes she preferred, so the funeral home staff could be notified and the body transferred.

Davis watched as Sheila was "puttin' on her show" again. Davis thought her ability to cry hysterically, stop crying and chat a while, and then return to more crying, was less than sincere. Davis didn't stay long at the emergency room. After a few minutes, while the coroner and Sheila were still talking, Davis left to drive home.

On the way home, Davis tried to put the pieces of the puzzle together. He kept wondering why Freda Weeks hadn't opened the door and gotten out of the car when the fire started. Sheila Bryan had said that her mother was okay when she went to get help, so why didn't Freda Weeks open the door and run from the car when it started smoking?

Sheila Bryan had not said that Freda Weeks was an invalid, only that she had Alzheimer's. Surely Freda Weeks' mind wasn't so tangled in the Alzheimer's maze that she couldn't figure out how to get out of the car. If her mind had been that bad off, then there would have been no point to taking her on a Sunday drive to visit the old family places, he thought.

And why had Sheila Bryan left her mother in the car? Why hadn't she taken her with her? If the woman was too feeble to get up the embankment, why didn't Sheila open the car door and leave it open for her mother? The heat was unbearable that day. Didn't Sheila think about how hot it had to have been in that car?

And when she saw the smoke, why hadn't she raced back to the car?

Like many people who were at the scene that day, Davis thought about what he would have done if he had seen his mother in a smoking car. He knew he wouldn't have been able to get down that embankment fast enough to snatch that door open, grab his mother, and pull her out.

Davis decided this story did not make a lot of sense. By the time he got back to the house about 4 p.m., he was hot and tired and had lost his appetite completely. He walked straight to the den and his big, old easy chair and plopped down. When Jeanne came in the room, he told her what he had been thinking all afternoon but had not told anyone: "That woman killed her mother."

46

CHAPTER FIVE

Sunday, August 18, 1996

If Investigator Donald Davis was a bear of a man, Coroner Rodney Bryan, at age thirty-four, was a bigger bear. Standing six-foot-four and weighing almost three hundred pounds himself, Bryan had become coroner for Colquitt County in February 1995, when he was appointed to the position by the probate judge after the untimely death of the elected coroner.

The job seemed a natural fit for Bryan, who had worked in both law enforcement and emergency medical services. He had liked the coroner position so much that after his appointed term expired, he ran for the position and was elected in November 1996, several months after the death of Freda Weeks.

Under Georgia law, the primary function of the coroner is to conduct death investigations in situations where a person has died of something other than natural causes. The coroner, like the medical examiner, has to determine both the manner and cause of death.

The cause of death was fairly simple to determine, in that people died if one or more of three organs (lung, heart, or brain) no longer functioned. Prior to modern technology, lung and heart failure were the only two causes of death. But once people were able to be kept alive through extreme measures, with equipment that could keep their heart and lungs functioning, the concept of "brain death" was added.

Determining the manner of death was far more complicated. Essentially, the manner of death fell into one of five categories: natural death, suicide, homicide, accident, or undetermined.

Bryan, who would always seem embarrassed by the fact that he truly enjoyed his work, said he liked putting the pieces of the puzzle together to explain the manner and cause of a person's death. Once he had the puzzle figured out, he would then write up the deceased's death certificate and

47

complete his coroner's death investigation report.

In rural south Georgia counties, the coroner's position was never intended as a full time job. For Bryan, the position was an adjunct to his job as the Emergency Medical Services (EMS) Director for Colquitt County.

Prior to Freda Weeks' death in August 1996, Bryan had worked as an auxiliary deputy with the Willachoochee, Georgia, police department and as a deputy with the CCSO. He had received his EMT certification in 1981 at Crisp County Technical School and had continued his education and gone on to become an EMS instructor at the police training facility in Forsyth, Georgia. He had then returned to Forsyth in December 1994, to take the forty-hour basic coroner's course. As coroner, he had no office to speak of and worked out of his personal vehicle with a pager.

Sunday was a day for socializing. People began the day by socializing at Sunday School and church, and then returned home to socialize with extended family members over Sunday dinner. For those who had not met their socializing quota, Sunday afternoons could be spent at Wal-Mart. Because there were no large shopping malls or entertainment possibilities like those found in Atlanta or larger towns, and because, as a rule, people in south Georgia did not work on Sundays, Wal-Mart shopping always seemed a good option.

On August 18, 1996, Coroner Rodney Bryan was shopping at Wal-Mart in Moultrie when his pager went off at 12:49 p.m., alerting him to the fatality on Livingston Bridge Road.

Shane Gay, an RN in the emergency room at Colquitt Regional Medical Center in Moultrie, had paged Bryan. Because there was no 911 system in Colquitt county at the time, Bryan would typically get pages from the sheriff's office, police department or emergency room. Once the ambulance had arrived at the scene on Livingston Bridge Road, the ambulance driver had alerted the hospital of the fatality and the hospital had then paged Bryan.

It was Bryan's job as coroner to respond to the accident scene, officially pronounce the victim deceased, oversee the transport of the body, and begin his manner-and-cause-of-death investigation.

Coroner Bryan went to the back of the ambulance and briefly interviewed Sheila Bryan. Sheila told Rodney Bryan that she and her mother were just riding along, talking, and she ran off the shoulder of the road. Sheila told Coroner Bryan that, as she had come around the curve in the road just before the bridge, she had failed to negotiate the curve and had ended up on the shoulder, and when the car had gotten to the guardrail at the bridge, in order to dodge the guardrail, she had turned the car down the embankment. Sheila told Coroner Bryan that she had been unable to rescue her mother because of the steep embankment and because the doors on the car had locked.

If this account told by Sheila Bryan differed from the accounts told to Chris Gay or Donald Davis, Coroner Rodney Bryan was not aware of it.

After his interview with Sheila Bryan, Coroner Rodney Bryan pronounced Freda Weeks dead at 1:16 p.m. He then took photos of the accident scene and the body, and had Week's body transported to the morgue at Colquitt County Regional Medical Center.

Under Georgia law, an autopsy was called for in the death of Freda Weeks. When Coroner Bryan reached the hospital, he called Dr. Anthony Clark, the regional medical examiner, to request the autopsy. He was told that the medical examiner was out of town on vacation. A little after 3 p.m., Bryan then called the state crime lab in Atlanta, as was his custom when the local medical examiner was not available. After explaining the death, as he understood it, Bryan was told by the Atlanta staff that an autopsy was not necessary. The Atlanta medical examiner told Bryan that he could use Sheila Bryan's statement for identification purposes. He then instructed Bryan to be sure blood was drawn from the body to submit for a toxicology report, which Bryan did.

Bryan would later explain that, at the time, it had not seemed to him that there was any problem with the case. It appeared to him to have been a car accident in which the deceased had been accidentally burned to death. Under those circumstances, an autopsy did not seem necessary.

Satisfied with the decision about the autopsy, Bryan had spoken with Sheila at the hospital, explaining to her that there would be no autopsy and that her mother's body would be released from the hospital morgue to a funeral home as soon as Sheila was able to make the arrangements.

Certain that his responsibilities as coroner had been met, Bryan needed only to complete his coroner's report and sign the death certificate once he received it from the funeral home. As far as he was concerned, the car accident on Livingston Bridge Road was a slam dunk. No problem.

Of course he was wrong, very wrong. The Sheila Bryan case was about to take Coroner Rodney Bryan places he had never been before, and places he never wanted to revisit.

Sheila Bryan arrived at the emergency room of Colquitt Regional Medical Center at 3:07 p.m. and was seen by the emergency room physician, Dr. Pamela Gouth, ten minutes after her arrival. Her vital signs were taken and her blood pressure was reported to be 150/94 with a pulse rate of 110.

Patient information gathered at the emergency room included her age (forty-three), that she was married, that she had not had any previous mental health treatment, and that she was not taking any medication.

The patient's chief medical complaint was of an injury sustained in an automobile accident: a bruised left forearm and an elbow that was tender to the touch.

Dr. Gouth found Sheila to be in an emotional state, and it appeared to the doctor that Sheila was in shock and unable to answer all of her triage questions. Besides the emotional state of the patient, Dr. Gouth also had to deal with the patient's cousin, Danny Weeks.

When Dr. Gouth tried to ask Sheila medical information, Danny interceded and asked Dr. Gouth, "Don't you see that she's upset, that her nerves are shot? Can't you just give her something for her nerves?"

Dr. Gouth tried to ignore the young man and attend to her patient, but Danny would not be put off: "Can't you give her something for her nerves? Just stop asking her questions."

Surely by the time they had reached the emergency room, Danny Weeks' own nerves were about shot. Fiercely protective of family, he had spent all afternoon in the blazing sun trying to comfort his cousin Sheila, to no avail. It is little wonder that his exasperation had begun to show.

With GSP trooper Chris Gay present, Dr. Gouth then drew blood for an alcohol and drug test. The blood specimen was drawn until the vacuum tube was full, at which time the blood was placed in a sealed kit, and the specimen was given to trooper Gay.

Dr. Gouth then sent Sheila to the x-ray room, where Dr. Michael Whittle x-rayed her arm and determined that there was no apparent injury, at least as determined by the x-ray. Dr. Whittle concluded there was "no bone or joint abnormality noted," and the result of the x-ray was "a radiographically normal elbow and forearm."

Dr. Gouth made her diagnosis: "contusion of the left forearm and elbow and grief reaction." She applied a sling to Sheila's arm and prescribed Motrin tablets to be taken every six to eight hours for the pain in her arm, and Xanax for her nerves.

Sheila Bryan was discharged from the hospital at 5:40 p.m.

CHAPTER SIX

Monday, August 19, 1996

Investigator Donald Davis was madder than a wet settin' hen. As big and as strong as Davis was, that was not a good thing.

Davis came into the CCSO office on Monday morning following the Sunday afternoon accident on Livingston Bridge Road and wrote up the statement Sheila Bryan had made to him at the back of the ambulance. It seemed everyone in the office had heard about the accident and they were talking about it; Davis talked about it, too.

One of the people in the office who had heard about the accident was Robby Pitts, the CCSO investigator who had loaned Davis his car the previous weekend. For whatever reason, Pitts decided he was interested in having the case, so he went and talked with Sheriff Billy Howell about it.

CCSO's policy was that the case belonged to the investigator who had been on call the weekend of the accident, the same investigator who went to the scene of the accident. But policies, like rules, were made to be broken.

Robby Pitts went to Davis' office and said the sheriff had given Pitts the case, assuming the State Fire Marshal's Office made it a case. Fortunately for everyone, Davis handled his anger by sulking. Davis decided he would not speak of the case again. He was through with it. Over and done. Davis decided that if Pitts wanted the case, then, by God, Pitts could have the case. *But,* he thought, *the little moron can just figure it out for himself; he won't get one whiff of information from me.*

The reason the sheriff had given the case to Pitts would depend on whom you asked. Pitts would say it was because the case promised to be complicated and he was the senior investigator at the CCSO. Davis would say it was because Pitts kissed the sheriff's ass on a regular basis.

It was the end of any friendship between Donald Davis and Robby Pitts. And while many friendships would be strained or broken during the course of the case, the relationship between Pitts and Davis was the first shot fired across the bow.

In January 1997, just four months after the death of Freda Weeks, Sheriff Billy Howell, who had lost his re-election bid the previous November, was replaced by Sheriff Jack Lanier. When Sheriff Billy Howell left, Pitts left the CCSO with him, ending his involvement in the Sheila Bryan case.

But the truth of the matter was, no one could really take anything away from Donald Davis that he did not want them to have. And, regardless of what Pitts said, or what the sheriff said, or what anyone said, the case belonged to Donald Davis.

Sheila Bryan had lied to him. He was sure of it. As with all of the suspects who lied to him, he meant to get her. Davis was persistent and would doggedly hang on to the case, one way or another.

Many years later, when all had been said and done and the Sheila Bryan case had come to its bitter end, Donald Davis would be there. In fact, he would be one of only two men in law enforcement who would be involved with the Sheila Bryan case from start to finish – alpha and omega.

There were just thirty-six certified fire investigators in the state of Georgia in 1996, and Ronnie Dobbins was one of them; in fact, Ronnie Dobbins *was* number thirty-six. To become a certified fire investigator, a candidate had to pass the requirements of the International Association of Arson Investigators (IAAI), which is quite a lengthy process.

The would-be-certified fire investigator is awarded points for various activities, such as investigating fires and attending training courses. Each applicant must have one hundred fifty points before they can take the certification test.

By the time the Sheila Bryan case came along, Dobbins had become certified and had investigated over five hundred fires. He had attended courses on arson investigation all over the United States. Prior to joining the State Fire Marshal's Office, Dobbins had been in the U.S. Coast Guard and had studied fire investigation there as well.

In 1998, Ronnie Dobbins would be named Fire Investigator of the Year for the State of Georgia. The award was given by the Georgia Arson Control Board. Dobbins was an exceptional investigator who was widely respected for his dedication and determination in ferreting out arson.

Like Coroner Rodney Bryan who had no office to speak of, Ronnie

Dobbins, who, by August 1996, had been an investigator with the State Fire Marshal's Office for ten years, also worked without an office. Dobbins worked a sixteen-county area of south Georgia from his car, using a beeper. Sometimes the local fire departments would find temporary office space for him at the fire station when he was working a case in their area.

When Georgia State Patrol Trooper Chris Gay placed the call to the regional headquarters for the State Fire Marshal's Office in Albany about the vehicle fire on Livingston Bridge Road, the Albany staff had, in turn, called Ronnie Dobbins.

When Dobbins got the call about the vehicle fire involving Freda Weeks, he went to Blanton's impound yard to take a preliminary look at the Mercury Cougar. Dobbins looked the car over in much the same manner Gerald Psalmond had before him and ended up at the same place: the fire looked suspicious. Understanding what would be involved in a thorough inspection of the car, including removing carpet, floor mats, and upholstery for testing, Dobbins decided he had better hold off until he got in touch with law enforcement and the insurance carrier on the car.

Trooper Chris Gay had told the Albany staff that Georgia Farm Bureau was the insurance carrier on the Cougar, and that meant Dobbins needed to call Paul MaGahee. Dobbins knew MaGahee, who was one of several arson investigators employed by Georgia Farm Bureau Insurance Company. MaGahee, like Dobbins, was a certified arson investigator – one of the thirty-six – and Dobbins knew MaGahee would want to be present for the total inspection of the car.

Dobbins placed a call to MaGahee, who told Dobbins he felt sure Georgia Farm Bureau would also want to call in a private investigator, to avoid any perception that the inspection would be anything less than objective.

The certified fire investigators all knew each other. They had a lot in common, and they worked together on various cases. When MaGahee told Dobbins Georgia Farm Bureau would want to call in a private investigator, Dobbins knew without being told exactly who MaGahee meant: the top arson investigator in the state, their old buddy, Ralph Newell.

Ralph Newell was the guru of arson investigation in the state of Georgia and he had his own company: Newell Investigative Services, Incorporated. Newell's office was in north Georgia, Gainesville to be precise, but he worked all over the United States.

Newell had personally trained most of the certified investigators in the state and had investigated thousands of vehicle fires. If there was something fishy with the Mercury Cougar, no one doubted Newell would find it. Hell, when it came to arson, Dobbins and MaGahee both knew, calling Newell in was like putting a bloodhound on a bleeding convict.

"I'll call you back when I find out when Ralph can cut loose and head to Moultrie," MaGahee said.

"Sounds better than snuff," Dobbins said.

"Right, and half as dusty," MaGahee agreed. They both laughed. It was a south Georgia joke.

Ralph Newell was a busy man and the case was put on hold, awaiting Ralph Newell's schedule.

CHAPTER SEVEN

Monday, August 19, 1996

The door that opened into Ralph Newell's world was purposefully inconspicuous. Located in a strip mall behind a service station in downtown Gainesville, his office had all the outside pizzazz of a CIA office in Bethesda, Maryland. What was behind door number 330 – which had no sign to give passers by a hint of the bustling activity a few feet away behind the door – was left to the imagination. Newell kept his private investigations very private.

Beyond the locked door was a world Newell had made to his liking. Through many years and many experiences, some of them painful, he had created his world of arson investigation and staffed it with his family and friends – people he trusted. No one entered his world without first winning Newell's trust.

Newell counted the other thirty-five certified arson investigators in the state of Georgia as his friends, and he trusted them to enter his world. Newell called Ronnie Dobbins "Dobberhead" and liked to reminisce about the practical jokes he had played on his good friend over the years. Paul MaGahee had worked for Newell as an assistant in his business for five years, and Newell and MaGahee spoke in arson shorthand.

When the telephone rang behind the unmarked door in Gainesville, and Newell's office manager and daughter, Lisa, took the call about the Sheila Bryan case, it was, as much as anything else, an opportunity for Newell to touch base with his old friends Dobbins and MaGahee.

Newell didn't need the work. By 1996, his business had mushroomed almost beyond his ability to manage it. In an effort to "tame the beast," Newell had only recently worked out a schedule that afforded him some measure of sanity. He would be on the road traveling to various cities across the country on Monday through Thursday, and he would return home to Gainesville on Thursday evenings. Friday was his day to spend with his lovely wife, Patty, and to play golf. The weekends were his family time, and time he spent at the Methodist church teaching a Sunday School class. He worked with the young people in the church and he and Patty enjoyed entertaining at their home. Newell's daughter, Lisa, and son, Scott, had filled his life with four grandchildren, and Newell made time for them in his weekend schedule as well – although it was not unusual for Newell's grandchildren to be running around in his office while he alternately took telephone calls and looked at coloring books.

The world of arson investigation was an ugly, dirty world, and Newell had years before determined that long-term survival in that world required balance and diversity.

"You need a hobby that is very different from the work you do," Newell said. So he had taken his own advice and found one: cooking.

His fantasy was to attend an international culinary school, but meanwhile, he settled for cooking for the young people at his church and making his own wine and beer for friends. If you got to know Ralph Newell well enough, he would share one of his favorite recipes with you: Beer Can Chicken.

Newell was a man who enjoyed life and packed as much into every day as he could. He liked to laugh and joke and have a good time. He had filled his life with family, friends, and interests that kept him involved and committed to his life passions. He was a man who was intense and funny – and also sentimental in ways one might not expect.

If he knew you well, he would talk to you about his experiences in the army. If he trusted you, he would tell you about the reunion of his army buddies he recently held, and why he organized the reunion. But he could not speak of it without tears streaming unashamedly down his face. It was a tender spot, a hole in his heart that would never heal.

Newell served in Vietnam and in 1966, there were forty-six men in his platoon. He was the leader of a long-range patrol unit that was called in for search and rescue missions. They had been on their third trip into the IaDrang Valley when a helicopter was shot down and his platoon sent in to rescue the crew. It was an ambush. An entire regiment of North Vietnamese opened fire on his platoon. The firing pinned his men down for four and a half hours, and Newell's best friend was killed as he attempted to rescue Newell. In all, almost half of the platoon – twenty-two men – would die that day before they were evacuated. The men who were not killed were almost all injured, including Newell. Newell was sent back to Fort Benning, and after three or four months in the hospital, he was put on limited duty training recruits.

Nearly thirty years would pass before Newell decided to bring the remaining men from the platoon back together again. He had to use all of his investigative tools just to locate the twenty-four survivors who had spread out across the country, one as far away as Anchorage, Alaska. Eighteen of the twenty-four attended the reunion and reminisced with Newell about the good times, and the bad.

There were some areas of Newell's life that he didn't joke about, and Vietnam was one of them. And when it came to the subject of arson, Newell didn't play with that either.

Newell had not intended to be an arson investigator but his first experience with the subject had so intrigued him that he ended up following the arson cases and intrigue that went with them for a lifetime.

It all began in the early 70s when he was working in law enforcement in Gainesville, Georgia, and he got a call one evening to respond to a burning car in Hall county. When Newell and the other officers reached the scene, the new Plymouth Duster was still burning. After the smoke cleared, they found a man's body inside the car and a hammer by the body. In the back seat were two five-gallon gasoline cans. About twelve feet from the car was a gasoline-soaked wallet. Newell and the other officers thought perhaps there had been a robbery that had turned into a murder. The autopsy of the victim determined that the man had been alive at the time the fire was set; he had burned to death.

The case fascinated Newell. It took six weeks of an intensive investigation to determine exactly what had happened out on that lonely stretch of road: the man had committed suicide. Strangely, the man had been not only suicidal but also fanatical about being cremated, and so he had solved both problems by burning himself to death.

"It was a weird case," Newell said, "but, I would learn, most arson cases are weird."

Eventually, Newell began working all the arson cases in the sheriff's department. He recalled a case where he was called out to a domestic dispute to find a house blazing and a woman standing in the middle of the road with her hair melted to her head. He went into the burning house looking for the woman's son. He entered through a window but could not find the man in his search of the house. Exiting back through the same window, Newell found the body of the man lying right under the window. "I had actually stepped over the man when I went in," Newell said. When he tried to move the man, the man's skin came off.

There was nothing at all pretty about death by fire, Newell said, having seen the ugliest it has to offer.

"Most people don't want to believe what has happened in an arson case. And most of the time it is about money," he said. Newell said that it was not hard to prove arson; it was hard to prove who did it, "because people don't want to believe it."

His experience with arson over the years had taught Newell that when it came to arson, human nature was basically stupid and, he said, "People continually surprise you at the stupid things they will do." The amateur arson cases were not a challenge to his investigative techniques. It was the arson pro who challenged Newell.

"He's the guy who commits arson, and you know he did, but you can't prove it," Newell said.

But most arson cases were of the amateur variety. They were like the case in Forsyth county where the man used four gallon-jugs of gas, poured gas in every room of his house, and poured gas by the lit pilot light on the heater.

"Of course he blew himself to bits," Newell said. "One gallon of gasoline has the explosive capability of twenty-four sticks of dynamite. The explosion was so great it actually lifted the roof off the house. Pretty stupid."

The cases that bothered Newell the most were the ones that involved children. He remembered a case in south Florida where a two-year-old had been killed in a fire.

"Acetone had been poured on the crib mattress," Newell sadly recalled. "Acetone, which is found in fingernail polish remover, is as explosive as gasoline."

Over the years, as Newell gained more and more experience in arson investigation, he learned that he also had to acquire the ability to communicate his knowledge in a courtroom, to a jury who typically knew nothing of arson. Eventually, he became an expert witness. His deep, rich baritone voice, which could serve him just as well as a radio commentator, would prove to be an asset in the courtroom. In time, he learned the importance of speaking directly to the jury, not to the lawyers who were asking the questions. He learned how to pace himself, how to handle cross-examination, and even how to dress.

Although certainly a man of money and means, Ralph Newell rarely entered a courtroom in a suit.

"I always wear a sports jacket and a pair of slacks that don't match," he said. Newell did not see his attire as being misleading; he saw it as a means of relating to the working-class jurors he was speaking to. He liked to tell the story about the time he wore an old pair of shoes that had a hole in the bottom of one of them. Unaware of the silver-dollar-size hole, Newell had crossed his legs while on the stand, and the hole in his shoe had been exposed for the jurors' viewing. After his testimony, the lawyer had complimented Newell on the added touch. Newell had thought it was funny – but it was a lesson he never forgot.

Newell liked to tell the story of a case that happened in Cullman, Alabama. It was a criminal case in which he was to testify about the arson. Newell was in the prosecutor's office, and the defendant had been brought into the adjoining room. When the man was told that he was being charged with arson one and arson two, he retorted, "That's a God damn lie. I didn't set but one fire!" Newell still laughed about that one.

Because of his knowledge of arson and his ability to testify, in time Newell would become a formidable expert witness – so formidable that once he was listed as a witness in a case, the opposing lawyers would immediately begin a campaign to discredit him, or get him off the case if they could. It would prove to be the same in the Sheila Bryan case.

Ralph Newell needed the Sheila Bryan case like he needed another hole in his shoe. He had a long list of clients, and Georgia Farm Bureau Insurance was just one of the names on the list, which included seven different vehicle manufacturers, insurance companies, individuals, attorneys, and other types of manufacturers.

Ford Motor company was Newell's largest client. Whenever Ford had a death or injury case involving a fire, they would call Newell in to investigate. Over the years, Newell's investigations had cost Ford millions of dollars. If he went into a Ford case and found them liable he would tell them so. His phraseology would be short and to the point: "You have serious exposure." To the Ford executives, this translated, "Settle the case immediately." In one case alone, Ford had settled with the plaintiffs for $900,000.

When Ford discovered they had problems with the ignition switches on some models of their cars – the switches catching on fire – they called Ralph Newell to be part of a task force to investigate the problem. Again, Newell delivered the bad news: "Yup. The switches were a problem." Newell's investigation led to a national recall that cost Ford Motor Company millions of dollars. But they had not hired Newell to tell them what they wanted to hear, they had hired Newell to tell them the truth.

In fact, it was Newell's integrity and unwillingness to bend the truth that had built his business. He worked for himself and always delivered the unvarnished truth as he saw it. If his clients didn't like Newell's answers or the fact that it would cost them money, well, they could always get a second opinion. Nobody owned Ralph Newell's soul; it wasn't for sale.

He approached each case the same way. He went into the arson investigation without knowing the names of the parties involved and with no knowledge of the circumstances surrounding the case. He didn't want to know. Sometimes he had to ask law enforcement not to tell him anything. He wanted his investigation to be objective; he wanted the scene of the fire to tell him what had happened. He would read the evidence at the scene and make his determination. Only after he had completed his investigation did he get involved in the surrounding facts of the case and all the many nuances.

Newell prided himself not only on his integrity, but also on his ability to not become personally involved in his cases. He had been in the business for many years, and he knew exactly what his role would be in a case, where it began and where it ended.

Through the years he had come up with maxims that guided him along his professional path, some of them serious and some not.

"Never trust a person with thin lips," was one of his sayings. And, although he would never explain where he had come up with that insight, he nevertheless held to it, at least somewhat seriously.

But, like so many other people who would be pulled into the Bryan case, Ralph Newell was about to embark on a long journey, rife with thin-lipped people, who would call his integrity into question and cause him to become more personally involved in the case than he had ever dreamed possible.

In fact, when the dust had settled, and everyone, including Sheila Bryan, had packed it in, Ralph Newell would still be personally involved in litigation.

It was going to be an ugly case. But when Newell talked with MaGahee about accepting the assignment from Georgia Farm Bureau, all Newell was concerned about was finding a place on his schedule to fit it in. In hindsight, it would have been smarter just to say he was too busy to fool with it. But this was old Dobberhead and his pal MaGahee, whom Newell had housed and fed and trained and looked upon almost as he did one of his own children. He would enjoy working with Dobbins and MaGahee, so he worked it out.

CHAPTER EIGHT

Tuesday, August 27, 1996

Coroner Rodney Bryan was between a rock and a hard place.

It had not taken long for the "slam dunk" accident on Livingston Bridge Road to become a problem. When Bryan met with Medical Examiner (ME) Anthony Clark about the accident, Clark told Bryan his information was incomplete and he would have to get more details in order to complete his reports. And the ME did not think the right decision had been made about the autopsy.

In truth, the ME said a lot more than that to Coroner Rodney Bryan, but some of those issues would be kept between the two of them, for the time being anyway.

Bryan would have to look into this further and continue his manner-and-cause-of-death investigation, which he had thought was a no-brainer. He needed to know exactly what happened before the fire in the car, and the status of Freda Weeks' health, including all of her known medical conditions.

Coroner Bryan knew only one person who could give him the information: Sheila Bryan.

Rodney Bryan called Donald Davis and asked him to ride with him to the Bryan's house on Maple Street in Omega. Davis grinned like the proverbial Cheshire Cat and accepted the invitation.

Davis and Bryan were friends. They had gotten to know each other when Bryan worked as a deputy sheriff with the CCSO. Eventually, Bryan went to work with EMS, but Davis still saw him on a frequent basis over work-related matters.

Rodney Bryan swung by the CCSO office, they got in Davis' car, and the two of them made the short trip up Highway 319 to the Bryan home.

When they pulled up to the house on North Maple, Davis was surprised. Davis had a theory that usually worked for him. He thought that the way a person dressed was a pretty good indicator of how they lived; if they dressed poorly, their living quarters were likely to be poor, and vice versa. So, based on the only time he had seen Sheila Bryan's attire, which had been at the accident scene, he wasn't expecting the attractive, middle class home they stopped in front of.

It was the nicest house on the street. A yellow brick, ranch-style home, Davis thought it looked to be about two thousand square feet. It was an attractive, well kept home with a manicured and pleasingly landscaped yard.

Sheila answered the door, nicely dressed Davis noted, and let the coroner and investigator in the house. Davis took a seat in the den directly across from Sheila's husband, Karlas. The Bryan's youngest daughter, Karrie, had been present when they arrived, but Sheila sent her daughter to her room and told her to stay there. While waiting for Sheila, Davis noted that the attractively decorated home was Spic-and-Span clean. No, this time his theory did not appear to have been accurate.

Rodney Bryan was asking the questions and, according to Donald Davis, he was just along for the ride.

Coroner Bryan asked Sheila about her mother's medical history, especially in light of her statement about the Alzheimer's. Sheila told the coroner that her mother had become "easily frustrated with things," and that she had fallen several times the previous month. Bryan wrote in his notes that Sheila told him that her mother, because of her age and mental state, had begun to "need help with things."

The coroner also wanted to know what prescription medications Freda Weeks had been taking. Additionally, Coroner Bryan discussed the subject of Freda Weeks' dental work, and Sheila told Bryan that her mother "had worn dentures for years." In the midst of the chat, which both Investigator Davis and Coroner Bryan had thought was a friendly, informal talk, Davis said, almost casually he thought, "Tell me again what happened."

As Davis took notes, Sheila gave most of the same information she had given Davis nine days earlier when he had interviewed her at the back of the ambulance. But this time, she added and changed some information. When he returned to the CCSO, Davis would once again write up Sheila Bryan's statement in his stilted style:

My mother, Freda Weeks, and I were riding around looking at places we used to live. We were just riding down the road talking and I looked off. The next thing I knew we were in the ditch. I heard my mother say my name, "Sheila!" when we were going down the ditch bank. When we stopped at the bottom of the ditch I couldn't get my car to switch off. I got out and tried to get the battery cable off so the car would stop. I couldn't get the battery cable off so I went back to the side of the car and tried again to get the car to shut off. Mama was sitting in the car with a dazed look on her face. She was wearing her seat belt. I think I got the car turned off. I told mama I was going to get help and I said I would be right back. I shut the driver's side (door) and it locked. I went around to the passenger side of the car but I couldn't get the door open. I told her that I was going to get help. I climbed the ditch bank to go for help. I knew that there was a woman I knew that lived just up the road. **The car wasn't smoking when I got to the road.** *I made it across the bridge and a car was coming. I waved it down and they stopped. I didn't know that in the car was my cousin Danny Weeks until he got out. I told him we needed help, that mama was in the car in the ditch and I couldn't get her out.* **When we got back to the car it was smoking.** *I didn't see any fire. Danny made me sit down on the road and he went back and got some water to put on the car. When he got back the car was on fire. He made me stay about half way down the bridge. His wife went and called for help. I didn't hear anything that sounded like an explosion.*

Sheila also added that she had gone to get gas in her car before she and her mother left her residence on their drive.

Davis took note of the fact that during the entire rendering of this, what he considered a new-and-revised version of what had happened out on Livingston Bridge Road, Sheila had not shed one tear.

Davis had understood from Sheila, when he had talked with her at the ambulance, that she had tried to lift the hood and couldn't. This time, she said she got the hood up, but was unable to get the battery cable off. She had added the part about her mother calling out her name as they went down the ditch bank. She also added the part about her mother having a dazed look on her face. And this was the first time Davis had heard about the car doors being locked.

But the major change that bothered Davis was that, in this version, Sheila had not seen the smoke when she got up to the road. She had seen the smoke after she had flagged down Danny Weeks.

Bryan and Davis were only at the house about thirty minutes. When they left and got in the car neither of them spoke. They just looked at each other, and shook their heads.

Rodney Bryan had expected Sheila Bryan's memory, which might have been clouded at the time of the accident when he first spoke to her, to have cleared in the nine days since the accident. But Sheila had not been able to clarify many of the questions Rodney Bryan had asked. He was still very uncertain of Freda Weeks' medical condition at the time of the accident. He was worried that he still didn't have enough information to complete his reports.

If Coroner Bryan was worried and mystified, Investigator Davis was deeply troubled. Davis considered consistency an indicator of truth. "The truth don't change," he would always say. But he now had two versions of what happened from Sheila, and the two versions didn't match in some significant ways.

While this version of what had happened answered some questions, it also raised more questions. Sheila Bryan was claiming that she had been locked out of the car, which explained away why she had not raced down the embankment to get her mother out when she saw the smoke. She was locked out of the car, so there was no need to race to the car.

But how was that possible? Where was the key? Did she leave the key in the ignition when she got out of the car? Even if she had left the key in the ignition, and the doors were locked, when she discovered that she could not unlock her mother's passenger side door, instead of telling her mother she was going to go get help, why didn't she say, "Mama, open the door"? She had said her mother was okay, only with a dazed look on her face, so why wasn't her mother able to open the car door from the inside? Her mother had not been trapped in the car. Davis had seen the car himself, and he knew there was no reason Freda Weeks could not have opened the car door herself. The car had not been damaged and there was nothing blocking either door.

And why would the car door lock when she closed it? What was the deal with that? And why, all of a sudden, did her mother have a dazed look on her face? What did that mean?

Davis wondered about Sheila attempting to take off the battery cable when the car would not turn off. *How many women would think of that?* he wondered. Most of the women he knew, including his wife he felt sure, couldn't tell a battery cable from a tree stump. They would just sit there and let the motor run until it gave out of gas or some man came along to help.

Although he had not corrected her, Davis knew that Sheila had made a wrong assumption. Taking the battery cable off would not have turned the car off. Because of the electronics in newer model cars, that was a valid assumption. But Sheila was driving an older model car, and the 1987 Mercury Cougar would not have immediately shut down if she had disconnected the cables.

But how do you reconcile, he wondered, *a woman adept enough to think to unhook the battery cable, who, at the same time, couldn't figure out how to get her mother out of the car? And why would the car motor not turn off anyway? Better yet,* Davis thought, *why didn't she just leave the car running? It had an air conditioner. Why wouldn't she leave the car running with the air conditioner on for her mother? She hadn't planned to be away from the car long. She had told her mother she would be right back. So, on such a hot day, why not leave the car running with the air on?*

And she had said she was talking to her mother, and had looked off. *Looked off at what?* Davis had to wonder. There wasn't anything on that stretch of road to look at except some trees and fields, which she must have seen a thousand times in her life.

And why did she bring up the subject of an explosion? Had she expected an explosion? Or worse, had she purposefully left the gas filler lid door open *planning* for there to be an explosion?

Davis knew that had also been a wrong assumption – maybe a *big*, wrong assumption on her part. Davis knew that cars exploding from open gas tanks was mostly television drama. Except on direct impact to the gas tank, cars rarely exploded.

And what did she mean when she said Danny Weeks had "made" her sit on the road while the car was burning? Her mother was in the car, down in the ditch, burning, and she was sitting on the road while Danny ran to get water, because he "made" her. What had the man done? How could he have made her sit there?

The more he thought about Sheila Bryan's story, the more troubled he became. Here was a woman who paid great attention to detail, as evidenced by the meticulousness of the home he had just seen, who, in a very short period of time, had forgotten to put the gas cap on the car, had forgotten to close the gas filler lid, had run off the road for no apparent reason, and had somehow gotten herself locked out of the car. Donald Davis had heard plenty of stories with holes in them, but this story had holes the size of the Grand Canyon.

As Davis and Bryan drove away from North Maple, and as they discussed the accident and Sheila Bryan, neither could have guessed where this case would take them. Nor could they have guessed that this visit, which had included Davis as a spur of the moment gesture of friendship, was later going to be viewed as an "interrogation" of a murder suspect.

Davis knew one thing. If Sheila Bryan had been officially considered a murder suspect that day, and if it had been an interrogation, he damn sure would have gotten a lot more answers to his questions.

When Donald Davis returned to his office at the CCSO, he broke the vow he had made to himself and talked to Robby Pitts about the case, telling Pitts about the two versions Sheila Bryan had given about what had happened the day of the accident. Like the straw that broke the camel's back, the latest conversation with Sheila Bryan moved Pitts to a decision: it was time to get the case moving. Pitts got on the phone and called Ronnie Dobbins in Adel. After talking with Dobbins, Pitts talked with the sheriff about calling in the GBI.

CHAPTER NINE

Wednesday, August 28, 1996

When John Heinen walked into a restaurant, people would stare at him and whisper to their dinner companions, "What's the GBI doing here?"

It wasn't that John Heinen was well known. At age twenty-nine, he was too young to have forged much of a reputation. It was just that John Heinen looked exactly like who he was: a GBI agent.

Maybe it was the black Crown Victoria with the tinted windows and two small radio antennas that gave him away. More likely it was everything about him – his persona. He had the clean cut, clean shaven, attractive, all-American-boy look found on cereal boxes. His light brown hair was short and perfectly trimmed. His white shirts were starched, and his dark colored suits usually had the GBI insignia pin on the lapel. In a pinch, a person could use his shoes for a mirror.

His demeanor was as no-nonsense as his questions were exacting and precise. Not so much as a hint of a smile creased his face. When he wanted information, which he often did, he would target the source of his inquiry like a bird dog eyeing a quail.

John Heinen was proud to be a GBI man and the GBI was proud of John Heinen. He was the pick of their litter.

Born in Greensboro, North Carolina, to Richard and Madonna Heinen, John Heinen was the youngest of six children. His family had moved to Atlanta when he was about six years old, and then when Heinen was in the fifth grade, his family had moved north to Gainesville, GA. The Heinen family settled in a home on Lake Lanier, complete with a dock and boat.

His father was a Talon zipper salesman, and with six children, there was little time or resources to waste. Richard Heinen provided the comfortable lifestyle for his family through hard work and long hours on the job, going above and beyond what was required of him – a trait that his youngest son observed and eventually emulated. Heinen's father traveled a great deal, worked on weekends and, when he was home, spent long hours in his home office.

After graduating at the top of his high school class, Heinen attended the University of Georgia in Athens as a business major. "Those classes were just so dry and so boring," Heinen would say later. He began filling up his class schedule with criminal justice electives. No one in his family had ever been in law enforcement, and Heinen did not consider the profession for himself, either.

But the criminal justice classes fascinated him, and after he had loaded so many of them onto his schedule, one of his academic advisors suggested that maybe he really ought to change majors. Heinen did change to a criminal justice major, all the while telling himself – and his father – that the coursework was just preliminary to attending law school.

In his senior year at UGA, as part of his graduation requirement, Heinen had to complete an internship with a criminal justice agency. He chose the Georgia Bureau of Investigation.

It was just one of those things. Like two strangers who glance at each other across a crowded room and fall instantly in love, their whole lives changed forever because of an inexplicable attraction, John Heinen fell in love with the GBI.

The internship that was supposed to last one quarter lasted longer for John Heinen because he couldn't bring himself to leave the place. He stayed right through Christmas holidays and then continued on through spring break. And all the while he was there, he was trying to figure a way to get into the agency so that he didn't have to ever leave again.

Heinen graduated Summa Cum Laude from the University of Georgia with a bachelor of arts degree in criminal justice in 1989.

Heinen knew the GBI did not like to hire applicants who were just out of school; they liked candidates who had some experience and some maturity to go with it. So, after Heinen graduated in 1989, he took a job with the Clarke County police department in Athens as a patrolman. A college town, Heinen thought it was a fun place to police.

After almost two years, Heinen decided it was time to make his move. Along with some four hundred other GBI wannabes, Heinen put in his application. It would be a long process, which began with a background check and a series of oral and written tests, followed by a polygraph test and interview after interview. Then there were psychological and medical examinations. Only the squeaky clean would pass the muster.

"I had my heart set on it," Heinen would say. "I don't know what I would have done if they hadn't picked me." But they did pick John Heinen in September of 1990. Of the four hundred applicants, there had been only a dozen who made it through the application process. The selection came just one week before Heinen was to report to the Georgia Public Safety Training Center in Forsyth where he would enroll in the GBI's sixteen-week training course. There were forty-four students enrolled in the class, most of them already GBI agents who were seeking promotion.

"You gotta really want it," Heinen would say, "because I knew going in this was going to be poverty pay." Starting salary for Special Agents today is still less than $30,000 a year.

The GBI basic training course was both physically and mentally demanding. Every aspect of law enforcement would be covered, from interviewing suspects, to crime scene procedures, to driving, to shooting. Classes were held in both the mornings and evenings, and physical training, much like the army's basic training, as well as the practical exercises, were held throughout the day. John Heinen loved it. In fact, he considered it fun.

Near graduation from the GBI training course, each agent opens an envelope that holds the name of his assigned location. The agent candidate opens the envelope in front of the entire class. When Heinen opened his envelope and read Thomas county, his classmates chuckled. Heinen was excited at first, but not for long. He had thought it was Thomson, near his old stomping grounds in Athens, but it was Thomasville and Thomas county. Heinen had no idea where that was; he would have to ask directions.

But the truth was, Heinen would have followed the GBI to Zimbabwe if that is what they wanted. He was proud to be a GBI Special Agent, so he packed his bags and headed for south Georgia.

Thomasville is the headquarters for region nine of the GBI, which covers the ten southernmost counties: Mitchell, Colquitt, Decatur, Grady, Thomas, Brooks, Lowndes, Echols, Seminole and Early. The eight agents working out of the Thomasville office were supervised by the Assistant Special Agent In Charge (ASAC), John White.

Heinen moved up the ranks quickly. After eighteen months in Thomasville, he was promoted to Special Agent Senior, and within another three years, he had been promoted to the top rank for field agents: Special Agent Principal (SAP).

The morning of August 28, 1996, Heinen had spent in Colquitt county working on a home invasion case in which an elderly couple in Moultrie had been beaten and robbed. Afterwards he had assisted GBI Crime Scene Specialist Ken Collins with the recovery of some human bones found in Moultrie. He was on his way to Thomasville to instruct at the shooting range when ASAC John White told him to return to Moultrie to meet with Robby Pitts.

It was almost 3 p.m. when Heinen sat down with CCSO Investigator Robby Pitts in Pitts' office. Heinen knew Pitts and most all of the other deputies and investigators with the CCSO. He had worked other cases with them, and when he wasn't working with them on a case, he made a point to stop in and find out what they were up to.

Heinen asked Pitts to brief him on the case and then looked over the accident report filed by Chris Gay.

"Did anybody get pictures of this?" Heinen wanted to know.

"Yeah," Pitts said, "Both Rodney Bryan and Chris Gay took photos."

"Did you get any statements from Sheila Bryan?"

"Donald Davis interviewed her at the scene and then he talked to her again yesterday."

"Let me read the statements." Heinen noted the discrepancies in the two statements taken nine days apart.

"Where's the car? Has anybody looked at it?" Heinen asked.

"The car's over at Blanton's and Ronnie Dobbins and Ralph Newell are looking it over."

"Who's Ralph Newell?"

"He's a fire investigator hired by Georgia Farm Bureau."

"He's not law enforcement?"

"No."

"What do Ronnie and this Mr. Newell think?"

"They think it looks suspicious. It appears that the fire started in the front, driver's side floorboard. There was no damage to the car other than the fire, but the fuel door was open and the gas cap was off."

"Let me see the autopsy report."

"There isn't one."

"What do you mean there isn't one?"

Pitts explained how it had come about that there had been no autopsy done on Freda Weeks and said she had already been buried at Weeks Chapel cemetery. Pitts could see that Heinen wasn't happy and he tried to make some amends. "We did do a blood draw for toxicology," Pitts said.

"So what's your next move?" Heinen wanted to know. The question was more a gesture than anything else, because everyone understood that as soon as Heinen showed up at the CCSO, he would be the lead investigator on the case. The ball had gone from Georgia State Trooper Chris Gay to CCSO Investigator Robby Pitts, and then to GBI SAP John Heinen. Once with Heinen, the ball would stay in his court for the duration, however long that took, and Heinen did not plan to drop any balls.

Investigator Donald Davis sat in his office smiling.

"Well, we got Newell and the fire marshal's folks here and we're ready to go over the car. That's why we called you," Pitts said.

"Hold up," Heinen said, seeing that things were moving a little too fast. "It might be all right for Dobbins and Newell to be out there looking at the car, but if this is a criminal investigation, you had better get a search warrant."

Pitts knew Heinen was right. Heinen called Ken Collins to come to Moultrie. If they were going to look at the car, Heinen wanted the GBI Crime Scene Specialist on board.

By 5 p.m., Heinen and Pitts had completed the information for the search warrant of the 1987 Mercury Cougar displaying Georgia tag TLT317. Both Dobbins and Newell's suspicions of arson were noted on the warrant, along with the discrepancies in the two statements obtained by Donald Davis.

By 5:30 p.m., they had the search warrant signed by the judge authorizing them to search the vehicle for any blood, incendiaries, accelerants, or evidence pertaining to the crimes of arson or murder.

It was going to be a long afternoon. The 1987 Mercury Cougar had a story to tell if someone knew how to speak the language. Ralph Newell and the state fire marshals knew how to speak the language of arson. Heinen and Collins and the CCSO investigators knew the language of murder. Maybe, between them, they could determine what had happened in the car just after noon some ten days before.

They were certain of one thing: if it was arson, it was murder.

CHAPTER TEN

Wednesday, August 28, 1996

Before the end of the day they would look like the dirty dozen. The twelve people gathered around the 1987 Mercury Cougar at Blanton's impound yard brought with them a lot of expertise and faced a dirty job: going through the car inch by inch.

Ronnie Dobbins and another state fire marshal, Keith Bell, were there. Paul MaGahee, the arson investigator with Georgia Farm Bureau was there, along with their private investigator, Ralph Newell. Fire Chief Gerald Psalmond and GSP Trooper Chris Gay had come for the inspection. And, of course, John Heinen and Ken Collins with the GBI were there. From the CCSO, Robby Pitts and other investigators were also present.

Investigator Donald Davis was there, although he had no official reason to be present. "Let's just say I was curious," he would explain.

This is the group of people who Karlas Bryan, Sheila's husband, would later refer to as "the junkyard gang."

Because Newell was the senior investigator, and because the other arson investigators respected his skills, Newell was the unofficial leader of the car inspection. Newell would photograph almost every piece of the Cougar they inspected.

However, because Ralph Newell was not in law enforcement, and because Heinen did not know him, Heinen was suspicious of Newell. For that reason, Heinen decided, he would watch Newell closely and would play devil's advocate.

The systematic inspection of the car began with an overall viewing of the outside of the vehicle. As was apparent to everyone present, there was no impact or accident damage to the car and no fire damage to the front of the car. The rubber spoiler and front bumper had no scratches or impact damage, as one would have expected if the car had been in a serious accident. All the tires were inflated and in good condition, and none of the hubcaps were missing. The burn patterns on the hood of the car showed that the fire had been in the passenger compartment and had moved outward.

Walking around the outside of the car, the investigators looked for any indication that the fire had come from underneath the car. Newell said that if it had originated underneath the car, the fire would have rolled out from underneath, up under the rocker panels and out to the side of the car. There was no indication of a fire originating underneath the car.

They looked at the gas tank area and made some of the same observations Psalmond had made the day of the fire. Newell told the other investigators that it was important to note that the oxidation, or burning, in the gas tank area had been above the open hole of the gas tank. Newell said this indicated the gas vapors came out of the gas tank, ignited, and burned, which was not unusual if the gas cap was not on. Dobbins explained that gas itself didn't burn; only the gas vapors actually burn.

"How can you be sure the gas cap didn't blow off?" Heinen wanted to know.

Newell patiently explained that as the heat started expanding the fuel, it could blow off the gas cap. But when the gas cap was blown off, the liquid gas would also rush out of the tank and you would see evidence of the gas coming out of the tank and down the side of the car, and there would be burn patterns below the gas cap. There was no such evidence of that on this car.

They moved to the roof of the car. The roof had sagged, which indicated to the investigators a very hot, intense fire with flames. The flames had made direct contact with the roof of the car, Newell said, causing the roof to actually sag and draw towards the fire. The part of the roof with the greatest sag was directly above the driver's seat and toward the passenger seat in the front, which Newell said meant that this was the area of greatest heat. Newell measured the sagged roof line at its deepest point, and it measured one and one quarter inches, which indicated to Newell that there had been a tremendous heat concentration from below.

Having inspected the outside of the car, the investigators had a wrecker come in and lift the car so they could get a good look at the underside of it. They checked the fuel lines and the exhaust system, including the catalytic converter. All the fuel lines were intact, and the catalytic converter evidenced no malfunction and appeared to be in pretty good shape. They checked the oil pan and transmission pan and the power steering hoses, the brake lines, and the transmission, coolant, and vapor lines. They checked the electrical wiring and electric fuel pump. They spent a considerable amount of time under the car but could not find anything that would cause a fire, or any evidence of fire damage or impact damage.

When they finished looking underneath the car, they moved to inspect the engine compartment. There was a small amount of radiant heat damage that had come though the bulkhead of the firewall, the part of the car that separates the engine compartment from the interior of the car where the passengers sit.

Dobbins explained that although people called it a firewall, it was not really a firewall, because fire could penetrate it. He pointed out the openings where the wires go through and said that where wires can go through, fire can go through. The wiring harness that went through the cowling of the bulkhead, where the firewall was located, was examined and appeared to be in good shape. Most of the hoses and all of the wires were still intact.

They looked at the battery and saw where the cables were still intact, as were the terminal posts; the battery did not appear to have been tampered with. They checked the fuel system, fuel line connections, wiring harness, heat producing devices and air conditioner dryer unit. They could find nothing amiss in the engine compartment that would have caused a fire. It still appeared that the fire had originated in the interior of the car and moved outward to the engine compartment area.

Next, they moved to inspect the trunk. The trunk was locked and since the investigators didn't have a key, they had to force the trunk open. When the lid opened, it provided their first surprise of several to come.

There was nothing in the trunk but the spare tire and jack on the left hand side. To the investigators, it looked like it had been cleaned and vacuumed out. They found the total lack of any object, other than the spare tire and jack, both odd and telling.

Dobbins pointed out that the trunk was located directly above the fuel tank, but there was virtually no heat damage inside the trunk.

When they had finished looking at the trunk, they went to the front of the car to look at the windshield area. The base of the windshield was still present and had sagged and melted inward. Newell said the windshield glass had fallen from the top of the roof line through to the inside of the car. This indicated to the investigators that the glass had popped out very quickly from the heat inside the car.

"How do you know it fell from the top and not the bottom?" Heinen wanted to know.

Dobbins explained that in an engine fire, or a fire in the engine compartment around the firewall, the windshield glass would separate first from the base of the windshield, where the wipers are located. In this fire, Newell said, the glass separated at the roof line, and showed Heinen what he was talking about.

Newell said because the windshield glass had separated the way it did, it indicated to him a fire that got very hot, very fast, inside the car. All of the windshield glass had fallen into the car, into the seats and the floorboard.

"When we get inside the car, we'll look at the windshield glass, and that will tell us something, too," Newell said.

Newell said the windshield glass was one of the most important indicators in a fire. The way the windshield glass broke out meant something to the fire investigators – it would indicate whether or not the fire had originated under the dashboard.

"How's that?" Heinen asked.

Newell said, "Just like in ignition switch fires, the fire comes out of the back of the dash and starts burning holes through the windshield, and the windshield will sag in irregular pieces, and not a constant piece and evenly across as with this windshield."

Getting ready to enter the car, they moved to the driver's side door and first inspected the window on the driver's side. They looked at the window track assembly and saw what Psalmond had seen the day of the accident: the window had been rolled down about six inches at the time of the fire. "If the window had not been rolled down," Newell explained, "all of the glass would have fallen inside the car." There was a portion of the window glass still attached to the top of the driver's door.

Newell pointed out that the Cougar had a keyless entry system, as well as a key lock assembly. The keyless entry was located just above the door handle in an elongated box.

Newell explained that on the Cougar, you would have a coded number, usually about three digits, which you could punch in to open the door without the keys. He explained the coded system required a small computer chip with a memory. It was electrically operated.

"You punch the right numbers, and it will either lock or unlock the car," he said.

"Without a key, right?" asked Heinen.

"Yup, without a key," Newell said.

In order to determine if the driver's side door had been locked, or unlocked, at the time of the fire, they had to look at the door track assembly. The track assembly is a sleeve with a rod in it. If the rod was in the up position, the door was unlocked. If the rod was in the down position, the door was locked. The rod in the Cougar was spring operated and was in the up position.

"Let me look at that," Heinen said. He wanted to see it with his own eyes. Sure enough, the driver's side door was unlocked. Davis wanted a close look, too.

"How can you be sure it was like this during the fire?" Heinen asked.

Newell explained that the fire causes the spring in the metal to lose its tension. "If its in the unlocked position, it can't move after that. Oxidation, which is just a fancy way to say rust, locks it into place. If it's locked, it can't unlock itself for the same reason."

Next, the investigators looked at the driver's door threshold and found a bigger surprise.

At the base of the A-pillar, at the front of the driver's door, on the threshold plate and rubber seal, there was an irregular burn pattern that ran across the aluminum strip, over to the floorboard area. Newell explained that with the door completely closed, as it had been when the firemen got to the car, this area would have been a protected area. The irregular burn pattern led from the door, across and up the console towards the passenger's seat.

Newell said the burn pattern indicated to him that prior to the fire, the door was open, then an ignitable fluid had been placed in the floorboard of the car, and when it was ignited, it had burned the rubber seal, and then the door was slammed shut. Newell explained that the rubber seal around the base and the top of the door serves as a protectant to keep the wind and rain out, and was both air tight and water tight.

"Nothing happens to the rubber seal during a fire if the door is closed," Newell said. Again, Heinen, and the CCSO investigators, wanted to take a long look at the threshold area.

Next they inspected the passenger's side door. They could not tell if the door had been locked or unlocked because of the damage done by the Hurst Tool when Freda Weeks had been extricated. They looked closely at the threshold of the passenger side door. There were no burn patterns on the rubber or plastic of the threshold. In fact, it was in excellent condition. "The door was closed on this side of the car when the fire started," Newell said.

Once they got to the inside front of the Mercury Cougar, they began by looking at the two front seats. Looking at the passenger seat, they noted that even though Freda Weeks' body was in the front passenger seat, hers was the seat back with the heaviest oxidation, or most burning. Newell pointed out that there was heavy oxidation on the front section of the driver's seat, moving toward the passenger side.

Looking at the back of the two front seats, again, the oxidation or burning was much more severe on the passenger seat where Freda Weeks had been located.

The passenger seat was tilted rearward, as if someone had been lying down or asleep.

Next, Newell looked very carefully at the windshield glass, which had fallen inside the car to the front floorboard and seats. The glass was not "sooted up," which told the investigators that the fire inside the car had not been a smoldering kind of fire. If it had been a smoldering fire, the glass would have had a lot of soot on it from the carbon buildup. But this had not been a slow, smoldering fire. The glass was clean. Newell told the investigators the windshield glass had popped out quickly and fallen inside the car and there had been no time for the soot to build up.

The arson investigators removed all of the debris from the passenger side of the car. They found only one personal effect: a change purse between the console and the front passenger seat.

Looking in the passenger seat, they noted that the seat belt had been fastened at the time of the fire. The male and female parts were still locked together, although the nylon webbing had been burned away.

Newell also found the remains of an adult diaper in the passenger seat. The diaper had been burned around the edges but the seat of the diaper was still intact.

What they found next gave them further pause.

They found a piece of terrycloth towel-type material lying across the console and onto the passenger seat. In fact, there was a large quantity of this material located in and around the passenger seat, as if it had been draped over Freda Weeks. Newell handed the remaining portions of the material to Heinen, to be examined at the GBI crime lab.

Next they examined the electric seats, in particular the wiring. Newell found no shorts in the wiring.

"Are you sure?" Heinen wanted to know. "How do you know that?"

Dobbins explained that if there had been shorts, they would have found some beading of the wiring. He told Heinen beads are small goblets of metal that form on the end of the wires. There were some wires that showed some sharp points, where the wires had been burned completely through, Dobbins said, but most of the time this was an indication that external heat had been applied to the wire.

"Look," he said to Heinen, "See these wires? Some of these still have the covering on them." The electric seat wiring was eliminated as the cause of the fire.

"What would you expect to find if the fire had started under the seats?" Heinen asked.

"If the fire had originated under the seats," Newell answered, "You wouldn't see these burn patterns. Fire burns upward and outward, and the car was sitting at an angle, with the tail end up. If the fire had started under the seats, all of the fire damage would have been in the back seat. But the fire damage is not in the back seat area, it is in the front floorboard area." The answer satisfied Heinen.

It was time to take a close look at the front floorboard area, but first all the debris had to be cleared out. The steering wheel column had fallen into the floorboard. The steering wheel itself had collapsed, along with part of the steering column, which held the key lock assembly. All of this was lying in the floorboard and had to be removed in order to see the carpet and padding.

While they had the key lock assembly out of the car, they looked it over as well. Newell explained the ignition switch on Ford vehicles and showed Heinen where the key portal was located. The key portal is a round, metal ring that the key slides into. There was no key in the key portal.

The investigators began a search for the key. They looked over every square inch of the front floorboard and in the debris that came out of the floorboard. There was no key.

"Maybe the key burned up in the fire," Heinen suggested.

Newell said, "In all of my career, I have never seen a Ford key melt. There was no key in this car at the time of the fire." Newell also said that in the Cougar, the transmission had to be in Park to remove the key.

Newell explained to Heinen that, typically, the car key was on a ring with a lot of other keys: house, other vehicles, shop, office, etc. If the key had been in the car anywhere, they would have found it, he was certain.

All eyes were on the carpet and padding in front of the driver's seat. Newell pointed to the weaving, irregular burn patterns, indicating to him that some type of ignitable fluid had been placed on it.

"Explain that to me," Heinen said.

Newell explained that carpet is normally self-extinguishing and very hard to ignite because it has a fire retardant chemical applied to it when the car is made. This car had a floor mat, carpet, and padding, and they had all been treated with a fire retardant. Normally, Newell said, carpet burns across, not down. He showed Heinen where the fire had burned down into the carpet and padding, all the way through the bottom layer of padding to the metal floorboard.

"If the fire had been from anything other than an accelerant, it would have burned across, not down," Newell said. "Besides," he added, "You don't find this same burn pattern on the passenger side floorboard, and it is the same material."

Newell showed Heinen where the fire had burned from the driver's side floorboard across to the passenger side. He explained that the console area is also carpeted, with the console placed down over the carpet. "The hottest area of the fire was the floorboard, across the console, to the passenger seat," he said.

Next, they looked at the dashboard wiring, which took a while. They found most of the wiring still intact. The major portion of the wiring still had the plastic wire covering and the damage to the wires appeared to be external. There had been a lot of direct fire to the dash assembly, but most of the wire had been protected under the dash area. There was nothing there to cause a fire.

"What about a cigarette?" Heinen asked. "Could that have started a fire?"

They took the ashtray out and examined it closely. There were no cigarette butts in the ashtray.

"But wouldn't the butts have been burned up in the fire?" Heinen persisted.

"If there had been cigarettes butts, they would still have been recognizable, because butts generally don't burn," Newell said. They inspected the cigarette lighter which was still intact, and it showed no evidence of malfunction or shorting.

Next they looked at the glove compartment. Like the trunk, there was nothing at all in the glove compartment. "This is very unusual," Newell said.

"Why?" Heinen asked.

"Because most people keep the car manual, insurance information, and other stuff in there. Even after a fire, most manuals are still there."

"They are paper – wouldn't they burn up in the fire?" Heinen asked.

"They're like a phone book," Newell said. "It's so thick air can't get between the pages."

Dobbins said he had been to several houses and vehicle fires where they found books. "The house or the vehicle would be totally destroyed," he said, "but we were able to find the manuals and things like that. They were compacted together and the air couldn't get to them."

Newell said that even if the manual had burned, they would have found some residue of it, and there was none.

They only had the back seat area left to examine. It was getting late in the day, and they were all glad they were coming to the end of the inspection. The car had held a lot of information – and surprises. But the biggest surprise of all was in the back seat.

While cleaning out the debris from the back seat area, in the floorboard directly behind the driver's seat, they found the remains of a claw hammer.

"Hold it right there," Heinen said.

CHAPTER ELEVEN

Wednesday, August 28, 1996

Dr. Anthony Clark had not been the least bit amused with what Coroner Rodney Bryan had told him two days earlier when he had returned from vacation.

Clark decided that was the problem with going on vacation – when you got back, everything was so backed up and screwed up, you wished you'd never gone to start with. He usually took his vacation the first two weeks in August, but this year he had been delayed, so he had not returned until Monday, August 26. That was the first time he heard about the Freda Weeks case.

He had enjoyed his vacation with his family in Connecticut. Clark's parents and all of his wife's family lived in Connecticut, and he always looked forward to spending time with them and catching up on family news. But all of the good times were washed away when he returned to his desk at the GBI crime lab. Although it was true that his office always looked a little jumbled, after a vacation, the mounds of paper on his desk were stacked ever higher.

And he had some "customers" waiting. That's what the ladies in the front office called them. He called them "stinkers." As the medical examiner for twenty-seven counties in southwest Georgia, Clark usually handled about 350 autopsies a year, or about one a day. The cooler could only hold three bodies, and so he couldn't fall too far behind without a problem developing pretty quickly. Normally keeping up wasn't a problem, but after a disaster, like a tornado, or when he had been away from the office for any length of time, things could get out of hand.

He was still playing catch-up when Rodney Bryan came to talk to him about Freda Weeks. Clark knew if he had not been on vacation, he would have done an autopsy on Freda Weeks. But that was what might have been. He had been on vacation, and the autopsy had not been done, and there were red flags on the case popping up everywhere.

It had been a bad call on the autopsy, and it didn't matter at this point who was responsible. The fact was, there were some big problems, and Clark only knew one way to correct the situation: exhume Freda Weeks and do the autopsy. Clark tried very hard not to get himself in a situation like this. It was upsetting to families to have the graves of their loved ones disturbed, and he always hated having to put them through the additional trauma.

As the medical examiner, he had a lot of concerns about the Freda Weeks case. His main concern was the results of the toxicology reports.

The blood had been drawn from Freda Weeks' body at Colquitt Regional Medical Center on August 18, the day she died. The hospital had a quick turnaround on their lab results, and he sometimes used the hospital's lab when he needed "a quick one." Coroner Bryan had received the results of the toxicology test the following day, Monday the 19th.

Coroner Rodney Bryan could not believe the results of the toxicology report. The report said Freda Weeks had no carbon monoxide in her body. None, as in zero, zip.

All fire victims had carbon monoxide in their bodies. Carbon monoxide was a by-product of a fire and fire victims breathed it in. There was no doubt in Rodney Bryan's mind that Freda Weeks was a fire victim. Hell, she had been a crispy critter. He had seen that with his own eyes.

Bryan decided the lab at the hospital had made a mistake. He went to the hospital and retrieved the vial of Freda Weeks' blood and took it to the crime lab to be tested there. He was sure the GBI crime lab staff would get the problem straightened out. The crime lab's result was the same as the hospital's: there was no carbon monoxide in Freda Weeks' blood.

This was the problem Coroner Rodney Bryan presented to ME Anthony Clark when Clark returned from Connecticut. Clark and Bryan's first and overriding concern was, if Freda Weeks didn't die from the fire, what did she die from? They both knew that if you had no cause of death, you couldn't have a manner of death. And now they had no idea at all how Freda Weeks had died, and she was already buried.

Clark knew that most fire victims he saw, and he saw a lot of them, would have a carbon monoxide reading of between 50% and 86% in their bodies. His rule of thumb was, if the carbon monoxide level was 20% or less, he would start looking for other causes of death. Cigarette smokers could have as much as 10% carbon monoxide levels in their body just from smoking, and cigar smokers might have more.

In older people like Freda Weeks, it could get a little trickier. Depending on what her medical condition was, a level of 22 to 23% might cause her death, and maybe as little as 15%, if she had a bad heart. But Freda Weeks didn't have any carbon monoxide, so it was all a moot point.

Beyond the concern about the carbon monoxide levels, Clark was concerned about the identification of the body. They didn't have any DNA, and Coroner Bryan had based the identification of the body on Sheila Bryan's statements. But the fire had been suspicious, and the State Fire Marshal's Office had been called in, along with the insurance company investigators. They only had Sheila Bryan's word that this was the body of Freda Weeks.

Clark was well aware that arson was sometimes used to cover the tracks of murder. He had seen enough cases where the victim had been stabbed or shot to death, and then the body burned to destroy any evidence of the crime. Forensic science was way ahead of that game, but criminals didn't always know that.

Without an autopsy on Freda Weeks' body they were nowhere, which was a bad place to be when a case was being investigated. Clark had told Bryan he'd better get to Omega and talk to Sheila Bryan and see what he could find out about Freda Weeks' medical condition. They would get that information and see where to go from there.

Bryan had come back and told him he had not been able to get much information from Sheila Bryan, at least not the information they needed to get this mess straightened out. It had been a long shot, anyway. Clark told Bryan he had better call over to the sheriff's office and let them know the situation that had developed with Freda Weeks.

GBI Agent John Heinen had no idea what was taking place a couple of miles west of him at the GBI crime lab. And it was just as well. He was knee deep in a murder case, and one more complication at that point was not what he needed.

He had known he had a murder case on his hands as soon as the investigators looked at the front floorboard and made the final determination: the fire was incendiary, meaning it had been purposefully set by someone.

Although he had been skeptical of Ralph Newell going into the inspection of the Mercury Cougar, Newell had impressed Heinen with his vast knowledge of both vehicles and arson. Heinen had asked Newell an untold number of questions as they went through the car, and Newell had answered each and every one of Heinen's questions in great detail and to Heinen's satisfaction. More than that, Newell had taken the time to carefully show Heinen what he was talking about. Everything Newell had told Heinen was reasonable from a common sense approach, as well as from the fire investigation training Heinen had received.

Newell would submit a written report of the investigation of the 1987 Mercury Cougar to the Georgia Farm Bureau Insurance Company and to the State Fire Marshal's Office. Heinen would wait for the written report and Newell's official conclusions.

But it had been more than just Ralph Newell's word that Heinen had to rely on. Not one, but two state fire marshals had come to the same conclusion as Newell. Neither Dobbins nor Bell had any doubt that the fire had been intentionally set. The three arson investigators stood together in total agreement. And then, of course, there was Fire Chief Gerald Psalmond, who also agreed with the findings. Four experts in the field of arson investigation had said the fire was incendiary. That was good enough for Heinen.

But the claw hammer had thrown all of them. It had been completely unexpected, and everyone had stopped dead in their tracks as soon as they saw it.

This car had been cleaned out. Nothing in the trunk, nothing in the glove compartment, and only a change purse inside the car. The investigators all knew that often enough arsonists cleaned out the cars or houses they burned before striking the match. It was a foolish thing to do, but the arsonists, who couldn't bear losing sentimental things or other objects they viewed as valuable, would remove them from the crime scene before committing the crime. Cleaning out cars or houses was just one of the things that arson investigators looked for at a crime scene. It was just another indicator that a crime had been committed.

So now, they had this Mercury Cougar that had been cleaned out, but there was a claw hammer left in the back floorboard. No one could help the sinister thoughts that came to mind. Had Sheila Bryan hit her mother in the head and knocked her unconscious before setting the fire? It certainly had to be considered as a possibility in light of the fact that her mother had not gotten out of the car of her own volition when the fire started.

Even though the inspection of the car proved that Sheila Bryan had lied about the car doors being locked, there still was no explanation for why her mother didn't exit the car of her own accord. The claw hammer might be the answer to the riddle.

In John Heinen's mind, there had never been a question about the fact that an autopsy needed to be done on Freda Weeks. Earlier in the afternoon, when he had heard from Robby Pitts that no autopsy had been performed, Heinen knew that if the investigation of the car proved to be arson, he would ask for an autopsy. He would have done that even if they hadn't found the claw hammer.

Heinen was the kind of person who lined up the pencils on his desk in neat little rows and had the clothes in his closet hung by color. He was compulsive about doing things the right way. And in a criminal case, the right way was to have an autopsy of the victim. It was as simple as that to John Heinen. The discovery of the claw hammer, which he had turned over to Robby Pitts to be placed in the evidence locker at the CCSO, was just one more reason to ask for the autopsy. But that would come later. At the moment, Heinen had some other fish to fry.

Where was the key to the car and where was the gas cap?

Both Donald Davis and Chris Gay had talked with Sheila the day of the staged accident. Neither one of them recalled Sheila having a purse with her. Where was her purse? If she didn't have her purse with her when she got out of the car, shouldn't it have been in the car? Or was the change purse they had found in the car what she had taken for a purse that day? The only thing in the change purse was a few coins. But Chris Gay said that Sheila had produced her driver's license and her insurance card. No one could recall if the outfit Sheila was wearing had pockets.

The car key was missing. The gas cap was missing. And, if an accelerant had been used, where was the container for the accelerant? Assuming the accelerant had been put in the car right before the fire was set and Danny Weeks had shown up, where had Sheila put the container? It had to be somewhere.

What had been the accident scene was now a crime scene and John Heinen knew he had to go there right away. Psalmond had told him about the search for the gas cap on August 18, but Heinen knew he had to go and look for himself. It was getting late, and Heinen wanted to search the area before it got dark.

Accompanied by the criminal and arson investigators, Heinen went to Livingston Bridge Road. There was nothing there to indicate that an accident had happened or that a crime had ever been committed, nothing to mark the place of Freda Weeks' death.

The investigators made a diligent search and found nothing.

Heinen reasoned that if Sheila had accidentally left the gas cap off, perhaps it was at the gas station in Omega where she said she had filled up with gas. He would have to find out. As for the key, maybe she had put it in her pocket or in her sock or in her shoe. But the fact that he could not find the container for the accelerant led Heinen to wonder if Sheila had done this alone, or perhaps if someone else had been involved and had helped her. Maybe that person had carried off the accelerant container and possibly the gas cap and car key. Heinen was sure now that none of those objects were at the crime scene or in the car.

After the search, Heinen headed back to Thomasville. It had been a very long day. It had started with the robbery of the elderly couple in Moultrie and ended with the search on Livingston Bridge Road. Heinen would not learn about the results of the toxicology report until the next day.

CHAPTER TWELVE

Thursday – Tuesday, August 29 – September 3, 1996

When Heinen caught the Sheila Bryan murder case, it wasn't like he didn't have anything else to do. The truth was, he had a full plate before the case came along.

He stayed at his desk in his Thomasville office all day Thursday, the 29th. Meticulous about his documentation, Heinen had to begin a file on the Sheila Bryan case and document what had happened to date. But he also was facing a theft trial and had to prepare for it.

Friday, the 30th had not gotten off to the best start. In the wee hours of the morning, he had been called out to investigate an armed robbery at a convenience store. Heinen worked that case from 2 a.m. until 4 a.m., and then at 9 a.m., he met with GBI Director Milton Nix.

It was an important meeting.

Heinen was planning to take a leave of absence from work to attend Harvard University. The idea had started innocently enough, born more out of idleness than farsightedness. Heinen had been in Valdosta, waiting for the jury to return in another case, and had passed the time reading the *Criminal Justice Newsletter* from the University of Georgia. He read where the Department of Justice had a scholarship available for a criminal justice employee to attend Harvard. It had made Heinen laugh to think of a south Georgia boy like him going to an ivy league school.

Although he had thought it was an unlikely chance he would be chosen, he nevertheless made some calls and started the long process of admission, which included writing numerous essays. The cost to attend graduate school at Harvard ran about $40,000, and even with the scholarship, Heinen would have to round up additional grants and scholarships in order to afford to attend the school.

But Heinen had seen it as a once in a lifetime opportunity, and he had not wanted to miss out. He had always thought that he would get his master's degree, so that when he one day got tired of "chasing the bad guys," he would have a degree which would allow him to pursue other avenues, possibly teaching. He planned to get a degree in management, and he didn't think a degree from Harvard in Public Administration would hurt his career with the GBI.

When he was offered the DOJ scholarship and was accepted to Harvard, Heinen had thought hard about it before he had committed himself. It would mean eating a lot of peanut butter and jelly sandwiches, working a part-time job, and making up the rest of the costs with loans that would take him years to pay off.

It was a year-long program and he was scheduled to begin classes in June of 1997, only nine months away. He was in the middle of some cases, including the Sheila Bryan case. He would have to get as much done on the case as his schedule would permit before he left for Harvard.

It wasn't until after lunch on Friday the 30th that Heinen had been able to return to Moultrie and the Sheila Bryan case. He went over to tie up some loose ends and to do some general nosing around. The following Tuesday, after lunch, Heinen worked on getting the paperwork done for the exhumation of Freda Weeks.

In late afternoon, Heinen and Pitts went to Tifton to meet with Jim Albritton, co-owner of Albritton-Jones Funeral Home, the one responsible for the services and burial of Freda Weeks. It was a brief meeting. Jim Albritton explained that Freda Weeks had been buried at Weeks Chapel cemetery in Colquitt County, a small, country cemetery located next to the church. Albritton told Heinen and Pitts that he would assist in any way possible with the exhumation and would point out the exact grave where Freda Weeks was buried.

The exhumation would require a court order from the Superior Court of Colquitt County and would have to be signed by Superior Court Judge Frank Horkan.

Heinen met with Assistant District Attorney Charles Stines in Moultrie to prepare the petition for the disinterment of the body. The petition would be submitted on behalf of the Colquitt County Coroner, Rodney Bryan, and would state the reasons the exhumation was required. Judge Horkan signed it that afternoon.

Although the investigators had originally thought they would have Albritton-Jones handle the exhumation, they changed their minds and went with Cobb Funeral Home in Moultrie. The funeral home would also have to have a permit signed by the Georgia Department of Human Resources.

By late afternoon, Heinen and Pitts had all their ducks in a row and were ready for the exhumation to take place on Thursday morning. He was so preoccupied with paperwork and procedures, it had not crossed Heinen's mind that the court petition for the exhumation would be filed with the Clerk of Court in Moultrie, and that soon enough, a reporter with the *Moultrie Observer* would check all papers filed at the clerk's office, and that the reporter would consider the exhumation of Freda Weeks a big story.

For Colquitt County, it was a big story. Exhumations were a rare occurrence, and the reason for the disinternment – "foul play" – only made it sound all the more interesting.

The *Moultrie Observer* had already run an article headlined, "Car Wreck, Fire Kills Woman; Accident Happens Close to Crosland." In the article, written by Charles Shiver, which was run on Monday, August 19, Shiver had quoted Coroner Rodney Bryan and Colquitt County Volunteer Fire Coordinator Gerald Psalmond. The basic information of the accident had been reported and Psalmond was quoted as saying, "The fire's cause has not yet been determined." That same day, the *Tifton Gazette* had carried a briefer article about the accident, and had also quoted Coroner Rodney Bryan, as well as a Georgia State Patrol official.

The court papers filed on the exhumation were the first indication to the local press that an investigation into the death of Freda Weeks on Livingston Bridge Road was underway, and that law enforcement was looking at the incident as more than an accident.

By Wednesday afternoon, the word was out. By Thursday, the day of the exhumation, print and electronic media were fully engaged in the story. Jim Albritton would say of the exhumation, "It looked like a three ring circus out there. I have never seen so many reporters and television cameras in my life." The local media coverage at the exhumation was only a hint of what was to come.

CHAPTER THIRTEEN

Wednesday, September 4, 1996

It was the right thing to do. John Heinen would make a courtesy call to the home of Sheila Bryan and tell Sheila that they were going to have to exhume her mother's body and do an autopsy.

But other than the fact that it had been the right thing to do, Heinen wanted to get a look at this woman he now considered a suspect in a murder investigation. It was one thing to have a name, and quite another to have a face to go with the name. It helped him to have the picture of the suspect's face in his mind as he worked the case.

Was she tall? Short? Fat? Skinny? Did she look her age? Did she look older? Younger? Was she attractive? Unattractive? None of those things mattered as far as the investigation was concerned, although if she became a defendant in a murder case rather than a suspect, all those things would be taken into account by the attorneys on both sides of the case. What went on at a trial was quite different from what went on in an investigation, and Heinen knew that all too well. As the suspect in a murder case he was investigating, Sheila Bryan was Heinen's adversary. And it was always good to be able to size up your adversary.

In the smarts department, it didn't look like Sheila was hitting any home runs. She had told too many versions of what had happened on August 18, 1996. She had clearly lied about the car doors being locked. She had left a claw hammer in the back floorboard. And there were probably another dozen things she had done that day that had made the accident suspicious.

More than anything else though, Heinen was curious to see a woman who was suspected of killing her mother. That kind of woman was a rare breed, and he figured he might only see one of them in his entire career.

It was almost 5 p.m. when Heinen and Robby Pitts pulled up to the house on Maple Street in Omega. Heinen had called ahead and told Sheila that he was coming up to see her. He had not told her why he was coming, just that she could expect him in the next few minutes.

When they pulled up to the house, Sheila and her husband, Karlas, were standing in the driveway waiting on them. Heinen and Pitts got out of the car and walked over to where Sheila and Karlas were standing. As soon as the investigators approached the couple, Sheila and Karlas started waving their hands and saying that they were not going to answer any questions, and they had a lawyer, Craig Webster, and not to bother to even try to ask questions.

Heinen told them that he had not come to ask them questions. He told them he had come because he wanted them to know that Freda Weeks' death was being investigated by the CCSO and the GBI, and that Freda Weeks' body was going to have to be exhumed and have an autopsy performed. He said he was simply making a courtesy call to let them know the situation.

The Bryans' reaction to the information about the investigation and exhumation shocked both Heinen and Pitts.

Karlas was clearly mad, and he appeared to Heinen and Pitts to be intoxicated. Karlas said in a loud, angry voice, **"Just do whatever the hell it is you gotta do and get on with it. We've got $100,000 riding on this. The insurance company isn't going to pay out until the investigation is over. So get it over!"**

Sheila started to cry, but appeared to agree with Karlas. Heinen thought she definitely looked more mad than sad.

With their mission having been explained, Heinen and Pitts got back in the car and left. As soon as they got in the car, they looked at each other and said simultaneously, "What $100,000?"

Heinen was not far enough along in the investigation to concern himself with motive, but now, strange as it was, the suspect and her husband had handed him the motive on the proverbial silver platter.

In the smarts department, Sheila and Karlas Bryan had just struck out. Telling a GBI Agent and a CCSO Investigator that you had $100,000 riding on someone's death was about as stupid as it got. Nevertheless, that is what had just happened. Heinen and Pitts couldn't get over it.

Heinen, who would never forget Karlas' words that day, knew he was going to be doing some talking to the insurance companies.

Why had she gotten a lawyer? It had only been a little over two weeks since Freda Weeks' death, and Sheila Bryan already had a lawyer. But until that very moment, Sheila had not known that there would be a criminal investigation. Heinen suspected Sheila's lawyer had been hired to collect the insurance money. He doubted she had hired a criminal attorney to represent her before she was sure there was going to be a criminal investigation. Well, that cat was out of the bag now.

The presence of an attorney in the case so early on presented a new wrinkle. Even if the attorney was not a criminal attorney, Heinen knew his chances of asking Sheila all the questions backlogged in his mind were not likely. Still, he knew he would try.

For the first time Heinen had to think about Sheila's husband. Karlas had made it clear he was a player in this. Until just that moment, Heinen had not given Sheila's husband a lot of thought. Karlas certainly had acted like he was the one calling the shots. And Sheila hadn't said or done anything to change that impression. Heinen decided he wanted to know more about Karlas, but that would have to wait a little while. He had the autopsy and a few other things in line ahead of that. One of those things was to find out about the $100,000. And if money was the motive in the case, Heinen needed to know more about the Bryans' financial situation.

They appeared to be living the middle class lifestyle. The house appeared to Heinen to be as nice as or nicer than any of the houses on the street. Maybe they were some of those people who tried to keep up with the Joneses and ran up credit card debt. Heinen had no idea what the situation was, but he intended to find out.

As far as what Sheila looked like, Heinen had almost forgotten his curiosity after the statement from Karlas. She had struck him as short and average looking. Maybe a little hefty. Truly, there was nothing exceptional in her appearance one way or another. She looked like any of the hundreds of women he passed on any given day of the year. But he had a face to go with the name now, and that helped.

The exhumation and autopsy of Freda Weeks was scheduled for the next day. The next thing Heinen needed to do was find out what had caused the death of Freda Weeks.

CHAPTER FOURTEEN

Thursday, September 5, 1996

The Georgia Bureau of Investigation operates six crime labs located across the state of Georgia in Atlanta, Augusta, Columbus, Macon, Savannah and Moultrie.

The crime lab in Moultrie, which is officially named the Southwest Regional Crime Laboratory of the GBI's Division of Forensic Sciences (DOFS), was built in 1994. It could pass for just another red brick office building if it weren't for the dozen stainless steel exhaust stacks on the roof: six exhaust stacks on the north side and six on the south side. There is something a bit sinister looking about the exhaust stacks, and it is these metal protrusions on the roof that tips a person off that this building is not your typical office building.

It is not a particularly large building to house office space, laboratories and a morgue. The morgue, where the autopsies are performed, is a relatively small area, long and narrow, measuring approximately 20 by 12 feet. The room is actually T-shaped, but the leg of the T is quite small. It accommodates the area where the X-rays are read.

Within this small space is housed all of the necessary paraphernalia and equipment needed to investigate the bodies of people who have departed this life for a variety of reasons. The room is kept quite cool, about 50 degrees, and is brightly lit.

Dr. Clark, who runs the lab, says he does not worry as much about AIDS as he does Hepatitis, and works with three pairs of gloves on his hands. He wears the paper gown but does not wear the mask most medical examiners use. The main purpose of the mask is to help with the wretching smell that fills the room when a body is being worked on. According to Dr. Clark, Vicks VapoRub is generally put in the mask to help cover the body odors, but he does not like the smell of Vicks and has become accustomed to the smells of the bodies. He works with a handheld cassette recorder into which he dictates his findings.

In 1996, Dr. Clark had been working as a medical examiner for six years and had been at the crime lab since it opened. A trim, dark-haired man of thirty-eight with friendly features and manner, Dr. Clark had been the first regional medical examiner for the GBI. Later, the GBI would add another regional ME in northwest Georgia.

Dr. Clark had become interested in forensic science from watching the television show "Quincy" when he was a boy. In high school, one of his teachers had been a mentor to him in the anatomy classes. He was good in math and science, and he had enjoyed the subject matter. He had originally thought he would become an engineer, working in hospitals, but eventually he had gone to medical school. When his plans to practice general surgery had not worked out, he returned to his old interest in pathology.

He liked his job, especially the interaction with law enforcement and the opportunity to go to court and present evidence. He was especially proud that he could talk to the jury without using "doctor words" and could get them to understand the information. He looked at it as teaching the jury. Another thing Dr. Clark prided himself on was his objectivity.

The morgue had been quite crowded on the day of Freda Weeks' autopsy. In addition to Dr. Clark and his two assistants, there were six other people in the room: Coroner Rodney Bryan; Hal Suber and Robby Pitts, with the CCSO; and John Heinen, Ken Collins and John White with the GBI. John White would videotape the autopsy proceedings for the GBI.

Dr. Clark welcomed the presence of law enforcement at his autopsies. He felt the exchange of information was helpful, both for him and for the law enforcement personnel. Many times law enforcement was able to give him information about what had happened to the victim, which helped him to interpret some of his findings. It was not unusual for law enforcement to bring photographs of the crime scene to the autopsy to help clarify information for Dr. Clark. And by the same token, Dr. Clark was able to answer questions regarding his findings for law enforcement as he moved through the autopsy procedure.

Typically, a full autopsy, such as the one to be performed on Freda Weeks, took approximately two to three hours to complete. It was not a pleasant two to three hours, and Dr. Clark recognized that most people, even those in law enforcement, could not always handle the sights and smells of the autopsy procedure. Therefore, he had made an informal rule: Anyone who made it through the first half hour was listed on his report as having been present during the autopsy.

The procedure was certainly gruesome and typically began with an external examination and then the opening of the chest area, the abdomen, and the head, followed by the neck. Other areas of the body would also be opened, depending on the circumstances of the person's death. Dr. Clark recognized the sensitivity of the families involved with the victim, who most of the time would still have to get through funeral ceremonies. He said he tried his best to leave the hands, neck and face intact, as those were the areas of the body shown during open casket funerals. That, of course, would not be a concern with Freda Weeks.

The crowd had begun gathering at Weeks Chapel Cemetery on Cool Springs Road before 9 a.m. Although the crowd numbered almost one hundred people, only seventeen were there on official business. The rest were civilian onlookers, family members or media.

Sheila and Karlas Bryan were not present for the exhumation of Sheila's mother. After learning of the exhumation from Heinen the day before, Sheila had called Jim Albritton and asked him if he would be sure and attend the exhumation and see that everything was handled properly. Albritton had assured Sheila that he would carry out her request.

Once the casket containing Freda Weeks' remains had been unearthed, it had been placed in the back of a GBI van and transported to the crime lab in Moultrie. The reporters had their copy, and the television crews had their footage. After the 6 p.m. evening news, most everyone in south Georgia was wondering why the CCSO and GBI were digging up that poor little old woman's grave. They figured something must be terribly, terribly wrong to go and dig her up like that.

The body of Freda Weeks, encased in the casket, arrived at the crime lab at 11:20 a.m., via GBI van number 635. The body was photographed in the casket, to record the state of its arrival at the morgue, and then placed on one of the stainless steel tables and weighed on the in-ground scales. Finally, the body was placed in the cooler, where it remained until 1 p.m., when Dr. Clark began the autopsy procedure with the law enforcement personnel present.

While one of his assistants photographed Freda Weeks' body, Dr. Clark began his procedure with a general narrative, which he dictated into his microcassette tape recorder:

This is an 82-year-old white female who reportedly died in a car fire several weeks ago. No examination was done at that time, though blood was drawn. The blood carbon monoxide level was negative. The arson investigators determined the fire started in the passenger compartment and not from the engine and/or catalytic converter. Because the cause of death is undetermined and the vehicle fire is of a suspicious nature, an exhumation was performed today.

Prior to beginning the external examination of the body, Dr. Clark took and read X-rays and dictated that the heat of the fire had caused the broken bones of Freda Weeks' left femur and anterior chest wall. These bones had broken into many small pieces, like a jigsaw puzzle. He also identified a "foreign body" in the area of her left hip.

As Dr. Clark began the external examination of Freda Weeks' body, he dictated:

The decedent is removed from the secured ground casket and the remains are contained within a black disaster bag. Accompanying the body are the following articles: an unopened package of pantyhose, an unopened pair of stockings, pink panties, and a pink dress. Numerous brown plastic bags lie over the body.

Dr. Clark explained to the men gathered around the table that the extra bags were put there by the funeral home staff to help contain the body odor. The body had not been embalmed because it had been burned too badly. The items of clothing inside the casket were obviously brought by the family to dress Freda Weeks. But again, because the body was so badly burned, it was not possible to dress her, so the funeral home staff had simply placed the clothing in the casket with her.

Dr. Clark continued his examination and dictation:

The body has been sprinkled with formalin powder, and the powder has been distributed over the surface of the body bag. Thick socks of indeterminate color are encasing the ankles and feet and have been heavily charred.

The socks were the only remnant of clothing on the body. Although the socks were burned, they were recognizable. Her toenails were painted with red-pink nail polish.

Dr. Clark continued to describe the white female as measuring 58 inches in length and weighing 78 pounds. Less than five feet tall, Freda Weeks had lost at least half of her body weight during the fire, possibly more. Having suffered what Dr. Clark called "thermal amputation" of her limbs, the body of Freda Weeks had been well on its way to being cremated in the fire.

The average size body can be reduced to ashes, cremated, when placed in a 1500-degree Fahrenheit oven for one to one-and-one-half hours. Dr. Clark estimated that in a small confined area such as a car, with an intense fire, it would have taken less than twenty minutes to cause the severe burning evidenced by Freda Weeks' body.

Dr. Clark described Freda Weeks' face as being "heavily charred." The eye orbits, nasal bones, and upper and lower jaw had been burned to destruction. He dictated that "the flesh is essentially gone from the entire head." Of course all of her hair had been burned away. Clark documented she did not have her natural teeth and was not wearing dentures.

The rest of the body had not fared much better. He continued:

...the anterior chest wall, the breasts and thoracic cage have been charred off with exposure of the underlying lungs and heart. A triangular portion of skin is identified in the anterior upper abdominal wall. Otherwise, the rest of the abdominal wall is charred away, exposing the underlying abdominal cavity.

The body was not as badly burned on the back, buttocks, and back of the thighs because she was seated and the flames could not get to these areas as readily. The genitalia were badly burned and, in some areas, burned away.

Dr. Clark dictated that "the soft tissues lying between the thighs and upper portions of the shins have been completely charred down to the bone." Only the feet and top portions of the shins, closest to the feet, were spared from burning. "The arms are heavily charred, with fractures of the left radius and humerus and heavy destruction of the musculature," he said. The right hand was in what Dr. Clark referred to as "the classic pugilistic posture," meaning that the hand was balled in a fist, the wrist flexed with elbows bent, and the upper arm raised.

In regards to any other injury to the body, Dr. Clark dictated that "in general, the remains display severe thermal injuries, but no obvious sharp or blunt force injuries or gunshot wounds. The fractures of the long bones are associated with heat injuries."

Dr. Clark then began the internal examination of the body by making a Y-shaped incision in the chest area.

He described the body cavity as having been "violated by the intense heat." The underlying body organs were "cooked," but not charred. The stomach and the right ovary had been burned away completely.

Dr. Clark then took the heart out of the body and weighed it. He examined the heart in some detail and found evidence of severe "atherosclerotic disease." The left main coronary artery exhibited an 80% to 90% blockage. The left anterior descending coronary artery had a 95% to 100% blockage. The other arteries appeared to have only minor evidence of disease. He noted that "clotted blood was contained throughout the aorta, and its branches and veins and the surface of the heart is stained with blood."

Dr. Clark then removed and examined other body organs. The right and left lungs were burned. He dictated, "Only a small amount of soot is distributed within the upper airways and extends slightly into the left main bronchus." The lungs had no lesions on them and appeared to be free of disease.

The right and left kidneys had been moderately-to-severely burned. There were large areas of the kidneys that evidenced fibrosis. The urinary bladder was empty. The fallopian tubes and left ovary were identified and examined. The spleen appeared free of disease. The liver had been burned, and there were patchy areas of disease noted.

Dr. Clark then examined the head. He used a saw to remove the top portion of the skull and found a "20 cc. clotted epidural hematoma" in the area of the back of the head. He dictated that the skull had "heat-induced linear fractures on the posterior left parietal skull. The brain is cauterized [burned]."

In the neck area, Dr. Clark found that the left adrenal gland had a yellow, egg-shaped mass, but the right adrenal gland and the pituitary gland were disease free. Dr. Clark said the yellow mass on the left adrenal gland was a relatively common finding in adults and really had no medical significance.

In his examination of the musculoskeletal system, Dr. Clark found that "the diaphragms are modestly charred." There was scoliosis of the spine, and the left hip area had a "1.3 gram fragment of brass-colored metal." The piece of metal was preserved as evidence. Although Dr. Clark could not identify the small piece of metal, he thought it might have been an artifact from the vehicle.

Sections of the heart, kidneys, liver, left adrenal gland and lungs were examined under the microscope. The lungs showed sections of "diffuse pulmonary edema and congestion of the vessels. The bronchi display cautery [burn] effects of the mucosa and marked congestion."

Dr. Clark explained to Heinen and the others present that the congestion in Freda Weeks' lungs had not been from a "cold" or pneumonia. Under the microscope, a viral type of infection was easily identifiable. He said that the congestion and edema [water retention] in the lungs was from the underlying heart disease or congestive heart failure and/or had been caused by the inhalation of hot gases. Clark said that thermal injury by hot gases could very well have caused the congestion and edema he saw in Freda Weeks' lungs.

Dr. Clark dictated his opinion:

*This 82-year-old white female, identified by circumstances as Freda Weeks, most probably died from a cardiac dysrhythmia/standstill due to severe coronary atherosclerotic disease, exacerbated by the stress of thermal injuries sustained in a motor vehicle fire. The autopsy examination did not reveal any significant blunt or sharp-force injuries or gunshot wounds which may have contributed to or caused the death. Only a slight amount of soot and cautery effect is discovered in the upper airways and the left mainstream bronchus. The blood carbon monoxide level was negative. **These findings support the conclusion that the decedent was probably alive at the start of the conflagration [fire], but was very quickly overcome by the heat and hot gases that resulted in a sudden cardiac death.** Whether or not the decedent was conscious cannot be determined from the autopsy examination. The state and insurance fire investigators have determined that this is a set fire [arson]. Because of the suspicious nature of the car fire, the manner of death will remain undetermined until further information comes to light, which may modify this opinion.*

Dr. Clark listed the cause of death as "probable cardiac dysrhythmia/ standstill due to coronary atherosclerotic disease exacerbated by thermal injuries." He listed the manner of death as undetermined.

It was almost 3 p.m. by the time Freda Weeks' body was loaded back into the GBI van and returned to Weeks Chapel Cemetery. The crowd had left the cemetery and only a few people were present to attend the reinterment. The Cobb Funeral Home employees returned Freda Weeks to her grave, hopefully to rest in peace, finally, and everyone left the area by 4 p.m.

CHAPTER FIFTEEN

Thursday, September 5, 1996

After the autopsy, in the late afternoon, John Heinen headed for his home in Thomasville, and Donald Davis headed for his thinking room. They were both mad and needed some private time.

When Davis needed some thinking space, he would leave his office at the front of the CCSO and go down the hall to one of the empty interrogation rooms. It was a quiet place, away from the crowd out front, where he could put his thinking cap on. He had heard about the toxicology report and autopsy results, and he needed to sit a spell and try, once again, to figure out the pieces of this puzzle.

Davis was not at all happy with his friend Rodney Bryan. Bryan had gotten the toxicology report and kept the information to himself. It was pretty important information to know, but Bryan had not shared it with him, not on the day they went to Sheila's house or even the next day. Davis had learned about the toxicology report from Heinen.

But more than the lack of information sharing, Davis was mad that Bryan had agreed with Dr. Clark's opinion that the manner of death was undetermined. *Undetermined my ass*, Davis thought. *It was plain cold-blooded murder, that's what it was. What did those guys need, a videotape of Sheila setting the fire?*

Davis told himself he needed to put himself in check. He had to get a grip and go over the facts of the case. He started at the beginning: the day of the accident.

He knew now that Sheila had not been locked out of the car. She had lied. There was no doubt about that. As far as he knew, people only lied for a couple of reasons: to protect themselves or someone they loved. He decided that Sheila had lied to protect herself.

If Sheila had not set the fire, what reason would she have had to lie and say she was locked out of the car? Davis couldn't think of any reason.

Davis thought the fact Sheila had lied about being locked out of the car was damning evidence. Whenever he lost his focus, he would go back to those two facts: the car door was unlocked, and she had lied about being locked out.

He thought about Danny Weeks and decided they needed to talk to him as soon as they could. Danny was Sheila's cousin. Would he lie for her? Or would he tell the truth? Had Danny been in on it? Or had he just been unlucky enough to have happened by at that exact moment? Assuming Danny Weeks was innocent of the arson, Davis figured that Danny showing up right after Sheila set the fire must have shook her up quite a bit. Not only had a car come by a little too early, but her cousin was in the car. *Now there was a stroke of bad luck for Sheila. Yessireebob, she had run a little short of luck there.*

With the gas tank full, and the gas cap off, and the filler lid door open, she obviously had planned for the car to explode into smithereens. But she hadn't wanted Danny, or herself, to get blown up in the process. She must have kept Danny away from the car as much as she could, Davis guessed, but how had she done that?

Davis decided that Sheila Bryan was a woman with balls. It had taken balls to set the fire and to do what she had done out on Livingston Bridge Road. There was no doubt in his mind about that. She knew the area. She had grown up around there. She knew that Sunday morning, before church let out, there would not be much traffic on that road. People were either at home or already at church. That was pretty much a given.

Davis figured Sheila must have been running later than she had planned. For some reason, which he didn't know, she had gotten mighty close to the noon hour, when traffic would pick up on Livingston Bridge Road. And that is how she had ended up with Danny appearing right after she set the fire. Davis figured it had probably freaked her out.

As far as Davis was concerned, the terrycloth material they found in the car was the most intriguing piece of evidence. He thought possibly the material had been used as a conduit, to move the fire from the floorboard over to the passenger seat where Freda Weeks was located. Probably, he assumed, there had been accelerant placed on that material as well. There had been so much of the material that initially Davis had thought it was a blanket wrapped around Freda Weeks. But the terry-type material indicated that it was more likely a beach towel, a large beach towel.

What possible explanation could she have for wrapping her mother in a beach towel? he wondered.

Every time Davis pictured Freda Weeks burned up in the car, and then pictured Karlas telling Heinen to hurry up and get the investigation over so he could collect his $100,000, Davis got so mad he wanted to put his fist through the wall, or better yet, through Karlas' head. Any way he looked at it, Davis found the statement about the $100,000 pretty damn callous.

Davis figured Sheila and Karlas might have been in it together. It looked like a man's crime anyway. It had all the touches of a man at work, not a woman.

Davis wondered if Karlas had just driven off when Danny Weeks appeared. Maybe. If Karlas had been in on it, Davis wondered why Karlas had not been the one to stay on the road with the car on fire, instead of Sheila. There must have been a reason, and he intended to find out what that reason was.

Davis didn't think the two of them together were smart enough to pour piss out of a boot.

He wondered about the insurance. How could they get $100,000 worth of insurance on an 82-year-old woman? Davis thought that sounded pretty improbable, but that's what Karlas had said.

Heinen and Pitts had said Karlas was intoxicated when they saw him. Davis figured Karlas was probably about half lit and was running his mouth off. He had seen Karlas just that one time when he and Rodney Bryan had gone to Omega. Now when he thought about it, Karlas had that alcoholic look about him. *Who else would be snockered before 5 in the afternoon except an alcoholic?* he wondered.

WHERE WERE HER SHOES? All of a sudden it hit Davis like a bolt from the blue. Freda Weeks didn't have on any shoes. They had not found any in the car, and she didn't have on any at the autopsy.

He tried to think of any little old ladies he knew who would go for a Sunday afternoon drive and leave the house without their teeth, their purse, or their shoes. He couldn't think of any. Why, it was ridiculous.

That was the problem with Sheila Bryan's story, he thought. *The more you knew, the more ridiculous it became.*

Davis decided this case had more twists and turns than a bad stretch of Georgia road. His mind had ended up back where it had started days before: Why didn't Freda Weeks get out of that car? The autopsy report had shown that she had not been hit in the head and knocked unconscious. If she had lost consciousness, it had been after the fire started. And Sheila had said her mother was okay before she left the car.

In Davis' book it was a despicable crime. To kill your own mother – for $100,000 no less – had to be barely a notch above killing a child. He had not the slightest shred of sympathy for Sheila or Karlas. He just hoped they would get what they deserved.

As for his friend Coroner Rodney Bryan, Davis figured his day would come when he would appreciate some information sharing. *Well, just good damn luck.*

After the autopsy, Heinen had gone home to follow his cleansing routine. He had been present at a number of autopsies in the past and had developed a way to deal with the lingering odor. The smell would cling to his clothes, skin, hair, and mucous membranes, and it was hard to get rid of the stench.

When he got home, he went to his back porch and stripped. He would leave his clothes outside for a day or two before bringing them in to wash. Then he would take several showers and then he would go jogging. He had to get the smell out of his sweat glands, so he would be sure to jog every day for about a week. Finally, after all the showers, washing and jogging, he would be rid of the smell, but it would take a few days.

After completing his initial cleansing routine, Heinen sat down to think about the case. It was a brain tease all right. Just when he thought he knew the time of day, it took a new turn. Usually when a case started like that, it stayed like that. And Heinen would have to figure his way through each twist and turn.

It had made Heinen mad that Clark had not put "homicide" in the box for manner of death. Clark had clearly understood that four arson investigators had said the fire was incendiary. And Clark himself had said Freda Weeks had most probably been alive when the fire started. So what else did the man want?

And then there was the claw hammer. Originally, he had had no doubt that Freda Weeks had died from the fire, but then, after the claw hammer, he had wondered if she had been knocked unconscious, or killed with the hammer, before the fire. But the autopsy proved differently. He was back to her being killed in the fire, but from heart failure caused by the fire. It was enough to make a person dizzy.

Heinen, who of course had stayed through the entire autopsy, had talked with Dr. Clark at length during the autopsy. Dr. Clark had told Heinen he had not expected to find a great deal of soot in Freda Weeks' lungs because the carbon monoxide level had been zero. The lack of carbon monoxide had told

Dr. Clark, even before the autopsy, that Freda Weeks had not lived long after the fire started.

Clark had reminded Heinen that the test run for the toxicology report was only for carbon monoxide and that fires gave off a lot of other toxic fumes, which had not been tested for. This was especially true, he told Heinen, if an accelerant had been used to start the fire.

Dr. Clark had said when an accelerant was used, there was typically a big WHOOOOSH from the super-heated gases when the fire started. That WHOOOOSH put out a lot of toxic fumes, sometimes even cyanide gas or other toxic poisons, and with Freda Weeks' heart as fragile as it was, that might have been all it took to cause her death. Just one quick breath and that would have been it for her. Even in people who did not have Freda Weeks' heart condition, those toxic fumes could cause a normal heart to go into arthymia and then stop.

Essentially, Dr. Clark had told Heinen he could not give him an exact answer as to when Freda Weeks had died. She could have been dead before the fire started, and the soot they had found in her lungs could have been just artifact, meaning it occurred after she was dead and resulted from the massive thermal injuries her body sustained during the fire. She could have died right when the fire started. Or, she could have died very soon after it started. Take your pick. Any of those answers would fit what Clark had found at the autopsy.

Heinen didn't like multiple choice. Heinen had hoped the autopsy would be more definitive. But they had what they had, and he would have to go from there.

Could he have a murder case with an autopsy report that listed manner of death as undetermined? Heinen didn't know.

Would the materials they had taken from the car to be tested for accelerants come back positive? Heinen didn't know.

What he did know was that he had put checking on the gas cap and finding out about the $100,000 worth of insurance at the top of his list for the next day. Maybe he didn't know where the case was going, but he knew where he was going: to the Georgia Farm Bureau Insurance Company.

CHAPTER SIXTEEN

Friday, September 6, 1996

Heinen planned a full day of work on the Bryan case, and he started with an interview of Danny Weeks at the CCSO office.

Danny Weeks told Heinen everything that had happened that Sunday, starting with the rattlesnake. Heinen asked about what time it was when Danny and his wife got to the bridge and saw Sheila. Danny said that he thought it was somewhere between noon and 12:30 p.m.

Danny told Heinen that Sheila had said the car doors locked automatically when the door was closed, and that she had tried to get the car door open but couldn't. He told Heinen that Sheila had stayed on the bridge when he went to get the bucket of water, and she had warned him that the car had just been filled with gas.

Heinen asked Danny how long a time period it was between returning to the car with the water, which is when Danny had said he first saw the flames in the car, and the arrival of the fire truck. Danny said he thought it had been about ten to fifteen minutes.

Heinen also asked Danny if he remembered seeing any doors or windows open, or the hood or the fuel door open on the car. Danny said he never saw the fuel door, because he thought it must have been on the right side of the car, and he had not observed the right side of the car. He said he thought the hood of the car was partially open.

Heinen wanted to know if Freda Weeks smoked cigarettes.

"No," Danny said, "Mrs. Weeks didn't smoke cigarettes."

Then Heinen asked him if Sheila Bryan appeared to be injured in any way. Danny said that her left arm was swollen, and he had accompanied Sheila to the hospital in the sheriff deputy's car.

Heinen was satisfied that Danny Weeks was being truthful about the events on Livingston Bridge Road that Sunday. He felt Danny had been fairly forthcoming about everything he had seen and heard that day.

With the interview completed, Heinen was ready to head to Tifton and talk to the insurance company.

Georgia Farm Bureau Insurance Company was founded in 1959, at a time when farmers and rural Georgians were having difficulty getting insurance coverage. The Georgia Farm Bureau Federation members pooled their money to create the company, which would grow to become Georgia's largest domestic property/casualty insurance company. With over 550 employees, the company had an office in each of Georgia's 159 counties. The home office was located in Macon.

Georgia Farm Bureau Insurance was committed to investigating and denying fraudulent claims. Six years before the accident on Livingston Bridge Road, the insurance company established a Special Investigation Unit to investigate suspicious losses. They had been successful in denying hundreds of claims, saving their policy holders millions of dollars.

The company did not consider insurance fraud a petty crime. It was one of the fastest growing industries in the United States, costing all sectors of the insurance industry $120 billion in 1996. Property and casualty insurance fraud amounted to more than $20 billion. The fraud perpetrated against the insurance companies cost its customers between 10 and 25 percent of the cost of an insurance policy.

Georgia Farm Bureau educated its customers to the variety of ways that insurance fraud is committed: faking an accident and the resulting injuries; reporting items stolen from the home when, in fact, the items have been moved to another location; phony break-ins; padding or inflating actual claims; misrepresenting facts on an insurance application; submitting claims for injuries or damage that never occurred; staging accidents and causing damage to property by fire.

Georgia Farm Bureau committed considerable resources to meet the need of combating insurance fraud. Like other insurance companies in the country, they were ever vigilant to find insurance fraud cases.

Right after lunch, Heinen and Pitts drove into Tifton to visit the Georgia Farm Bureau Insurance office for Tift county. There they met with insurance agent Tami Bostick and asked to see any insurance documents regarding the automobile owned by Sheila and Karlas Bryan that was involved in the reported accident. Bostick gave Heinen copies of insurance policy number APV 0462381-03-05.

Heinen and Pitts sat there a while studying the insurance policy. The owner of the policy was listed as Karlas R. Bryan, and the driver of the vehicle was listed as Sheila Weeks Bryan.

Lo and behold, there it was – the $100,000 Karlas had told them about. On May 28, 1996, just short of three months before the accident on Livingston Bridge Road, Karlas Bryan had increased his bodily injury limits from $25,000 to $100,000.

"Who made the change on this policy?" Heinen asked Bostick.

"Bobby Underwood made the change," she said, "but he is now working in our Monroe County Office." Bostick gave Heinen the telephone number for Bobby Underwood.

"Is there any life insurance coverage on Freda Weeks through your company?" he asked.

"No, no life insurance coverage," she said.

Heinen thanked Bostick and he and Pitts headed to their next stop in Tifton.

"How do you collect $100,000 on a car liability policy?" Pitts asked Heinen.

Heinen said he didn't know, but he would find out.

"I know this much," Heinen said. "Karlas obviously thinks they can collect that $100,000. And they've hired a lawyer to help them do it."

Before leaving Tifton, Heinen and Pitts went to the home of the Amoco station clerk, Judy Paulk, to find out about the gas cap and to confirm that Sheila had gassed up in Omega that Sunday morning. She said the work schedule indicated she had worked the Sunday of August 18, but she did not know Sheila Bryan by name and was not familiar with her car. Heinen described Sheila's car, but Paulk said she could not recall if the car had been to the station that day.

In Omega, at the Citgo gas station, they interviewed employee Teresa Massey. Massey said that she had been working during the day of Sunday, August 18, and that she knew Sheila Bryan and her car, a blue Mercury Cougar. Although Sheila was a regular customer at the station, Massey said that Sheila had not come to the station that Sunday.

When they got back to Moultrie and the CCSO office, Heinen headed straight to the telephone to call Bobby Underwood in Forsyth.

"I understand you are the Georgia Farm Bureau agent who increased the limits on Sheila and Karlas Bryan's vehicle that was recently involved in an accident," Heinen said.

"Yes," Underwood told Heinen, "I remember making that policy change."

Underwood explained that company policy dictated that agents are allowed to perform reviews on customers' policies once a year in order to suggest an increase.

"Did you suggest the increase?" Heinen asked.

After reviewing the Bryans' file, Underwood told Heinen that he had suggested that they increase their limits on their vehicle in October 1994 and October 1995, but the Bryans did not want to increase their coverage at that time.

"How did it come to get changed in May 1996?" Heinen wanted to know.

"In May, Karlas Bryan came into the office and increased the limits on the vehicle," Underwood said.

"Why?" Heinen asked.

"I don't know. There was not a review conducted at that time."

"Did you initiate the discussion about an increase?"

"I don't recall who initiated the discussion. I just know that it was not time for the annual review."

"So you don't know of any reason why Karlas would have come into the office and increased the coverage?"

"I do recall that at some point in time he had purchased a truck and a lake lot. But that's about all I can tell you."

Heinen thanked Underwood and concluded the conversation.

Now Heinen and Pitts had something else to think about. What did Karlas do for a living that he could afford a nice, big house and a new truck and a lake lot? Sounded like some mighty fine living.

No doubt about it – Karlas Bryan was a fella they wanted to get to know a whole lot better.

CHAPTER SEVENTEEN

Wednesday, September 11, 1996

It was way past time to talk to Sheila and Karlas Bryan. Heinen and Pitts had wanted to talk to them, so Heinen told Pitts to contact their attorney, Craig Webster, and see if he could get the interviews arranged.

Heinen had been curious about Craig Webster's practice, so he had checked him out. Webster was a civil attorney, not a criminal attorney, just as Heinen had expected. Heinen knew that lawyers, like doctors, all had specialty areas and, as a rule, civil attorneys didn't take criminal cases.

Webster's specialized area of practice was in personal injury, wrongful death, auto accidents, workers' compensation, insurance claims, and trial practice.

"If Sheila could find a way to make a workman's comp claim, she could hit all of his areas of specialization," Pitts said.

"True," Heinen agreed, "but she's got him working on four out of the six, anyway. Maybe, if she's lucky, she won't need his experience in trial practice."

Heinen and Pitts agreed that they had the time of day about Sheila and her attorney Craig Webster: She was going after the insurance money.

Pitts had ended up in a phone tag situation with Webster. That afternoon, while Heinen was sitting in Pitts' office at the CCSO, Webster returned Pitts' telephone call. Heinen listened as Pitts talked to Webster. When Pitts finished the conversation with the attorney, he told Heinen what Webster had just said.

"Webster said he thought this was a civil case, not a criminal case," Pitts said, with a smirk.

"Yeah, he thought it was an insurance case," Heinen said. "Did he ask you why it was a criminal case?"

"Yeah, that's when I told him that unattended deaths are investigated as a homicide, so that all the bases are covered. Webster said he assumed Sheila was a suspect in the case. I told him we wanted to talk to *both* Sheila and Karlas."

"What did he say?"

"He said he would talk to Sheila and Karlas about it, and that he might have to talk to another attorney about it."

"Because he isn't a criminal attorney, and they hadn't hired him to handle a criminal case; they hired him to collect the insurance money."

"That's what I figured, too. That's when I told him that the GBI was also investigating the case, not just the CCSO."

"When you gave him my name and telephone number, what did he say?"

"He said he would call you when a decision had been made about the interview."

"I guess we shouldn't sit here holding our breath."

"Probably not."

Eventually, Heinen was able to have a conversation with Webster, only to learn that Webster was no longer Sheila's attorney. She had left Tifton and gone lawyer hunting in Albany, forty-five miles northwest of Tifton. Her new attorney was Ralph Scoccimaro. Scoccimaro was also a civil attorney and Heinen assumed Sheila was still after the insurance money, obviously unconcerned about any criminal issues.

Brown & Scoccimaro was an established firm of trial lawyers composed of Scoccimaro, Jimmie Brown, and several other attorneys. Scoccimaro was a self-described "no-nonsense, hard-charging former Marine, who didn't like to take 'no' for an answer, especially from an insurance company." He was known for his successes in the personal injury field and had brought in some substantial verdicts and settlements for his clients.

Sheila would be in good hands with Scoccimaro as long as her case remained a civil case centering on the insurance money.

But, as Heinen would learn later, Sheila ran into some major legal obstacles very quickly. Georgia Farm Bureau Insurance, having learned that the automobile fire was deemed arson, had no intention of shelling out any money to Sheila Bryan. If Sheila wanted to discuss insurance money, then she was going to have to take a sworn deposition – in other words, answer questions about the accident, under oath, and with a court reporter present. And any statements she made in the deposition could be used against her even in a criminal case, if that came to pass. Under the advice of her attorney, Sheila would refuse to take the deposition that Georgia Farm Bureau Insurance was demanding. They would come to an impasse and Georgia Farm Bureau

Insurance wouldn't budge. Scoccimaro – who did not like to take 'no' for an answer from an insurance company – set his client on a new course: Sheila would sue Georgia Farm Bureau Insurance. Technically, Karlas Bryan would bring the suit, since he was the policyholder on the Mercury Cougar and had the right to sue and receive damages.

Eventually, when Donald Davis learned of the new development, he told Heinen, "See, I told you she had balls. Who else would sue the insurance company while they are being investigated for arson and murder except Sheila Bryan?"

Heinen had to agree, it did look, well, rather bold.

But the suit against Georgia Farm Bureau Insurance was not going to get Sheila and Karlas the $100,000. The deposition was just the tip of the iceberg as far as bad news about the insurance money. The Bryans had quickly found themselves in a legal sticky wicket.

The bodily injury insurance for $100,000 meant that the insurance company would pay up to $100,000 for each person, or for up to $300,000 for any number of persons, who would have been injured as a result of negligence or intentional acts of a driver of the Bryan vehicle.

The policy referred to Sheila Bryan as a named insured, since she was listed as a driver of the vehicle, and Karlas as the owner of the vehicle and the policy.

The coverage would not pay Sheila Bryan anything if there were an accident, but would pay someone that Sheila Bryan injured in the accident. Of course, if someone dies as a result of the injuries, that person's estate would be able to recover the benefits. Ordinarily, Sheila, who was Freda Weeks' sole heir, would be the one who would recover because of her mother's death, except for the fact that one cannot recover against oneself. Georgia law also has a statute that says no one can recover under any insurance claim for the death of someone they murder.

The $100,000 bodily injury policy that Karlas carried on the Mercury Cougar was for exactly that – bodily injury – and Freda Weeks had died, although certainly one might claim she had been injured prior to her death, however long that might have been. But Sheila had been the driver of the car that was in Karlas' name. Who was Sheila going to sue? Herself? Even assuming that the accident had not been staged and was not insurance fraud – not to mention arson and murder – Sheila was the person driving the car and the one at fault for the accident. In a normal case, Freda Weeks would have sued Sheila Bryan.

Legally, it was quite simple: Sheila could not make a claim against herself and collect the $100,000.

There are always legal loopholes, but few attorneys – at least those who value their good standing with the bar – would want to wade into those treacherous legal waters. It was possible that the administrator of Freda Weeks' estate could bring suit – but the administrator would be Sheila Bryan, Freda Weeks' only surviving child, and Sheila was back in the same position: suing herself.

When Heinen related that strange set of facts to Donald Davis, Davis almost convulsed with laughter.

"See, I told you they weren't smart enough to pour piss out of a boot," he told Heinen. Davis thought the Bryans had been hoisted on their own petard. Obviously, they did not have a good understanding of insurance policies – but most people didn't.

If Karlas had been driving the car, well, maybe they would have had a shot at the $100,000 – a slim shot, but still a shot. At least in that instance, Sheila, as the administrator of her mother's estate, could have sued her husband and not herself.

"That's just too damn funny," Davis said between snorts of laughter.

If Heinen was right, they had committed arson and murder for nothing, absolutely nothing. Davis laughed for days. But when he quit laughing, he got worried, and went back to talk to Heinen. Since the Bryans weren't going to be able to get the $100,000 after all, what did that mean as far as the motive in the case. If the Bryans' didn't get the money, then the prosecution had lost their motive – that's what Davis was worried about.

Heinen was able to reassure Davis that it really didn't matter from their point of view whether the Bryans got the money or not. The point was that they intended to get the money; Karlas had told them that himself and they had hired the lawyers to do it.

But Davis wasn't through with it.

"Don't you think anybody who was going to commit arson and murder would at least check out the legal situation with the insurance money before they committed the crime?" he marveled.

Heinen said, "Obviously not."

The lawsuit that Scoccimaro would file on Sheila and Karlas' behalf would be for the property damage to the Mercury Cougar.

Georgia Farm Bureau had not even bothered to answer Karlas and Sheila's lawsuit. When the suit went unanswered, the court in Dougherty County said that Georgia Farm Bureau had acted "in bad faith" and awarded Karlas the money for the loss of the 1987 Mercury Cougar. It was a few thousand dollars and no where in the vicinity of the $100,000 they had been after. It was all they would ever receive from the accident on Livingston Bridge Road.

Davis figured Scoccimaro had ended up with most of what little money they had been awarded.

"Maybe there is some justice in the world," Davis said.

Heinen would continue to keep tabs on Sheila's quest for the insurance money. Since Sheila had a habit of changing lawyers, and obviously did not want to speak to him, Heinen spoke with John Croley, the attorney for Farm Bureau Insurance Company. Croley told Heinen that the insurance company had continued to try to subject the Bryans to an examination under oath about the accident but had had no success. He also told Heinen that there had been a statute of limitations on the recovery for damages to the Mercury Cougar: one year. Croley said that any claim for damages on behalf of Freda Weeks had a two-year statute of limitations; that would make August 18, 1998, the last day the Bryans could file a claim for the death of Freda Weeks.

In December of 1996, Croley told Heinen that the Bryans had terminated the services of Ralph Scoccimaro and had hired a lawyer from Valdosta, William E. Moore, Jr.

Bill Moore was a criminal attorney but, like most south Georgia lawyers, he had a general practice. He had graduated from the Walter F. George School of Law at Mercer University where he had been selected as his class's Most Outstanding Trial Advocate. He had been in practice with George Saliba for over twenty years. Saliba, a graduate of the University of Georgia School of Law, had probably tried more cases than any attorney in south Georgia.

Moore and Saliba, along with Kent Edwards, had represented Maurice Cassotta in one of the most noted cases in south Georgia history. Cassotta, a Valdosta policeman, was accused of murdering his young son and the child's mother. The lead investigator on the case had been none other than GBI Agent John Heinen.

The trial was the longest and involved the most witnesses of any trial in Valdosta history. It had been carried simultaneously with the O.J. Simpson trial in 1995 by Court TV. Cassotta was acquitted and the popularity of Moore and Saliba was noted by *Dateline* NBC, Court TV specials, and ABC's *Inside Edition*. The one hour documentary re-run on Court TV was perhaps the most widely run production of a trial. When Cassotta was acquitted of both murders, the headlines of the *Valdosta Daily Times* had screamed, "INNOCENT!"

Already having experienced success in their careers, the Cassotta case catapulted Moore and Saliba to the upper echelon of defense attorneys in Georgia.

It did not make Heinen's heart beat with joy to know that Sheila had hired Moore and Saliba. He knew they were a tough defense team to beat. He knew because he had already tried, and lost.

CHAPTER EIGHTEEN

October 1996

John Heinen decided there must be some kind of universal law that said there had to be at least one major muck-up in any criminal investigation. He had hoped that the decision to forego an autopsy had fulfilled that universal requirement, but no such luck.

Brian Hargett, his GBI colleague in Columbus, had called from the crime lab there to tell Heinen that the test for the accelerant was negative. They were not the words Heinen had longed to hear.

Hargett and Heinen talked at some length about how that could have happened. Hargett told Heinen the test run at the lab was for petroleum-based accelerants, such as gasoline, mineral spirits, kerosene, charcoal lighter fluid, and heating oils – and while they were not water soluble, they were subject to evaporation. The samples had not been collected until ten days after the fire. If petroleum-based accelerants were present, they had been subjected to evaporation from the hot summer days in late August, when the Mercury Cougar had sat at Blanton's impound yard.

Heinen had learned that Karlas Bryan was a house painter, but that was after the samples had been sent to Hargett in Columbus. Acetone, which was an accelerant, and a common ingredient in paint cleaning products, seemed like a real possibility to Heinen, so he asked Hargett about the test for acetone.

Hargett told Heinen that the sample had not been tested for acetone, a very volatile substance. According to Hargett, the test for acetone was not a routine one, and without specific instructions to do so, the test was not carried out. In fact, Hargett said, *only* petroleum-based accelerants had been tested for, because there had been no specific request to test for other accelerants.

Heinen was mad. He had assumed that the staff at the crime lab would always go "the extra mile," without having to be instructed to do so. He was wrong.

Had Jamie Hinson not continued to pour water in the car after the main fire was put out, had the samples been collected the day of the fire, and had all the tests been run on the samples, well, there might have been a different outcome from the tests.

It was a muck-up. And like the autopsy decision, it didn't matter who was responsible, it only mattered that Heinen's case had just gotten immeasurably more difficult. Not only did he have a case where the GBI's own medical examiner had gone against convention and ruled the manner of death undetermined in an arson case, he now had a case where there was no scientific proof of an accelerant.

Although Ronnie Dobbins, Ralph Newell and Gerald Psalmond assured Heinen that most of their arson cases did come back with negative results on tests for accelerants, it did not go a long way in raising Heinen's spirits.

It was time to kick a rock. As he often did when he needed inspiration in a case, Heinen returned to the scene of the crime. Heinen stood on the shoulder of Livingston Bridge Road thinking about the case and Freda Weeks dying down in the ditch. As he stood there, he realized how wide the shoulder of the road was: very wide. He made a note to call in an accident reconstructionist and get it measured. Like so many of his cases, Heinen had too much to let it go, and not enough to make it easy.

While Heinen couldn't do anything about the results from the test for accelerants, he thought he had some ray of hope when it came to Dr. Anthony Clark. Although Clark had written his autopsy report saying the manner of death was undetermined, he had not signed off on it. And the report was not official until Clark signed it. Heinen felt confident that if Clark was made aware of all of the evidence in the case, Clark would change his mind.

When he returned to Thomasville, Heinen talked to his supervisor, John White, about his idea on dealing with Clark. White agreed with Heinen that he might consider calling all the parties together – including Clark – to discuss the case. Quite likely, when all of the evidence of arson was laid out, Clark would see things differently.

Heinen wanted to get more information before he called the meeting.

He contacted the Ford dealership in Moultrie to find out if the Mercury Cougar's doors locked automatically when the doors were closed, as Sheila had told Danny Weeks. Heinen learned that the doors did not lock automatically. Another lie. That made three lies Sheila had told Danny Weeks on the day of the accident: (1) the car doors were locked (2) the doors locked automatically, and (3) the key was in the car.

But something else had come up in the case that Heinen knew he had to check out: the car's ignition switch.

Newell had talked with Heinen about the problem with some of Ford's cars catching on fire from a defect in the ignition switch. And Newell had assured Heinen that the vehicle fire on Livingston Bridge Road was not an ignition switch fire. Nevertheless, Heinen, who liked to dot every i and cross every t, wanted to check out the problem of the ignition switches with Ford Motor Company. Unlike Newell, who had a direct line to the company, Heinen would have to initiate his inquiry through correspondence. Gina-Marie Stone, Ford's Litigation Assistant, wrote to Heinen, telling him that there had been a recall on 1988 – 1993 Mercury Cougars due to a possible short circuiting in the ignition switch which might cause a fire. The ignition switch in Sheila's 1987 Mercury Cougar was not included in the recall.

Wanting to be thorough, Heinen also requested of Stone the differences and similarities of Sheila's 1987 ignition switch and those involved in the recall. Stone told Heinen he would have to contact United Technologies Automotive (UTA), the company that manufactured the switches, to obtain that information.

The communication with Ford about its ignition switch problem would go on for months. But when it was over, Heinen felt confident the fire in Sheila's 1987 Mercury Cougar had not been caused by the ignition switch.

The meeting with Heinen, the arson and criminal investigators and Dr. Anthony Clark was held at the end of October. The men discussed the case in some detail, exchanging information and ideas. But Clark made it clear that he had no intentions of changing his manner of death finding from undetermined, although he did say that if the test for the accelerant had been positive, he would have changed it to homicide.

As the men filed out of the room, Heinen felt more discouraged than he had ever felt about the case. Although he kept his feelings to himself, one of the investigators, evidently noticing Heinen's glum mood, stopped at the door on the way out and told Heinen that before he gave up on the case he should find out about Gail Sullivan.

Who was Gail Sullivan and what did she have to do with anything? Heinen wondered.

CHAPTER NINETEEN

Thursday, November 14, 1996

Joyce Weeks sat at her L-shaped walnut desk with the banker's lamp turned on over her electric typewriter. She knew that most desks like hers were equipped with computer monitors and keyboards, but she was a middle-aged woman who had been reluctant to jump into the computer age. And why should she? Everything around her was old and smelled of paste wax and Pine Sol. The building she occupied was almost one hundred years old. Built in 1906 as a private residence, the home had been converted into a business site nearly a half century before. Once known as the Buck House, it was a Tifton landmark.

She liked her job as office manager, but she didn't care for the hustle and bustle of the business world any more than she cared for computers. True, she was a working woman, but most days this was a quiet, serene place to work. She liked it so much she had been there seventeen years.

Some people kidded her about working at a funeral home. They thought it was morbid. She felt differently. She felt that she was in a position to help people at a time in their life when they were fragile and vulnerable. She liked being helpful to people, and she prided herself on her ability to be of assistance during difficult times.

Of course there was always the sick humor: "Any body here?"

Although she didn't get many requests to look up information on funerals held at Bowen Donaldson from almost thirty years past, she was willing to try. She went to the back room where old files were kept and returned disappointed.

"I only found one notation," she said, apparently disappointed in herself for failing to be totally helpful. "At the bottom of the page, there was a handwritten note that said, 'Linda Gail Sullivan, Memorial Service, November 24.'"

Joyce Weeks apologized for the lack of adequate records and, only when it was a polite moment in time, returned to her typing.

Twenty-six years after her death, it did seem that Linda Gail Sullivan was all but forgotten by the people in the Tifton community. At Bowen Donaldson Home for Funerals, she had become little more than a postscript.

When most people did speak of Gail Sullivan now, they didn't recall her name; she was "that woman who had been killed at the drive-in." So if she was remembered at all, she was mostly remembered for her death, not her life, as short as it had been.

The story of Gail Sullivan's brief life and death had been saved on microfiche at the Tifton-Tift County Library on Love Avenue. On October 31, 1970, the *Daily Tifton Gazette*, as it was known then, had carried the engagement announcement of Gail Sullivan. The announcement, which was headlined "Wedding Plans Are Announced," ran under a small 3" by 5" picture of Gail Sullivan.

It was a formal picture in which Gail was wearing what looked to be a graduation gown, black, with a sharp V neck. Her head was tilted to the left and she had a slight smile on her face. Her hair was dark and styled in a "bubble" with bangs across her forehead. Her dark eyes were somewhat sad. The overall impression the picture gave was of an attractive, contemplative young woman.

The announcement read:

> *Mr. and Mrs. Clarence D. Sullivan of Los Angeles, Cal., announce the engagement of their daughter, Gail, to William Arthur Rampey Jr. of Lakeland, Ga. He is the son of Mrs. William A. Rampey Sr., of Lakeland. Miss Sullivan is a hair stylist at Town and Country Plaza and Mr. Rampey is a timberman in South Georgia. Wedding plans will be announced later.*

The wedding plans would never be announced. Two weeks after her engagement announcement had run in the newspaper, Gail Sullivan had been killed, and the next announcement had been of her death.

The story of Gail Sullivan's death appeared on the front page of the Saturday, November 14, 1970, edition of *The Daily Tifton Gazette*. The headline read, "Woman Is Killed At Marbro; Tift Man Held; Charges Ahead."

But the story didn't begin with Gail's name. It began with the name of the man who had killed her. The story read:

Karlas R. Bryan, the 22 year old son of a Tifton farmer and an employee of Tifton Aluminum, is to be charged today with murder in the Friday night shooting of a 21 year old Tifton woman.

Miss Gail Sullivan, a hair stylist from Lenox who worked at Town and Country Shopping Center, died about 9:45 p.m. Friday after being shot in the head at the Marbro Drive-In on US 82 West.

Sheriff Tom Greer said the charges would be filed against the man today.

According to witnesses to the shooting, some hostile words were passed between Miss Sullivan and Bryan before the man wheeled around and grabbed a gun...stuck the gun up to the back of her head and pulled the trigger.

Sheriff Greer quoted Bryan as telling him that he "blamed the girl with breaking up his family." He said Bryan and his wife, Judy M. Bryan, 21, have a divorce suit pending.

Miss Sullivan earlier this month had announced her engagement to a Lakeland, Ga., man.

Miss Sullivan was born in Amory, Mississippi, and whose parents live in Westminster, CA, lived about an hour following the shooting. A single .22 caliber bullet went through the back of her head and lodged over the right eye.

According to the sheriff, Bryan surrendered to him at the jail and handed over to him the .22 pistol. He is being held without bond.

A friend of Miss Sullivan's, who was at the drive-in with the hair stylist, said Bryan parked his car in the rear of Miss Sullivan's car.

He added that the two exchanged heated words. The witness said he and Miss Sullivan were going to the concession stand to call police and that as they passed the Bryan car, Bryan made more comments.

The witness quoted Miss Sullivan as saying, "What are you trying to do, threaten me?" He wheeled around and grabbed a gun...stuck the gun up to the back of her head and pulled the trigger. She moaned and fell to the ground. He jumped into the car and squealed off.

According to another witness, the night watchman tried to stop Bryan as he sped away from the drive-in.

Funeral services, by Bowen Donaldson, will be announced after the arrival of her parents, brother and sister.

Records at the Tift County courthouse revealed the short, ugly story of the marriage of Karlas and Judy Bryan.

Karlas, who had just turned eighteen years old that March, married Judy Mathews on September 3, 1966, in Eufala, Alabama. She was seventeen years old. Some nine months later, they would have their first child, William Matthew.

A little over two weeks after the birth of Judy and Karlas' first child, Judy's parents, Cyrus E. Mathews and Louise L. Mathews, deeded them a home at 3009 Ivy Drive in north Tifton. The doting grandparents of William Matthew had given the young couple a home at no cost to them. The warranty deed stated that the home was given "in consideration of love and affection for their daughter and son-in-law."

The small, red brick home was located in a well-developed subdivision, and was situated on a nicely landscaped lot, and had a fenced backyard and a carport.

There were probably few couples as young as Karlas and Judy who had the privilege of living in, let alone owning, such a fine home in which to raise their growing family. Life should have been good for Karlas and Judy. He was working for Tifton Aluminum and she was working as a receptionist in a dentist's office at the Town and Country Shopping Plaza.

It was through her work at the Tifton shopping mall that Judy Mathews Bryan would eventually meet and befriend Linda Gail Sullivan, another mall employee.

*Betty Johnson*** knew both Judy Mathews Bryan and Linda Gail Sullivan during that time. Betty had worked as a dental hygienist in the office with Judy, and she was a close friend of Gail. In fact, it was Betty who had introduced Judy to her friend Gail.

"Gail was just a lot of fun to be around," Betty would say. "She always had a laugh and a joke and it was hard to be in a bad mood when Gail was around. I didn't know anybody who didn't like her, except, of course, Karlas."

Betty said that Karlas was jealous and possessive and "he was always coming in the dentist office checking on Judy."

After work hours, Betty spent a lot of time with Gail. She frequently went to Gail's house in Lenox to play cards.

"We had some great card games," Betty would recall. "We'd laugh and joke and cut the fool and have ourselves a good old time. Of course, we were young and we liked to party. We'd make our own fun."

A little over a year after the birth of William Matthew and the acquisition of the home on Ivy Drive, Judy and Karlas had their second child. A daughter, named Marni Michelle, was born July 11, 1968.

By the time Marni Michelle was six months old, court records reflected the first signs of a disintegrating marriage. On January 13, 1969, Karlas' name was taken off the deed to the house when he deeded the house on Ivy Drive to Judy for "the love and affection of his wife."

But Karlas' financial interest in the house may not have been without cost to Judy. On April 21, 1969, Judy borrowed $12,000 against the house from Tifton Savings and Loan.

By October of 1970, the short, stormy marriage was coming to an end. On October 18, 1970, Judy took their two children and moved out of their home on Ivy Drive in Tifton. Considering the fact that it was Judy who owned the home that had originally been given to the young couple by her parents, it seems strange that it would be Judy and the children who would move, rather than Karlas. One can only assume that Karlas was intransigent, and the only way Judy could get out of his reach was to move herself and the children – while Karlas remained in their home. She must have wanted desperately to physically distance herself from her husband.

Friends and acquaintances of Judy would later say that when Judy moved out of her home on Ivy Drive, she spent more time in Lenox with her friend, Gail Sullivan.

Judy wanted a divorce; Karlas clearly did not want the divorce and was bitterly opposed to it. Judy hired Tifton attorney Seymour Owens to file the Complaint for Divorce in Tift Superior Court and handle the divorce trial. Karlas hired attorney Hilton S. Hutchinson to represent his interests.

The irreconcilable differences Judy Bryan would cite as cause for the divorce included the complaint that Karlas had "willfully inflicted bodily and mental pain such as reasonably justifies apprehension of danger to her life and health."

In court papers, Judy would spell out the specifics of the legal terminology. She said, "My husband has threatened me on one occasion with a gun and on many occasions he has cursed me and called me bad names. During the last few weeks that we lived together he continually fussed and nagged at me and made my life with him unbearable." Judy said that Karlas' behavior had affected her health and her nerves. She said, "I just could not stand it any more and I had to separate from him."

Through the wrangling with attorneys, by October 31, 1970 – the same day Gail Sullivan's engagement was announced in the Tifton newspaper – Judy and Karlas Bryan made a property agreement. In the agreement, signed by both Judy and Karlas and their respective attorneys, custody of their two children was given to Judy, with Karlas having reasonable visitation rights.

According to the agreement, Karlas was to pay Judy child support for the two children in the amount of $150 per month, or $75 per month for each child. The child support payments were to continue until the child turned twenty-one years of age, married, or became self-supporting.

Although the young couple had settled any property or custody issues, the divorce itself still loomed in front of them. At the end of October, Karlas was still contesting the divorce, and they faced a jury trial and what promised to be a nasty court battle.

On November 9, 1970, Seymour Owens filed court documents stating Karlas had thirty days to answer the Divorce Complaint filed by Judy Bryan. If he failed to respond within thirty days, Judy Bryan would be granted the divorce "by default."

On November 12, 1970, the day before Gail Sullivan was killed, Karlas had apparently thrown in the towel. That afternoon, Judy and Karlas Bryan, and their respective attorneys, signed an agreement that Karlas would not contest the divorce. No demand for a jury trial would be made. Judy would give evidence and testimony to the Judge of Tift Superior Court without notification to Karlas – and without him being present. The agreement about the property they had signed on October 31, 1970, would be the divorce settlement.

The marriage was over. All that remained were the formalities. Judy must have been greatly relieved, and Karlas must have been furious. The very next evening, November 13, 1970, Karlas went to the drive-in and killed Gail Sullivan.

CHAPTER TWENTY

Thursday, November 14, 1996

After Karlas' arrest for murdering Gail Sullivan, no other news of the murder case was forthcoming until Friday, November 20, 1970, when the *Daily Tifton Gazette* published a front page story stating that Karlas Bryan was still being held in the Tift County jail and continued to blame Gail Sullivan for breaking up his marriage.

While Karlas awaited his possible indictment on murder charges by a Grand Jury, Gail Sullivan's family had to deal with their young daughter's death.

On November 23, 1970, the *Daily Tifton Gazette* carried the information about the family's plans for Gail's funeral. Under the headline, "Memorial Rites Tuesday for Miss Gail Sullivan," the newspaper stated that Gail Sullivan would be buried in her home town of Amory, Mississippi, and a memorial service would be held for Tifton friends at Bowen Donaldson Home for Funerals. The short article also said that she was a member of the Baptist church and that she had only lived in Tifton for six months when she was killed.

In December 1970, the Grand Jury of Tift Superior Court handed down a murder indictment on Karlas R. Bryan. Tifton resident B.L. Southwell was the foreman of the twenty-three member Grand Jury panel.

William J. Forehand, who had been the District Attorney for Tift County since 1955, would try the case for the state. After serving as a DA for twenty-two years, Forehand would become a Superior Court Judge. He would continue serving the people of Tift County in that capacity for another twenty years, officially retiring in 1996.

By December, Judy Bryan was settling her affairs in Tifton and returning to Alabama. On December 8, 1970, Judy deeded the house on Ivy Drive back to her mother.

The divorce between Karlas and Judy Bryan would become final on January 15, 1971, as Karlas awaited trial for murder.

Judy had packed her belongings and taken their two children to Birmingham, Alabama. Eventually, Judy and the two children moved into a small apartment, and Judy got a job with a periodical publisher, making $80 a week.

By March 1971, Karlas had Tifton attorneys Emory Walters and Henry Bostick to defend him; Karlas' parents were divorced and, for whatever reason, they each hired an attorney for their son. The attorneys had begun filing motions in the case. On March 24, 1971, they filed a demand for a copy of the indictment and a list of witnesses who were to testify against Karlas. They also filed a motion for arraignment. At the arraignment, Karlas would plead *not guilty* and a date would be set for a jury trial. Judy Mathews Bryan would be a witness for the state and would have to return to Tifton to testify against her ex-husband.

It was a short trial with a quick and shocking verdict.

On April 8,1971, the *Daily Tifton Gazette* ran a front page headline: "Tiftonite Acquitted of Murder." Under the one-column headline, the *Gazette* reported:

> *A Tift County jury took less than two hours to deliberate over three days of testimony and evidence before acquitting a 22 year old Tift Countian of a murder charge here today.*
>
> *The jury returned its verdict at approximately 10 am, clearing Karlas R. Bryan in the fatal shooting last November 13 of Gail Sullivan, 21, a hair stylist for men.*
>
> *The defense wound up its argument late Wednesday and the case went to the jury about 7:10 p.m. Jurors deliberated approximately 30 minutes Wednesday night and returned to continue deliberations at 9 am today. The verdict was announced in an emotion-packed atmosphere, before a large number of spectators, relatives and friends.*
>
> *Bryan, who has been held in the Tift County jail for most of the time since November 13, was immediately released from custody.*

One of the key points in the defense case was that Bryan was under a great emotional stress at the time of the shooting.

A psychiatrist, testifying for the defense, said it was his opinion that Bryan did not know right from wrong at the time of the shooting.

The defense also used an unusual sequence of presenting its evidence and testimony by putting Bryan on the stand first to make a lengthy and emotional unsworn statement concerning events leading up to the shooting.

Miss Sullivan was killed by a single .22 caliber bullet fired into the back of her head on the night of November 13.

Edd Walker had been a deputy back then, and he had accompanied Sheriff Tom Greer to the drive-in movie theater the Friday night Gail Sullivan was killed. Edd Walker had begun his career in law enforcement on September 15, 1960, and when Greer retired in late 1972, Walker was elected Sheriff of Tift County the following January. He would serve as a much-loved and widely respected sheriff for twenty-four years, retiring on December 31, 1996. There was very little that went on in Tifton for thirty-six years that Edd Walker didn't know about.

He remembered Gail Sullivan.

"We hardly ever had any crime back then," Walker recalled. "Oh, you know, just the usual shine liquor and drunks on the week-end; that was about it."

So the Gail Sullivan case stood out in his mind. Murders were certainly a rare thing in the 1960s and 1970s, and when they did happen, unlike today, the sheriff's office didn't have investigators. The cases were generally turned over to the GBI. The sheriff's office would not have its own criminal investigators until around 1975.

"We weren't much on record keeping," Walker recalled. "Sheriff Greer had a yellow legal pad he would scratch some notes on and throw in his desk drawer. That was about all the record keeping that was done."

Edd Walker recalled that the man, Karlas Bryan, had been acquitted of the murder. "I can't really explain that," Walker said. "All I can say is the jury must have felt sorry for him and turned him loose. It ain't supposed to happen like that, but sometimes it did back then."

Walker credited the acquittal to Emory Walters. "Let's just say that if Emory Walters or Peter Zack Geer walked in the courtroom, you could be 99% certain their client was walking out with them," Walker said. "It didn't mean it was right – it just meant they were that good."

Other Tifton residents who recalled the case had another explanation for Karlas Bryan's acquittal: she was a newcomer from California and he was one of the good ol' boys; Tifton took care of its own. Today it would be called jury nullification.

Whatever it was called, and however it had happened, Karlas Bryan had murdered Gail Sullivan and had walked away free and clear. The only time he had served for her murder had been the few months he was incarcerated prior to the trial.

*Cindy Davis** would always remember Gail Sullivan's murder and Karlas Bryan's acquittal. Like Gail Sullivan, Cindy worked as a hairdresser at the Town and Country Shopping Plaza. The shop Cindy worked in was directly across the mall from the shop where Gail was employed.

Cindy got to know all of the girls who worked in the mall, and Gail was no exception. Even thirty years later, Cindy would remember Gail Sullivan. She had done Gail's hair that Friday afternoon, before Gail went to the drive-in that evening. She had put Gail's hair up in some curls, Cindy recalled. "It was Friday afternoon and Gail was excited about her plans for the evening. She was going to the drive-in with some of her friends and looking forward to a fun time," Cindy said. Cindy had been shocked and saddened to learn of Gail's death later that evening.

"The whole thing was very hush-hush," Cindy would say. "When people talked about it, they whispered."

The reason for the hush-hush and whispering about the case – and the reason for Karlas' acquittal – could be summed up in four words by *Jeremy Thomas**, the foreman of the jury in Karlas' murder trial:

"She was a lesbian."

Almost thirty years after the acquittal, and at age eighty, Thomas had no apologies to make about the verdict.

Sheriff Edd Walker told GBI Agent John Heinen that Karlas had gone to the drive-in that night after deciding that his wife was having an affair with Gail Sullivan. Walker told Heinen that Karlas had located his wife with Gail Sullivan at the drive-in and had shot and killed Sullivan, but did not harm his wife.

Karlas' defense had not been that he was innocent; he had pled not guilty by reason of insanity. Of course Karlas' insanity had been only temporary, and once the not guilty verdict had come in, he was evidently back to mental health. And Emory Walters, perhaps ahead of his time in defense strategies, had simply put the victim on trial: she deserved killing.

Betty Johnson agreed that there had been a lot of whispering in Tifton about the Gail Sullivan murder.

"Karlas killed Gail in cold blood; that's a simple fact," Betty said. "And after he got arrested, he put out the tale that Gail was a lesbian. But I knew Gail Sullivan real well, and if she was a lesbian, I sure didn't know anything about it. And I think I was close enough to Gail that I would have known."

Betty also said, "I knew Karlas. You can't tell me Karlas Bryan didn't know what he was doing. He knew exactly what he was doing. That's the biggest bunch of baloney I ever heard. Karlas always did what Karlas wanted to do, and Karlas wanted to kill Gail Sullivan, and he did."

"The rules in court were different back then," Judge Forehand said. "Defendants were allowed to get on the stand and make long, unsworn statements in their defense and the state could not cross-examine them." After Karlas' trial, the court rules were changed and today such unsworn statements are not permitted in the courts. Judge Forehand and Henry Bostick said that there was never any evidence in the trial that Gail Sullivan was a lesbian – only Karlas' words in his unsworn statement.

Many people in Tifton did not think the Karlas Bryan murder trial was Tift County's finest hour of jurisprudence.

Karlas was a free man and Judy sat in Alabama waiting for Karlas to send the $150 a month child support for William Matthew and Marni Michelle. It was a long wait.

After being acquitted of the murder of Gail Sullivan, Karlas had been busy establishing a new family. On November 24, 1971, Karlas and Sheila Weeks were married by J. Terrell Ruis, an ordained Baptist minister, in Omega, Georgia.

Sheila was eighteen years old and had just graduated from high school; Karlas was twenty-three years old and had already been married and divorced and had two small children.

In one year's time, Karlas had separated from his first wife, gotten a divorce, killed Gail Sullivan, gone on trial and had been acquitted of her murder, and met, courted and married Sheila Weeks. Quite an eventful year by anyone's standard.

The man who had killed Gail Sullivan for breaking up his family had started a new family within seven months of his acquittal for her murder. And he did not concern himself with any financial obligations he may have had for his young son and daughter living in Alabama with his ex-wife; he did not send any child support.

For two years, Judy Mathews Bryan had struggled to support herself and her two children without receiving any child support from Karlas. Finally, on August 30, 1972, Judy went through the "uniform reciprocal enforcement of support act (URESA)" between Alabama and Georgia to get Karlas to pay child support.

In court papers filed on that date, she stated that Karlas Rayford Bryan was living at 215 Chesnutt Avenue in Tifton and was working as a painter for Reverend R.M. Hobbs. She stated that she did not know what Karlas' income was at the time. She said that Karlas had made one payment for $150 of child support on November 1, 1970; that was the first and last payment he ever made. She stated that she had outstanding debts for a car for $1,000, a loan for $225 and a credit card debt of $325.

On September 8, 1972, Alabama Circuit Judge William H. Cole made a court order for Karlas to pay the support. On October 3, 1972, Judge Bowie Gray of Tift County Superior Court signed the civil action for the URESA petition and ordered the defendant, Karlas R. Bryan, to appear in court October 20, 1972 at 2 p.m.

At the court appearance, Karlas was ordered to pay Judy the child support as agreed to in their divorce settlement.

It wasn't long before Karlas was in trouble with the law again. On February 25, 1973, Sheriff Edd Walker had Karlas arrested for ramming his car into the back of another vehicle on Highway 35. Karlas posted bond to get out of jail the next day, but when he failed to appear in court his bond was forfeited and the proceeds were put towards his eventual fine.

CHAPTER TWENTY-ONE

Thursday, November 14, 1996

Somebody was going to have to sit on Donald Davis. That's all there was to it. Go in there and tie him to a chair and put some duct tape on this mouth. Something.

The man was livid. Banging around in there in that interrogation room. Why, you could hear him all the way down the hall and into the front office.

Heinen had talked to Davis and told him he was going to have to let it go. Heinen had said to let it go because there was no way it was going to get into the courtroom. It would be considered too prejudicial to the Sheila Bryan case. No judge on earth would ever allow them to bring out the Gail Sullivan murder. So the best thing they could do was to let it go and concentrate on the case they had now.

Davis wasn't ready to let it go. He wasn't even close to ready. It would be days before he could even calm down enough to think the thing through.

Davis would never be able to accept it. *What lawman could accept a thing like that?* he thought. *A criminal investigator wouldn't be worth spit if they could accept a woman being gunned down in cold blood. It didn't matter if it was 30 years ago or 300 years ago, it wasn't right and it would never be right. Go tell that to somebody else.*

In time, Davis had been able to calm his thoughts enough to think about the Sheila Bryan case in light of the Sullivan case.

This wasn't the all-American family they portrayed themselves to be, that was for sure, he thought. Davis decided the Bryans were living a lie, a big lie.

Yeah, Davis thought, *Omega was too small a town for nobody to know about the Gail Sullivan murder. Some of the people there knew. Maybe more than a few.* But Davis wondered if they knew the details of the case. He felt sure the people of Omega thought that since Karlas had been acquitted, he was innocent. Acquittal didn't mean innocence, but Karlas and Sheila had probably passed it off that way.

But Davis also figured some people knew the real truth, and the ones who knew the real truth were probably afraid of Karlas. *Why shouldn't they be afraid of Karlas? A man who could do what he had done was capable of anything. Hell, with Karlas' drinking and his capabilities, they were smart to steer clear of the man and the subject.*

Davis reasoned that if Karlas could gun down Gail Sullivan in front of God and everybody at the drive-in picture show, he certainly could burn up a little old lady for $100,000.

That was the problem with injustice. When a man got away with murder one time, it only made him bold, led him to think he could get away with it again.

Davis wondered if Freda Weeks would still be alive if Karlas had been convicted in the Gail Sullivan murder. It was something to think about. *Karlas should have been convicted and given a life sentence and still had his butt sitting in a prison somewhere*; that's what Davis thought.

Yeah, Karlas was in this Freda Weeks thing with Sheila – he was in it up to his eyeballs, Davis thought. *He was probably the one who had planned the whole thing. Planned it for three months, maybe more.*

Now, Davis thought he knew why Sheila had been on the road with the burning car. The Gail Sullivan case would have made Karlas a suspect right off the bat. Karlas had to stay in the background, had to have an alibi. That's why he had put Sheila on the road. Sheila didn't have a criminal record; he did.

Not that Davis thought any better of Sheila. She had married the man, knowing who he was and what he was. And she had gone along with the Freda Weeks plan. Not only gone along with it, but carried it out. And it had been her mother, not his mother, her mother. As far as Davis was concerned, she was just as low as Karlas, maybe lower.

They had nerve all right. Stand there with that big lie tucked under their belts in front of their nice, middle-class home and tell Heinen they wanted him to hurry up and get the investigation over so they could get their $100,000. Sheila Bryan had balls. Not little ones.

Donald Davis made himself a promise. Sheila and Karlas Bryan were not going to get away with murder this time. Whatever he had to do, however long it took, he was going to see to that. He was going to stay on them like a fly stayed on shit.

When they put the handcuffs on Sheila Bryan, he wanted to be there. It was the only thing he could think of that was going to make him feel the least bit better about any of it. He wanted Sheila's smiling face behind bars, and Karlas' too, if that was possible.

"All-American family, my ass," he said.

CHAPTER TWENTY-TWO

Thursday, December 19, 1996

On any given weekday morning during the school year, Walter Young could be found at the intersection of Highway 319 and Oak Street, strategically positioned at the one and only traffic light in Omega. People from outside Omega sometimes debated the need for even the one traffic light, but in Omega, it was a small point of pride and there was no debate.

Walter Young would stand at the intersection until all of the children were safely routed to their destinations and tucked safely away in school. His duties at Oak and 319 were akin to a school crossing guard.

He would always arrive at work early, before 7 a.m., and walk across the street and get himself a big breakfast of grits and eggs. While eating his breakfast at one of the two restaurants in Omega – a recent addition to the BP gas station that locals referred to as the "Omega Cracker Barrel" – he would catch up on all the local gossip. There was always a lot of gossip.

*Barbara** had gotten herself one of those SUVs, those vehicles that couldn't decide if they wanted to be a car or a truck. The thing had turned out to be a lemon and she had to take it all the way to Albany, about seven times, to have it looked at, but the fools still didn't have it running right.

*Jerry** had a pretty poor crop of pecans coming in. It didn't look like he was going to get up his tax money from pecans this year. That was a shame. But those dang pecan trees sometimes only produced a healthy crop every other year. Jerry might have to take up odd jobs to get the money for his taxes.

Old *Pete** had finally kicked the bucket. It was probably just as well. Lord knows the man had suffered. But how was Betty Jean going to keep up that place without Pete? Those kids of theirs weren't worth a tinker's damn. Everybody knew that.

*Ed's** cows wouldn't stay put. They kept getting out and running all over the road out there in front of his place. Dang near caused a traffic fatality Friday. Big old Cadillac Seville came barreling through there right when Bessie went on one of her walks. You should have seen that city slicker's face. You'da thought he'd seen a Martian. Ed got a good laugh out of that one. But you'd think Ed could find some way to corral that herd.

When Walter Young finished his breakfast, he would return to his office at city hall and check his messages that had come in while he was away from his desk. As the chief of police for Omega, he had a lot of messages. And headaches.

There might be a harder job then being the chief of police in a small town like Omega, but if there was, Young didn't know what it would be. It was a twenty-four-hour-a-day job with little pay and no job security – and a whole lot of aggravation. The salary for chief of police was just $25,000 a year, and his was an appointed position. He served at the behest of the Omega City Council. All he had to do was make them mad enough, and out the door he went. Here today, gone tomorrow. Just like that.

In December 1996, he had been chief of police for almost four years, but he had been a deputy in Omega for five years before that. He had learned how to walk the political mine field, but some days it was harder than others. This would be one of those hard days, he could tell already.

He was on a "crackdown" about parking in the alley behind the Post Office. People had parked back there for years. But the folks at the Post Office had complained and demanded that the No Parking sign be enforced. Young had ignored the situation as long as he could, but when the City Council told him to crack down, he did. Everybody was screaming bloody murder and half the people in town were mad at him and weren't speaking.

Young didn't worry a whole lot about that. It had happened dozens of times before, and he knew after a while they would get over it. But for the time being, all their anger was vented at him.

"What the hell you doin' puttin' a ticket on my car, Walter? Ain't you got nothin' better to do?"

The calls would come in hot and heavy. Young saw it as just another of many little episodes to get through, nothing more, nothing less.

"Sorry about that, Jimmy," he would say. "Everybody's gettin' 'em. You guys are just goin' to have to find someplace else to park."

Young had two police officers who worked under him, and he only had two police cars for the three-man force. He drove his own car around some of the time. He didn't have a jail. If he ever arrested anybody, he had to drive them into Tifton and put them in jail over there. But other than putting some of his townsfolk in the Tift County jail, he tried to keep some distance between his office and the Tifton police.

It wasn't like he had any major crimes to deal with in Omega. Mostly it was traffic offenses – some said Omega was a speed trap – and domestic disputes. Occasionally they had a break-in or a prowler, something exciting like that. At night, the officers checked every store every hour on the hour; there weren't a lot of stores. One time they had had a drug bust. It got in the *Tifton Gazette* and Young had laminated the article and hung it in his office, like a trophy.

Walter Young's office was tastefully decorated with "Mayberry" memorabilia. A large poster of Barney Fife hung on the wall next to his desk. In some ways, Walter Young thought of himself as a real-life Andy Taylor.

If there was ever a contest for the community most like the television sitcom community of Mayberry, Omega, Georgia, would probably get the prize. It is a small town where everybody knows everybody – and everybody's business. The chief of police not only knew everyone in town, he knew "the name of every dog and cat in town" as well.

His wife had lived her entire life in Omega and his three children, two daughters and a son, had been raised there. It was home. For better or worse, it was his life.

Overall he liked his police job, and he planned to stay, but just in case, he had covered some bases. Young owned and ran a cleaning business, which he worked nights and weekends. It was mostly commercial work done on contract, and his wife and several others worked in the business with him. Just one of his janitorial contracts was more than his police salary. In addition to the cleaning service, he owned and operated a car wash in Omega that was open on Thursday, Friday, and Saturday.

Young planned to retire at age fifty; in 1996, he was thirty-nine. He was poking money away for his retirement – and just in case he made the city fathers mad enough one day, he could walk away from his desk without so much as a financial hiccup. But his plans were to stay at his police job until he retired.

He had veered from his game plan a little to put in a swimming pool at the house. He considered it family entertainment, which there was a scarcity of in Omega, and, as he said, "I never buy anything I can't pay for."

But anything he bought, wore, drove, said – or even thought about, he sometimes felt – was grist for the mill in Omega. Everybody had an opinion about everything and everybody all the time. And he certainly wasn't left off the list of people to talk about. He was used to it and it didn't ruffle his feathers much.

When GBI Agent John Heinen showed up at his office just after lunch that day, Young knew he was going to be drawn into something he would just as soon stay out of. He knew about the accident on Livingston Bridge Road. He knew about the exhumation. He knew about the investigation. And he knew, for a lot of reasons, he would just as soon be left out of this. But as usual, he didn't get to stay out of anything that went on in Omega, and Sheila and Karlas lived in Omega, just one street over from his office.

When Heinen came into the office, Young got up and shook his hand, and went and closed the door. He always closed the door to his office when he was talking to someone; it was the only way to pretend he had any privacy at all. But he knew there were already Omega residents who had spotted Heinen's Crown Victoria and were wondering who was visiting Young.

"What can I do for you?" Young asked.

"I need to know some things about Sheila and Karlas Bryan," Heinen said.

"Like what?"

"Well, first, on the day of the accident, August 18, I want to know where Karlas was that day."

"He was at the lake," Young said. Young explained to Heinen that he had gotten a call at home that Sunday afternoon, telling him about the accident on Livingston Bridge Road. Young couldn't recall who had called him. But whoever it was had asked Young to deliver a message to Karlas and tell him that there had been an accident involving his wife and mother-in-law.

Young told Heinen he had driven over to the Bryans' house to talk to Karlas, but there wasn't anybody at home. He said he walked across the street to Michael Bennett's house and asked Bennett if he knew where Karlas was. Bennett told Young that Karlas was probably at Lake Mary in Tifton. Young knew that Karlas and Sheila owned a lake lot there, and, he said, he went back across the street to the Bryans' and saw where the jet ski was gone from under the carport where they usually kept it, so he assumed Karlas was at the lake.

Young said he then called the Tift County Sheriff's Office, and they told him they would find Karlas and deliver the message for him.

"Did they deliver the message?" Heinen wanted to know.

"As far as I know, they did," Young said. "You'd have to call them about that."

"Did you see Karlas at all that day?"

"No, the first time I saw Karlas was a few weeks after you had paid him and Sheila a visit."

"Tell me about that."

"Well, I just happened to drive by there and decided I would go and check on them, see how they were doing, after all the business about the accident. Just to see if they were okay."

"Were they okay?"

"Not exactly. Karlas was drunk. He was pitchin' a fit, like Karlas does. Said he wasn't going back to prison. Said he would kill himself first. Just carrying on to beat the band. So I left. No use in staying and listening to all that."

Heinen asked Young about Karlas' drinking and Young confirmed that Karlas had a problem in that direction. He let Heinen know that with the drinking problem and his temper, Karlas was not going to win any popularity contests in Omega. The people in Omega gave Karlas wide berth.

"Did you know Freda Weeks?" Heinen wanted to know.

"Yeah, I knew Freda," Young said.

"Tell me about her."

"Well, she lived back there in the trailer on their property. She had Alzheimer's and she would wander off and forget where she was. She could get around okay most of the time, but her state of mind wasn't too good. A couple of times I had to go over there. She fell one time and was just laying out in the road. That sort of thing."

Heinen thanked Young and told him he would follow up on the message about the accident with the Tift County Sheriff's Office.

"Glad to be of help," Young said. But he didn't mean it.

He knew when he was being put in a bad place, and this was definitely a bad place, in his view. The people of Omega might talk from sun up to sun down about each other, but they didn't abide talking to outsiders. It was like family. You might say derogatory things about a family member to other members of the family, but you didn't say those things to people outside the family. That's just the way it was.

Sheila and Karlas were the topic of conversation on many lips. But Young knew, better than anyone, that what was said in Omega was supposed to stay in Omega. They didn't want their business, even if it was about Sheila and Karlas, being toted out of town by some sharp-dressing GBI agent or anyone else.

And Young knew that Karlas and Sheila, although not exactly well liked by everyone in Omega, had some connections to the movers and shakers in town. And there was no way to tell where that might lead.

It wasn't like Sheila and Karlas hadn't been the topic of town gossip before. That had gone on for years, even before Young started working in the police department. But now, he knew, most of the gossip was coming out of Omega Baptist Church. Sheila had been the church secretary there for years, but she had resigned quite some time back. People still talked about that. She'd had to either resign or be fired, one or the other, that's what he had heard.

Young had heard a lot of talk about how Sheila had ended up leaving the church. Some people said it was because she was caught stealing money from the church. Some people said it was because she had run the pastor out of town by saying he had made sexual advances towards her. Some people said it was because she had taken a job at the Swannee Swifty store and was up there selling beer. Some people said it was because she was having an affair and was at the Swannee Swifty flirting with her boyfriend. Some people said it was because she wore her bikini out in the yard when she was mowing the lawn. Young didn't put too much credence in any of it, he heard so much.

But he did know that after the accident, Pastor John Spivey over at Omega Baptist Church had talked Sheila into coming back into the church. There were some folks who weren't too happy about that. They saw Sheila as trouble, and they didn't want her back in the church. Things had gone along pretty smoothly after she had left and they wanted things to stay like they were. But Sheila was back in the fold, and already trouble was brewing, Young knew that.

Young didn't much cotton to Pastor Spivey. They'd had a falling out a while back. Young had had the contract to clean the church, and it had been such a problem, he had finally just told Spivey he could clean the church himself. The bathrooms were the problem. All sorts of things thrown in the toilets. Just a damn mess is what it was. Young blamed it on the Hispanics who attended the church.

Omega had a large Hispanic population. Many of them were illegal aliens, so they never showed up in the census count. That was why the population was really bigger than what was ever shown in any population statistics. The Hispanics were called migrant workers but Young knew them to be Mexicans who never much migrated past Omega. For whatever reason, Omega had become the migrant worker capitol of Tift County. They worked farms all over Tift and surrounding counties, but they lived in Omega. And that meant they were Walter Young's worry. Most of them didn't speak English. It made his life a little too interesting sometimes, he thought.

Young was glad when Heinen left and took his questions with him. He had other things to worry about. He had to get that alley behind the Post Office cleared out.

CHAPTER TWENTY-THREE

Thursday, January 2, 1997

The last interview Heinen had scheduled for the day was after 5 p.m. with another one of the volunteer firemen who had been called out to the fire on Livingston Bridge Road.

Danny Griner gave pretty much the same information Heinen had heard already from the other firemen he had interviewed. They had come to the end of the interview when Griner said, just as kind of an aside, that a neighbor of the Bryans had told him that a fire had been reported at the Bryan residence in the past, and that $17,000 in insurance money had been collected on that fire.

Heinen's ears perked up.

"Tell me more about that fire," Heinen said

"Let me check on the information and I'll get back to you," Griner said.

Griner did get back to Heinen. He called him a few days later and gave Heinen the information he needed to check on the residential fire.

It was 8:44 a.m. on Wednesday morning, September 8, 1993, when the call came in to the Tifton Fire Department. Sheila Bryan made the call, telling dispatcher Mike Flippo that her house was on fire.

The alarm was put out and the fire engine arrived at the address on Maple Street at 8:50 a.m. In all, nine firemen responded to the scene of the fire: six volunteer firemen from Omega and three firemen from the Tifton Fire Department. Lieutenant Vick Stone had been the one in charge of the fire, and Bill Wade had completed the Incident Report.

By the time the fire department arrived, there was no fire, only smoke. The fire had self-extinguished.

Sheila reported that she had been cooking eggs, and that she had accidentally left the stove on, and that the bacon grease in the pan had caught fire.

There was smoke throughout the house, but the fire damage was in the kitchen. The microwave above the Jenn-Aire stove had been damaged as had one of the stove-top eyes. The wall behind the stove and the cabinets above it had also suffered some damage.

The firemen noted that the fire detectors were operating at the time of the fire and the house had no sprinkler system.

The firemen had used an ejector fan to clear the house of the smoke. They left the scene at 9:54 a.m.

Heinen would learn that the Bryans had collected approximately $17,000 from the insurance company for the grease fire. He would also learn that the fire had not been investigated.

Grease fires, in and of themselves, were not unusual. Heinen learned that one-fifth of all home fires in this country start in the kitchen because of the constant potential for fire there, and because the majority of kitchen fires involved oil or grease igniting during meal preparation. Professionals in fire prevention looked at cooking as being 730 *controllable* fires a year (cooking two meals a day for 365 days).

Heinen learned that what was unusual about the grease fire at the Bryan home was the amount of damages claimed. In 1993, the National Fire Data Center reported the average claim on a property loss during a fire in Georgia was $4,666 – considerably less than the Bryan's claim. The average amount of money paid on a grease fire claim was only a couple thousand dollars.

Heinen got a copy of the insurance claim filed by the Bryans and saw where the claim had been padded. According to the Bryans, the fire had caused them to find other lodging for almost a month which amounted to a claim for expenses totaling over $2,000. There were bills for dry cleaning, including the children's stuffed toys. Then, of course, there was an estimate for cleaning the house, which was several thousand dollars. And, after the cleaning, according to the Bryans, the entire inside of the house needed to be painted, resulting in another estimate for thousands of dollars. The Bryans had even wanted their kitchen linoleum replaced. Beyond all that, there were appliances to be replaced, as well as other contents, such as vitamins and spices. And not to forget an estimate to wash clothes.

"Expensive egg," Heinen said.

Heinen wondered if the Bryans had gotten a taste of "easy money" made off of the grease fire.

Heinen also learned of another insurance claim by the Bryans. That one was made on August 2, 1996, just two weeks before the death of Freda Weeks.

The Bryans had a jet ski and trailer stolen from under their carport. The Omega police had found the jet ski a short distance away from the Bryan's house on Maple Street. It was found on Flat Ford road, down in a ditch. The ski had been damaged and the Bryans had filed an insurance claim to have the ski and trailer repaired.

The Polaris jet ski, which was just three months old, had suffered considerable damage, according to Karlas Bryan's claim. He submitted a claim for over $1,500.

"Another ditch," Heinen said.

CHAPTER TWENTY-FOUR

Tuesday, January 7, 1997

Investigator Donald Davis stood on the dock trying to decide what to make of it. It was either an overgrown pond or an under-grown lake, one or the other. But whether it was a big pond or a small lake, the property at Lake Mary certainly had not lived up to his expectations of a "lake lot."

When Heinen had told him the Bryans owned a "lake lot," Davis knew that nothing would do but for him to make the drive up to Tift county and check it out. So there he was, standing on the dock Karlas and Sheila had built at their lake lot, and he was, as usual, mystified.

It wasn't just the size of the lake, which he estimated to be somewhere between thirty and fifty acres, that had surprised him. It was the location of the lake, more than anything else, that had bewildered him. When he had heard "lake lot," he had had visions of a rustic woodland and a place for Smoky the Bear and his friends to hang out. It was quite clear to Davis that Smoky would not be welcome here.

This was a thriving subdivision; a residential area where $100,000-and-up homes had sprung up along the lake's shore-line like mushrooms in a cellar. Instead of "lake lot," Davis thought Heinen should have said, "a well developed residential neighborhood in which middle and upper class homes have crowded next to each other on half acre lots to share a small lake."

These were the homes of Tifton's up-and-comers, the homes of working professionals and business owners.

Karlas Bryan's lake lot was located in north Tifton just two-tenths of a mile east of busy Highway 125 north, also known as Tift Avenue. The sound of traffic rushing along the main north-south highway drowned out any of the quieter sounds of Mother Nature.

Karlas' lot was at the narrow end of the lake's north side, closest to the highway. The north side of the lot was on 40th Street, a paved main road running east-west through the subdivision. To the south was the lake. Houses had already been built on both sides of the lot: to the east, a two-story red brick ranch style home; to the west, a two-story home with vinyl siding and stone.

Karlas' lot would have been completely barren if it were not for about a dozen yellow pines. The lot had been cleared, and there was no flora, certainly no fauna, to be concerned with.

It was obvious to Davis that Karlas had been planning to build a house on the lot. He had already run electricity, and the utility pole was about midway down the lot to the waterline. Karlas had built the boat dock Davis was standing on, had painted it rusty brown, and fitted it with a security light. Davis assumed that with these property improvements, the Bryan family had been able to enjoy the lake-front property while they awaited financing to build their dream home. Karlas had even gotten a jump-start on the care and maintenance of the lawn that was to surround the dream home: He had already put in an underground sprinkler system.

Davis was also aware that Karlas had purchased a pontoon boat and jet skis to complement the family cookouts and outings at the lake.

Davis thought about Freda Weeks moving to this place. Certainly the Bryans were not planning to leave Sheila's 82-year-old mother behind in Omega when they moved to Tifton and Lake Mary. Davis again compared Freda Weeks to the little old ladies he knew: None of them would have wanted to leave their homes and move to this place he was looking at. What had their plans been for Freda Weeks? Were they going to build a four-bedroom house? Would Freda Weeks want to trade in her spacious mobile home for a bedroom in this swanky neighborhood? Donald Davis would have laid bets that Freda Weeks would not have been happy about moving to this "lake lot."

This was choppin' in some pretty high cotton, Davis thought. How did a man who worked as a house painter and a woman who worked for minimum wage as a data entry clerk afford lake-front property, a pontoon boat, jet skis, a new truck, a couple of other cars, a large house in Omega – and two children? Davis knew where to find some of the answers to his questions: the Tift County courthouse.

The records revealed that Karlas had purchased the lake lot on March 7, 1995. He had paid Sunbelt Plantations, Inc., owned by A.N. Adcock, $20,000 for Tract 9 on Lake Mary. The tract of land contained .513 acres and had 100 feet on the water-front. Karlas had paid a premium price; $20,000 could buy a lot of land in Tift County, even in 1995. Davis noted that Sheila Bryan's name was not on the warranty deed.

Davis knew any kind of water-front property in land-locked Tift County was hard to come by. While irrigation ponds were prevalent, recreational bodies of water were almost nonexistent. Developers had long ago recognized that they could get a premium price for small lots on the few bodies of water existing in the county.

All of the lots for sale at Lake Mary were residential building lots, and they came with covenants or restrictions on the property.

Davis found the protective covenants for Lake Mary had been established in February 1978 by Leonard Morris and A.N. Adcock, when they had originally begun to develop and sell the lake-front lots. All houses erected on the properties were to have at least 1,800 square feet of heated area. If the house had an attached carport or garage, the house had to have at least 1,700 square feet of heated area, and all carports or garages were to be at least 200 square feet.

There were twenty-nine protective covenants in all, covering everything from types of animals permitted (only dogs and cats and household pets), to what kinds of garbage cans could be used and where they could be placed, to types of piers and docks that could be erected.

The records reflected that the deed to the lot had been satisfied, meaning paid off, by Karlas on October 18, 1995, about six months after he had originally purchased the property. On that date Karlas had paid A.N. Adcock $8,000.

Davis had to put his thinking cap on to figure out the money situation. He knew about the kitchen fire in September of 1993 that had netted Karlas and Sheila some $17,000, and he knew about the theft claim just a few weeks before Freda Weeks' death. Still, it looked to Davis like Karlas was a little shy of a load to buy the boat and jet skis and truck, etc. He kept looking.

Then he found it. Karlas' mother, Mary H. Bryan Brown, had died on July 23, 1994, just ten months after Sheila's grease fire. Mary Brown's estate had been probated on August 3, 1994.

According to the probate court records, Mary Bryan Brown had four children at the time her estate was probated: Kermit, age 47; Karlas, age 45; Myric, age 41; and Myra, age 33. Her two sons and her daughter Myric lived in Tift County; her daughter, Myra, lived in Bardstown, Kentucky. Kermit, the oldest son, had been named the executor of her estate.

In her Last Will and Testament, Mary Brown had bequeathed all of her household furnishings and her automobile to her four children equally. She had left her jewelry and clothing to be divided equally between her two daughters. All other property, including her home and monies, was to be divided equally between the four children. At the time of her death, Mary Brown owned a home in Tifton at 621 Prince Avenue.

Davis saw where the Prince Avenue home had been sold on February 22, 1995, for $46,500. Assuming that nothing was owed to the bank on the mortgage, that would come to $11,625 for Karlas, again assuming the money had been divided four ways, as his mother had instructed in her Will. The children had not gotten the money from the house until August 26, 1995, after everything went through probate court.

Davis sat down and drew himself out a time line:

Sept. 8,	1993	Fire; Karlas and Sheila get $17,000
July 23,	1994	Karlas' mother dies
August 3,	1994	Karlas' mother's estate is probated
Feb. 22,	1995	Karlas' mother's house is sold
March 7,	1995	Karlas buys the lake property ($20,000)
Aug. 26,	1995	Karlas gets approx. $11,625
Oct. 18,	1995	Karlas pays off the lake property; ($8,000) and plans to build a house
May 28,	1996	Karlas raises bodily injury insurance
Aug. 2,	1996	Theft is reported
Aug. 18,	1996	Freda Weeks dies

Davis thought it made an interesting picture. It appeared to Davis that all of the "extra" things Sheila and Karlas had purchased – lake lot, boat, skis, truck – had been gotten through two sources: insurance and death. Even the 1987 Mercury Cougar Sheila had been driving the day of the accident had been inherited; it was Mary Bryan Brown's car.

But what Davis found most thought-provoking in his time line picture was the lull of activity between October 1995 and May 1996. What was going on in that seven-month period?

Karlas had paid for the lake lot, put in the sprinkler system and dock and gotten the boat and skis. He was clearly ready to start living the good life at Lake Mary. So why wasn't there any construction on the dream home? Karlas did not strike Davis as the patient kind; he appeared to move quickly. But it was obvious no construction had ever begun. Why?

Davis figured the dream home had to be about 2,000 square feet of wonderfulness; that's what the property covenants called for and it was pretty clear those where the kind of homes that had been built around Lake Mary. Davis figured a 2,000 square foot home would cost at least $100,000 – the magic number – or maybe as much as $150,000.

So where was Karlas Bryan going to get $100,000 to build his dream home? Had he applied for financing and been turned down? Had he over-extended himself? What exactly was the hold-up on the $100,000 and the dream home? Karlas had had seven months to get those pieces together – the man who had managed to buy the lake property in about a week's time after his mother's house was sold – and yet he did not appear to have made any progress with the lake house.

Davis did not think it was just coincidental that Karlas had gone into Georgia Farm Bureau Insurance Company in May 1996 and raised his bodily injury coverage from $25,000 to $100,000. Even if he was going to raise the amount of coverage, he could have waited until the annual review in October. Davis had the feeling that Karlas planned to be well into his building phase by October 1996.

Davis decided that while he was in Tifton, he would find the house on Ivy Drive where Judy and Karlas had lived out their three years of marital bliss.

He was shocked when he found the house. It was located in the Lakeview subdivision less than half a mile by car from Karlas' dream-house-to-be on Lake Mary. Karlas could stand on his dock and throw a rock across the lake and break a window at 3009 Ivy Drive.

Davis wondered if that was just another strange coincidence. He decided this case just got curiouser and curiouser.

By early spring, Heinen was readying to leave for Harvard. And, because he was the lead investigator and he was leaving, he was pressed into making some decisions in the case. Heinen talked with Charles Stines, the Assistant District Attorney who would try the case if it went to trial, and they decided to take the case to a Grand Jury and let the people of Colquitt County decide what to do with it. Heinen would fly back to testify before the Grand Jury.

As far as what to do about Karlas, Heinen decided to let it go. But there was no statute of limitations on murder. No one close to the case doubted for a minute that Karlas was involved in the crimes. In fact, everyone, to a person, believed that he was the instigator. Sheila would take the rap while her husband walked away free and clear. *Must be hard on a marriage*, Heinen thought.

But he also wondered whether, if the Grand Jury brought back an indictment on Sheila, Karlas would let her take the walk alone? Perhaps an indictment would cause enough tension between this husband and wife to cause Sheila to step forward and talk. It was a hope.

Heinen would leave for Harvard and leave the case in the capable hands of Donald Davis and Charles Stines. There was still an awful lot to do if the Grand Jury came back with an indictment.

CHAPTER TWENTY-FIVE

Thursday, December 18, 1997

On Thursday, at 8:30 a.m., the Grand Jury returned a True Bill of Indictment against Sheila Bryan. She was charged with malice murder, felony murder, and first-degree arson.

Charles Stines notified Sheila's attorneys Bill Moore and George Saliba of the indictment and told them of the bench warrant being prepared for Sheila's arrest.

Moore made two requests of Stines: He wanted an agreement that Sheila could turn herself in to the police and would not have to be handcuffed and brought to the jail – like an ordinary criminal – and he wanted Stines to agree to a bond stipulation.

Stines did not have a problem with either of the requests from Moore. Stines did not see Sheila as a flight risk and did not feel that she was likely to endanger anyone else. Moore and Stines agreed on a $30,000 bond and for Sheila to turn herself in to the jail at the CCSO that afternoon.

Sheila got the bad news from her attorney and concerned herself with coming up with the $30,000 bond, which was really a financial agreement that she would appear in court to answer the criminal charges. Donald Davis knew the $30,000 bond would be a problem for Sheila. She would have to post a property bond, but for Sheila, Davis knew, that would not be easy.

To post a property bond, Karlas and Sheila would have to own property in Tift county, which they did: the lake lot in Tifton and the home on Maple Street in Omega. But when a property bond was posted, they would have to have twice the bond amount – $60,000 – plus $2,000 homestead exemption in clear, unencumbered equity in the property. Davis knew that Karlas and Sheila did not have $62,000 in equity in their two properties.

Davis knew, through his search of court records, that the Bryans had purchased their home in Omega on November 16, 1976, from Kenneth and

Mary Francis Napier. They had paid the Napiers $300 and had assumed a $17,100 mortgage with Tifton Federal Savings and Loan. Both Sheila and Karlas' names appeared on the warranty deed.

Davis knew the house he had been to on Maple Street in Omega was not a $17,000 home. It was clear to Davis that the house had been extensively enlarged and re-modeled, and, in its present state, was more like a $60,000 home.

From the court records, Davis knew the Bryans had paid off the $17,100 mortgage and owned the property free and clear by January 1979.

But on May 14, 1990, they had borrowed $25,000 against the house on a ten-year note that fell due on May 7, 2000. Then, on October 13, 1992, they had borrowed another $25,000, again on a ten-year note, which fell due on October 15, 2001. Both loans had been taken out with Citizens Bank of Tifton.

Within two years, they had gone from having their home paid for to being some $50,000 in debt. Davis knew that neither of the loans had been paid off at the time of Sheila's arrest. He assumed that a large portion of the $50,000 had gone to re-model the house.

But the issue of a bond was Sheila's problem to solve. For Davis, it was a good day; it was the day he had been hoping to see for seventeen long months. Still, he was disappointed he wouldn't get to see them slap the handcuffs on Sheila. He consoled himself with the idea that he would go next door to the jail and look at her behind bars when she got to the CCSO. If he'd had his way, she wouldn't have been eligible for a bond, but he wasn't the one calling the shots.

The bench warrant for Sheila's arrest marked the end of something – and the beginning of something else. It meant the end of the investigation and the control law enforcement had over the case. The case had now entered the legal system – and Donald Davis knew, as well as anyone, that could be a crapshoot.

It was after lunch, in late afternoon, that John Heinen met Sheila at the CCSO jail. It was there he officially served her with the warrant for her arrest.

Heinen then sat down with Sheila for the first time to ask her questions in order to complete the GBI's arrest record. She gave her name as Sheila Kay Weeks Bryan and said she had no aliases. Her date of birth was March 12, 1953, and she had been born in Cook County.

The arrest record indicated that her hair was brown and her eyes were blue. She was 5' 3" tall and weighed 195 pounds. She had two missing top teeth and three missing bottom teeth. She was working as a substitute teacher for the Tift County Board of Education and drove a 1990 white Honda Accord.

She listed her mother, father, and three brothers as deceased. Karlas was listed as her spouse. The GBI's term for "friend" is "associate," and Sheila named two "associates": Cindy Camp of Lenox and *Debra Pearson** of Omega. At the time, neither of the names meant anything to John Heinen.

Sheila had a bone to pick with Heinen: Why hadn't she been allowed to testify in front of the Grand Jury?

Heinen told Sheila he was sure that Charles Stines would have welcomed her testimony, and that Bill Moore or George Saliba could have arranged for her testimony, if that had been her wish.

Heinen took the opportunity to express to Sheila directly, rather than through her attorneys, that he would like to interview her any time she wanted to tell her side of the story. He told her that her attorney could make the arrangements for the interview. He also told Sheila that he had spoken with Bill Moore earlier that morning and had, once again, requested an interview with her.

When the booking procedure was completed, Heinen turned Sheila over to the jail personnel.

It was about 4 p.m. when Donald Davis finally got over to the jail to take a look at Sheila sitting behind bars. She was gone, and Davis was denied his one moment of satisfaction. *Burt Pearson** had arrived with Sheila's bond, and Sheila had never seen the inside of a jail cell.

How Sheila solved the problem of her bond would, again, be one of those questions where the answer to what actually happened depended on whom you asked.

Sheila said she had started thinking about the problem of the bond in the event of her arrest long before the arrest had actually come. She said she had met Debra and Burt Pearson at Omega Baptist Church years before, when they were all working in the Meals-on-Wheels program at the church. Sheila said she had discussed the problem about the bond with Debra Pearson, and Debra had told her, "Burt will post your bond, that's no problem."

Sheila would also say that it had been a bad decision to have Burt Pearson sign on her bond. Years later, in hindsight, Sheila would say that if she had it to do over again, she would not have let Burt Pearson sign her bond.

Burt Pearson said Sheila's explanation was a total lie. Burt Pearson said he never discussed the bond with Sheila, and Sheila had never discussed it with his wife, Debra.

Pearson said Karlas had come to him that day, crying and begging him to please post the bond so Sheila would not have to stay in jail. Pearson said he had posted the bond for Sheila because he had felt sorry for Karlas, and no other reason.

Pearson would also say that Karlas had worked for him off and on for twenty years, and that he had put food on the Bryans' table for many years, and that Sheila Bryan was an ingrate. Furthermore, Pearson said, Sheila Bryan was as guilty as the day was long and, if justice was done, Sheila would sit her ass in jail for a long, long time.

If anybody knew the truth, Burt Pearson was likely to be the one to know it.

Burt Pearson not only knew a lot about Sheila and Karlas Bryan, he knew a lot about arson and prison. He had only been out of federal prison a short time, on a conviction involving arson, when he went to the CCSO to bond Sheila Bryan out of jail.

And he had the money to do it. It would have surprised no one in Tift County if Burt Pearson had laid $30,000 in cash on the table – and never missed it. But he had not needed to do that. He could post a property bond.

His house, located just on the outskirts of Omega on Highway 319, looked like Tara from Gone With the Wind. The huge, three-story home with white columns sat far back off the road – and was an imposing structure even from that distance. His driveway was longer than Main Street in Omega.

No one told Ronnie Dobbins that Burt Pearson had signed on Sheila's bond or that there was any connection between the Pearsons and the Bryans. If they had, Dobbins would have let out one of his "Whooooooooopdeeeeeedoooos!" While people in Tift County knew Pearson as a businessman, Dobbins knew Pearson as a suspect. Dobbins had a thick file folder he kept in a filing cabinet on Burt Pearson and any time there was an arson case in Tift County, Burt Pearson's name always crossed Dobbins' mind. For Dobbins, arson in Tift County was synonymous with the name Burt Pearson.

CHAPTER TWENTY-SIX

Thursday, December 18, 1997

Charles Stines – everybody called him Charlie – had come to the end of his rope with District Attorney David Miller and, unknown to him at the time, the Sheila Bryan case was going to be the very last case he tried in the Moultrie office for the Southern Judicial Circuit, which Miller was elected to serve.

Stines was an Assistant District Attorney who had joined the DA's office in July 1987. Stines' office was located at the Governmental Building in Moultrie, and he generally tried most of the Colquitt County cases for the circuit. And since the Sheila Bryan case was a Colquitt county case, the case naturally had fallen to Stines. The case was not the problem; David Miller was the problem.

Like Omega Police Chief Walter Young, who served at the behest of the Omega City Council, Stines served as Assistant District Attorney at the behest of District Attorney David Miller, whose office was located in Valdosta.

For many years Stines and Miller had been close friends. They had socialized together, taking canoe trips in a group they belonged to called "Fellow Travelers." The group was made up of men who liked to canoe the rivers and backwaters of south Georgia and surrounding areas. They were a convivial bunch, and their motto had been, "no drunks, no motors and no women." Eventually they had to change the motto to "no ugly women" because, often enough, wives and girlfriends would accompany them on their journeys.

But somewhere along the line the friendship had fallen apart and their professional relationship along with it. As is so often the case, the disintegrating relationship had not come about over a major disagreement, but rather had whittled away over a number of small, and what might have been, inconsequential disagreements.

As best Stines would ever be able to recall, the first break in the relationship had come over a year earlier when Miller had announced that he was running for the DA position. At the time, both David Miller and Charlie Stines were working under District Attorney Lamar Cole; Stines in the Moultrie office and Miller in the Valdosta office. Stines had already promised Lamar Cole that he would support Jim Hardy – the senior man in the DA's office – for the job and so, when Miller came to Stines seeking his support in the election, Stines had told him that he was already committed to supporting Hardy. According to Stines, Miller did not take it well. In the end, Hardy decided not to run and Stines eagerly put his full support behind Miller. Miller ran as a Republican without any Democratic opposition and became DA – but the crack in their relationship was already there by the time Miller took office.

Shortly after Miller was elected, he had gone to Moultrie and called Stines and the other Assistant DA, Scott Gunn, in for a tail-chewing. He told them they were losing too many cases. Stines knew that Miller had no idea how many cases he had won or lost. Stines wasn't real sure himself, since he didn't keep a record, but he knew he had won eight of his last thirteen cases; he also knew he tried more cases than any other Assistant District Attorney.

Miller had ended up on Stines' case, eventually telling Stines that he thought he was "too close to law enforcement." Stines was tight with the men in law enforcement in Colquitt County; he liked them and they liked him. Stines counted on them to put the cases together and they counted on Stines to bring in a conviction. Miller told Stines that he allowed law enforcement officers and probation officers to tell him what to do. Stines said, hooey.

Sometimes Stines met with a group of prosecutors and law enforcement officers in Thomasville on Friday mornings. The group was called the South Georgia Intelligence Network. The group had been formed by Jim Hardy and attendance had been supported by Lamar Cole. But after Miller let Stines know that he did not approve, Stines quit attending.

But it didn't matter. It didn't seem that anything Stines did pleased Miller. They had differing opinions on many subjects. Stines thought that asset forfeitures should continue being handled by the Prosecuting Attorney's Council; Miller thought they should be handled through the DA's office. Miller wanted to hire a prosecutor to handle juvenile cases; Stines thought it was a waste of money because they only spent one-half a day a week on the cases.

The tension between the two men had built to a crescendo by the time

Stines took on the Sheila Bryan case.

But Stines was not a man to give up easily. A slender, muscular man of forty-nine with prematurely white hair, Stines had grown up poor and hard in the hills of North Carolina and he knew what it meant to tough things out. Nothing had come easily for Charlie Stines and when things did finally come his way, he didn't let go without a fight.

When he was a young man, a girlfriend of Stines' had made fun of his use of the English language. Stines had grown up in the poor, rural South and he was embarrassed by the fact that he did not speak properly. So he worked on it. And worked on it. But nevertheless, he would always be self conscious about his speech – always afraid that he would use incorrect grammar or an inappropriate word.

Too poor to afford a college education, Stines had found a way. Berea College in Berea, Kentucky, forty miles south of Lexington, offered a college education, tuition free, to the Appalachian poor. Stines went there in 1965 and graduated with a degree in political science in 1969.

After college he had gone into the Army and worked as a dog handler with the military police. He had spent a year in Vietnam and counted it as a positive experience in his life. "I made up my mind to read at least one good book every week while I was there," Stines said. And he did.

Once out of the military, Stines had gone to Appalachian State College in Boone, North Carolina on the GI Bill to get his master's in political science. To help with expenses, he had worked as a photographer for a newspaper and as a research assistant.

But in 1973, once out of college, Stines learned that a master's degree and a quarter could get you a cup of coffee. He went to work for Ryder Truck Rental in Jacksonville, Florida, in management and sales. Working in a manager trainee position, he found himself loading trucks. It was not what he had intended to do, but it was what he felt he had to do. He knew how to roll with the punches.

Stines had met Diane Sandefur, the woman who eventually would become his wife and best friend, during his senior year at Berea College, and when he worked at Ryder they saw each other frequently. She had written to him often while he was in Vietnam. Diane was teaching school in Moultrie. Stines bought Diane a ring for Valentine's Day and they were married in June of 1975.

Diane and Charlie Stines bought a house and settled in Moultrie. Stines took a job teaching eighth and ninth grade social studies. He continued teaching for the next six years.

The Stineses wanted to start a family, but when the doctor said that they would not be able to have children, Stines decided that he would point his life in another direction: he would attend law school. He had no sooner completed the application to be admitted to Campbell University in Buies Creek, North Carolina, than Diane announced she was pregnant with their daughter, Ellen.

Financially, it was rough.

"We lived from hand to mouth," Stines said. "It was really tough. People at our church in North Carolina would bring us meat and vegetables from their gardens, and somehow we made it."

Stines decided he would take the Georgia Bar exam in February, right before graduation, and without benefit of the usual review course and against the advice of the majority of his professors. Stines wasn't optimistic that he would pass the bar the first time out the gate and especially before he had even completed all the coursework, but he felt it would be good practice, and so he had signed on.

"It snowed the whole way from North Carolina to Atlanta," Stines remembered. "I didn't get there until about 10 in the evening and was scheduled for the exam early the next morning."

To Stines' never-ending surprise, he passed the Georgia bar on the first try and after graduation he and Diane returned home to Moultrie. Stines got a job as an attorney working for Doug Silvis in Thomasville, primarily working in real estate law. After a year and a half, Stines decided to launch out on his own, and opened a private practice in Moultrie.

"I made a living, that was about all," Stines said. And when, in 1987, he was offered the opportunity to join the District Attorney's office under Lamar Cole, Stines took it. He had found his calling.

When Stines first started work, then District Attorney Cole sat Stines down and told him never to take a case to prosecute that he didn't believe in.

"If you don't think they are guilty, don't try it," Cole had told him. "If you think they are guilty, give it everything you've got."

For the rest of his career, Stines would live and work by that piece of advice Cole had given him. But it would not always be easy. Prosecuting cases in a small community like Moultrie, where everybody knew everybody and many times were related to a defendant in some way, was not the way to win a popularity contest. But Stines didn't care about being popular, he cared about putting away criminals.

One of those difficult cases for Stines had been the Willie-Dell and Kirk Blount murder case. The two brothers had shot and killed a young man named Randy Lee. The two defendants were the sons of "Bull Blount" and were a prominent family in the black community. Judge George Horkan told Stines he had "no case." Horkan had recused himself from the case – because he had been a friend of the Blount family for years – and Stines went on to try the case and win a conviction on both of the Blount brothers; the convictions were upheld on appeal.

"I think that case cost me a lot of standing in the community," Stines said. But Stines did not ever allow his standing in the community to be a factor in determining what cases he would prosecute; guilt or innocence were his only considerations.

Another difficult case for Stines had been the Roger Dale Dean, Johnny Warner and Mario (Marty) Allen case, which was an arson case involving two trials. Dean was a nephew of the former sheriff of nearby Grady county.

It was a case where a restored plantation worth $475,000 had been burned to cover a burglary. Eventually Roger Dale Dean had "spilled his guts" about the arson, saying Clarence Allen, Mario's father, had set up the crime. Roger Dale Dean and Johnny Warner pled guilty. Mario Allen was tried and convicted of burglary and arson. Then, Marty's father, former deputy of the year, Clarence Allen, was tried and convicted of burglary and instigating the act. Stines won a conviction in the case, even though "Clarence had been my friend."

The Sheila Bryan case was Stines' first automobile arson case. And he would apply the same standard to the Bryan case as he had to all the others that had come across his desk in the nine years he had been an Assistant District Attorney: guilt or innocence.

His first involvement with the Bryan case had come on August 28, 1996, when Pitts had called him and asked him to come out to Blanton's impound yard where Newell and the rest were inspecting the 1987 Mercury Cougar. Stines had gone out to Blanton's and met with the investigators. Newell had gone over the entire car with Stines, showing him, piece by piece, all the evidence of arson.

"The man ought to be a professor," Stines said.

After talking with Heinen and Newell, Stines was convinced that the crime of arson and murder had been committed. He had no qualms about prosecuting the Sheila Bryan murder case. He would give it everything he had.

But, again, it was not without a possible personal cost to Charlie Stines.

One of his dearest and closest friends, and a long-time member of the "Fellow Travelers," was Franklin Sutton, who was a former state senator, and distantly related to Sheila. And Stines had been friends enough with some of Sheila's relatives that, in the past, he had attended the Weeks' family reunions. He had worked in the Colquitt County school system with Ernest Weeks, Sheila's uncle and the patriarch of the Weeks family. Endangering those relationships would not be a consideration. It never had been.

But what Stines did not know, and could not have known without the gift of precognition, was that it was his disintegrating relationship with David Miller that would cause the biggest repercussion in the Sheila Bryan case. In fact, later, much later, some would say that it was Stines' relationship with Miller that would work to Sheila's greatest advantage.

CHAPTER TWENTY-SEVEN

Friday, April 17, 1998

It was an expected deluge of papers but a deluge nonetheless. In one day, Sheila's defense attorneys had filed twenty-four pre-trial motions and Stines would have to attend to each and every one.

Many of them were what Stines thought of as "boiler plate" motions, meaning just the standard motions that would be filed in most any trial, but there were others that were worthy of his undivided attention.

Of some interest were the Motions In Limine (pronounced lem-ah-knee) which were motions for evidence to be included or excluded from the trial. There were three Motions In Limine in the stack of papers.

The very first motion filed was a Motion In Limine to keep any information about Karlas from the jury. In what was called a "prior difficulty with the law," the defense asked that the Court "instruct all parties to refrain from reference being made to the fact that Karlas Bryan ever had a prior arrest or trial." Additionally, aware of Heinen's interview with Omega Police Chief Walter Young, the defense wanted the statement Karlas had made to Young that he would kill himself before he would return to prison, also excluded from the trial. The defense stated that Karlas' remark to Young was "in question" because it "was made while under the influence."

Stines was not surprised or in disagreement with the motion. Stines knew that he could not introduce the evidence about Karlas without risking a mis-trial. He also knew, of course, that Judge Frank D. Horkan, who would preside over the trial, would grant the motion.

The second Motion In Limine was to exclude any comments or evidence concerning Sheila Bryan's unwillingness to be interviewed by any law enforcement agency prior to her indictment.

The third Motion In Limine was about Ralph Newell and Sheila's lawsuit against Georgia Farm Bureau Insurance. It was in this motion that the defense made clear who they held responsible for Sheila Bryan's indictment: Ralph Newell.

According to the motion, it was only after "a self-interested, independent, investigation by the Georgia Farm Bureau Mutual Insurance Company through its agent, Ralph Newell, that the decedent's body was exhumed in this case and the subsequent investigation led to the indictment of the Defendant."

The defense said in the motion that the initial investigation had determined the death was accidental and "only after Ralph Newell became involved in the case did the State pursue this matter as a possible homicide."

Stines understood from the motion that Ralph Newell was going to be the "bad guy."

The motion went on to say that Georgia Farm Bureau Insurance had been found liable on their automobile insurance policy and had "acted in bad faith in this case."

The Motion in Limine was not the only motion regarding Ralph Newell; there were several.

The Motion To Reveal Interest was about Ralph Newell and was hardly a surprise to Stines. The defense stated that Newell was biased because Georgia Farm Bureau Insurance Company had a financial interest in the outcome of the case, and yet Newell was going to be an expert witness for the prosecution. Further, the defense said, Newell had been employed by Ford Motor Company and the automobile which had burned in the accident was a Ford product.

The defense would go after Newell, but Stines had known they would. Stines didn't think Newell would give them much to work with and he had no problem disclosing anything about Ralph Newell they wanted to see. *Have at it*, he thought.

Of most concern to Stines in the pile of motions on his desk was a Motion To Suppress. The defense was asking the Court to keep out of the trial any statements Sheila made to law enforcement at the time of the accident. The reasons given by the defense that Sheila's statements should be excluded from the trial were that she was "disoriented, upset and visibly shaken," that she had not been given the Miranda warnings while she was in "a custodial interrogation-type setting," that she was "in need of medical attention and was repeatedly questioned in a custodial-type atmosphere by numerous authorities."

Of the twenty-four motions, the Motion To Suppress was the most serious and, if granted, could cause great damage to the prosecution's case. A large part of Stines' case was built around Sheila's prior inconsistent statements to

Donald Davis, Chris Gay and Rodney Bryan. If the motion was granted, he would lose that entire part of his case. Stines would have to fight that motion tooth and nail.

In the stack of motions there was also a motion to allow the defense to call an unlimited number of character witnesses for Sheila at trial and a motion for individual voir dire, the questioning of jurors, and their sequestration during voir dire.

The last motion had been a Motion To File Additional Motions. And, before the judge had ruled on the original twenty-four motions filed by the defense, the defense filed an additional motion asking for a jury view of the accident scene, bringing the number of pre-trial motions to twenty-five.

On May 7, Judge Horkan scheduled a pre-trial hearing for June 30, in which he would give his rulings on all of the motions to date. The trial was scheduled for August 31.

A fairly young, attractive man with a soft voice and even temperament, Judge Horkan was known to be firm but fair in the courtroom where he presided. A native of Moultrie, Horkan had gotten his law degree in 1983 from Samford University in Birmingham, Alabama. After law school, he had returned to Moultrie and engaged in private law practice until 1988 when he was elected State Court Judge. He served in that capacity until 1994, when he was elected Judge of the Superior Court for the Southern Judicial Circuit of Georgia.

A Jackson v Denno hearing would be held at the June 30 hearing presided over by Judge Horkan. The hearing would determine if Sheila's statements to law enforcement would come into trial.

A month before the pre-trial hearing, on May 29, the defense filed motion number twenty-six: Motion for Change of Venue.

A change of venue, meaning to move the trial to another location, is always a serious matter and always warrants careful consideration by all of the parties involved. In the motion, the defense laid out their case for having the trial moved out of Moultrie and Colquitt county, citing the extensive pre-trial newspaper coverage of the case.

Judge Horkan would add the change of venue motion to his list of motions to be ruled on at the June 30 hearing.

Stines knew that the change of venue motion came about because the information about Karlas' murder of Gail Sullivan had "leaked out." All the rest was fluff.

Of the twenty-six motions, only the Motion To Suppress was a real worry to Stines.

Stines had never tried a case against Moore or Saliba, and the pile of motions told him that these were good lawyers who were not going to leave any stone unturned in defense of their client. Stines would have to be in top form if he hoped to win this one.

His first hurdle would be to get through the Jackson v Denno hearing unscathed.

At the pre-trial hearing, Judge Frank Horkan gave his rulings on the twenty-five pre-trial motions filed by the defense in a court order dispensed to the attorneys on that date.

Horkan granted seven of the motions, most of them of the boiler plate variety, and also the Motion In Limine which excluded any testimony about Karlas' prior legal history – and, of course, the Motion To File Additional Motions, which had already been done in any case.

Three of the defense's pre-trial motions were denied by Horkan. He denied the motion to have an unlimited number of character witnesses, limiting the number to ten. He denied the motion for individual voir dire and sequestration of the jurors during voir dire. And he denied the Motion In Limine requesting that evidence in Sheila's civil lawsuit be permitted into trial.

Fourteen of the pre-trial motions had been complied with by the prosecution and were withdrawn by the defense.

Judge Horkan reserved his ruling on the change of venue motion and granted the motion for the jury view of the scene of the accident.

All that remained to rule on was the Motion To Suppress, which would come at the end of the hearing.

After hearing the testimony and the attorneys' arguments, Judge Horkan made his decision on the Motion To Suppress: denied. Horkan agreed with Stines that the statements were non custodial and that Sheila had been free at that time not to discuss the matter with law enforcement, that the statements were made freely and voluntarily and therefore should be admissible at trial.

Stines had won his first victory in the case and it was not a small one.

Two years after the accident on Livingston Bridge Road, they were going to trial. And everyone knew the case would rise or fall on the testimony of Ralph Newell.

CHAPTER TWENTY-EIGHT

Friday, August 21, 1998

It would have been easier to thread the proverbial camel through the eye of a needle than it would have been to get Charlie Stines to calm down. Ten days before the trial date, he was in all out "trial mode" and there was no turning back. Calm was not part of the picture.

He was a nervous wreck. He was always a nervous wreck before and during a trial. He paced. He mumbled to himself. He shuffled papers. He made telephone calls at all hours of the day and night.

One thing he didn't do was drink his grapefruit juice. The juice was a staple in his diet that helped him keep his trim physique. But when he was in "trial mode" he didn't eat or sleep – so the juice was out.

Stines knew he was a basket case and he tried to protect his long-suffering wife Diane and wonderful daughter Ellen from the agonies of his psyche: he stayed at the office as much as possible. He would sneak in the house late at night and fall in the bed, only to toss and tumble and get up bleary eyed the next morning to start the routine all over again. He was lucky if he got three or four hours sleep.

It was at times like this he questioned why he had ever thought he wanted to be a trial lawyer in the first place. All of his insecurities about his use of the English language would rear their ugly head and he would begin to question if he could even string two sentences together without butchering the King's English.

Like an obsessed madman he would type out all of the questions that he was going to ask his witnesses on the stand and then he would go over the questions with the witnesses, leaving them a typed copy. No surprises. Stines didn't think he was very good at ad libbing in the courtroom. He wanted everything in line, every t crossed and every i dotted long before anyone got to the witness stand.

And this case had brought on an unusually strong episode of Stines' trial jitters. Part of it was that he was going against two "hot shot" lawyers from out of town who he was not familiar with and he didn't know exactly what to expect from them. Part of it was that this was a high profile case getting lots of media attention. But the rest of the uneasiness had been brought about by the escalating tension with David Miller.

Just a few days before, things had come to a head with Miller. Only recently having accused Stines of not getting along with defense attorneys, Miller, in the next breath, told Stines that he was moving him out of the Moultrie office and into the Valdosta office because, "We need your strength and commitment in Valdosta."

Stines knew that was baloney. Stines knew the move was "punishment" for some real or imagined wrong he had done to Miller. Stines didn't want to move. He had been in Moultrie for all of his eleven years with the DA's office. Nevertheless, he had started packing his office. The whole thing smacked of banishment.

Stines' friends and colleagues at the Governmental Building where he worked had been upset to learn of Stines' impending move and they let it be known they were going to give him a big going-away party. According to Stines, when word had reached Miller of the planned party, he had gone to Moultrie and informed everyone that there would be no party. Miller had planned for Stines to leave town quietly; Stines' friends had planned to have the big party regardless of what Miller said. After all, *they* didn't work for Miller.

Stines tried to put all of that out of his mind and stay focused on the case at hand. He wanted to win this case – his last case in Colquitt County. Foremost, he thought Sheila was guilty of the crimes. He also wanted to win it because of Miller's accusation about his win-loss record. In some way, winning such a tough case, against difficult odds, would be a way of giving Miller the finger – in a quiet, professional sort of way, of course.

So he chewed his fingernails and typed frantically into the night, praying for no surprises and a break somewhere.

Bill Moore and George Saliba, who felt no need to give Stines a break, filed a few more Motions In Limine and they were humdingers.

The first motion was to exclude evidence in the trial of the prior insurance claims filed by the Bryans. Moore and Saliba did not want the jurors to know about the $17,000 grease fire.

The second motion was to exclude Karlas' statement to Heinen that they needed to complete the investigation because $100,000 was at stake. In fact, the motion stated that "unless a proper foundation is laid for the admissibility of insurance in this case, the defense objects to any reference to insurance, insurance proceeds or insurance policies."

In short, the defense was asking the Court to throw out the motive in the case.

Stines was worried about these two motions which had the capability of cutting the legs off his chair. Although the insurance issues weren't a big part of the case they were an important part – a part Stines didn't want to lose.

Who would believe a daughter killed her mother unless they are given some reason for her to do so?

In short order, Judge Horkan ruled on the latest pre-trial motions filed by the defense.

The evidence of the $17,000 grease fire and Karlas' statement to Heinen about the $100,000 were out.

It was a blow to the state's case. The only shred of motive testimony left would be Bobby Underwood's testimony about Karlas raising the insurance limits from $25,000 to $100,000 a few months before the fire. And Stines could only bring that in if he laid the proper foundation.

The motive in the case was starting to disappear. If Stines had a dog, he would have thought about kicking it.

Unknown to Charlie Stines, in Valdosta, Bill Moore was doing some nail chewing of his own. He had tried forty murder cases and never lost a one of them and he was afraid the Sheila Bryan case might break his winning streak. The problem that churned in his mind was that he just could not get a handle on the woman. He had spent hundreds of hours with Sheila, driving around the Livingston Bridge Road area, and in discussions in his office and in her home. But even with all that, he never had felt he had a real "fix" on her. Moore was so unsettled with the issue he had gone to extraordinary means to resolve it: he had requested that Sheila Bryan take a polygraph test. Later he would say that he could not discuss the results of the test – which, most people agreed, was lawyer-talk for saying she had failed the test. Moore prided himself on the passion that he brought to his cases, believing with every fiber of his being in his clients' innocence. But he was about to go into the courtroom with Sheila Bryan, never having been able to form an opinion. It made him extremely nervous.

166

In Omega, everyone was looking forward to the trial, at least they were looking forward to having the whole Sheila Bryan matter put behind them: they were sick of thinking and talking about Sheila Bryan.

"If you say one more word I am going to come in there and hit you on top of your pointy little head with this ruler. Now I mean it. You just hush up."

"What's wrong with talking about Karrie?"

"I'm sick of talking about Karrie, that's what's wrong with talking about Karrie."

"But Karrie can't help it."

"I know Karrie can't help it. But I would just like to get through one evening here without having to talk about the Bryans."

"What's wrong with talking about the Bryans?"

"That did it. Go to bed, young lady. Right now. I mean it. Get in that bed. Right now."

"I won't talk about 'em anymore, Momma. Really. Please. Just let me stay up and watch the Simpsons. Please."

It had been *the* topic of conversation and gossip for two years. Enough was enough. The residents of Omega had every confidence the trial and subsequent verdict would put an end to the entire subject. Regardless of the verdict, they were happy to think that the entire episode would soon be behind them.

Over the course of the two years it seemed that the entire town had coalesced into two factions: for and against or guilty and innocent. Opinions were based on newspaper articles and outright gossip as no one was privy to the investigation or the facts of the case in its entirety. But rarely did a lack of facts or evidence prevent anyone from having a strong opinion.

It had been a tense situation. And Karlas had exacerbated the situation, perhaps not intentionally, but the effect was the same.

Sheila Bryan Defense Fund jars had sprung up in stores around town. The large pickle jars sat next to the cash registers so townsfolk could put their change in the jars – or more if they felt so inclined. The object, of course, was to raise money for Sheila's legal fees.

For most of the store owners the pickle jars had been a hard call to make. Half of their customers fell in the guilty faction and half fell in the innocent faction. They risked offending and possibly losing half of their customers any direction they went. Some put the jars in, some didn't.

Tommy Lindsey, who owned and ran the town's pharmacy, had let the pickle jar in his store, telling his customers they could use it or not, it was up to them. He had been in business in Omega a long time, and he wanted to continue his business.

In the midst of all this bickering over the pickle jars – and much discussion about the Bryan's finances – Karlas had gone out and bought a brand new $30,000 crew cab truck. And drove it around town for all to see. It led to interesting conversations:

"Did you see that new truck?"
"Yeah, I saw it."
"Pretty nice, huh?"
"Sure 'nuff"
"This thing ain't slowed him down none."
"Don't look like it."

"Have you lost your ever-lovin' mind?"
"What's your problem?"
"You're my problem."
"I'm not anybody's problem."
"Yes you are, you're my problem."
"Why? Just because I want to help out?"
"You're helping out with our checkbook, that's what the problem is."
"I'm allowed to write a check."
"Writing a check isn't the problem, writing a check for the Bryans is the problem."
"So. They just need some help right now. That's all."
"I'll tell you what, I'll help them out when I get a new truck like Karlas has. How about that?"
"There's nothing wrong with your truck."
"It's not about my truck, it's about Karlas' truck."
"It's about your shitty attitude, that's what it's about."

"Where did these things come from?"

"Down at the store. They're sellin' 'em to raise money for Sheila and Karlas."

"Let me tell you something. If you want to go and throw away money then you just go and buy some lottery tickets, how about that?"

"I was just being neighborly."

"Well these neighbors are living mighty fine. They are the ones with the lot at the lake, not us. They are the ones with the boat and jet skis and new truck, not us."

"That's true."

"Well, it just doesn't make any sense to me to be shelling out money to the Bryans while they're over there living so high on the hog."

"You made your point."

"They spent every dime they ever got their hands on."

"That's the truth."

"Fixin' that house up. Buyin' this, buyin' that."

"Yeah, they sure did that alright."

"Never saved a penny."

"Not a penny."

"Now look at 'em. Askin' for handouts."

"Should have saved for a rainy day."

"Might be a lotta rain fore this is over."

"Might be."

If the situation in town was tense, Omega Baptist Church was the epicenter of distress.

Pastor John Spivey was beginning to recognize that he was in a no-win situation with his congregation. Those in the church who were convinced of Sheila's innocence appreciated his support of Sheila – and sometimes felt he should do even more. Those in the congregation who were convinced of Sheila's guilt did not think their pastor should be supportive and, in fact, resented everything he did in Sheila's direction.

He tried to sidestep the issue to no avail. When the subject came up he tried to change it. Or make a joke; but no one laughed.

The split in the church grew wider every day while Spivey watched and worried over the growing chasm.

Many of the church members felt that the church was being dragged into something it should never have gotten involved with in the first place. It made them furious that the pastor of *their* church was going to testify at the trial on Sheila's behalf.

"I saw Sheila today at the store."

"So?"

"She was smiling. Happy. In a good mood."

"Don't you think something might be wrong with that picture?"

"What do you mean?"

"I mean, it isn't normal to be in a good mood when you are going on trial for murdering your mama."

"She's a Christian. She has faith the Lord is going to carry her through this."

"Looks to me like Omega Baptist Church is going to carry her through this thing."

"You know, it wouldn't hurt you a bit if you ever entered the church door."

"Well, Sheila didn't enter it until she got arrested."

"You know that's not true."

"I know she wasn't in church that Sunday her mama got killed. I know that much."

CHAPTER TWENTY-NINE

Sunday, August 30, 1998

By all logic Freda Weeks should have lived her entire life in obscurity. She was a plain, simple, country woman who had spent her life as a homemaker.

But logic did not prevail when it came to Freda Weeks or to Freda Weeks' family. They had made headlines in the local press for decades. As tragic as any Greek drama, Freda Weeks' life of misfortune had started long before her life's journey came to an end on Livingston Bridge Road.

The newspaper accounts in the Sheila Bryan case had little to add to anyone's knowledge of the woman, wife, and mother who was Freda Weeks. She was generally referred to as "the elderly mother of Sheila Bryan," or "Sheila Bryan's 82-year-old mother."

It was not anyone's job to know anything about the victim in the case. To the lawyers, both prosecution and defense, she was simply the reason for the trial.

Freda Weeks was born Freda Mae Cable in MacEwen, Tennessee. It was a hardscrabble life from the very beginning. As a young woman, when she had met the love of her life, Zelmar Alvin Weeks, Freda Cable saw a brighter future. He was a cook in the Army and they courted and eventually married.

After they were married, Freda continued to live with her family in Tennessee while Alvin completed his military service. After his return home, it did not take a lot of persuasion for her new husband to convince her to leave her family in Tennessee and move with him to his family's land in south Georgia. Freda Weeks didn't have a lot to give up or leave behind in the hills of Tennessee.

Alvin Weeks' family had settled in the Reed Bingham area of Georgia in 1827, when south Georgia was mostly a wilderness area. The Weeks people were known to be honest, hard working, stubborn and patriotic. Many of them had fought in the War of 1812 and even more went on to fight in the Civil War.

The people of south Georgia were not all exactly "gung ho" about going off north to fight in the war, but they paid their patriotic dues. When Georgia seceded from the Union, those left behind suffered terrible hardships, including many in the Weeks' family.

The family historian, Hazel Weeks, tells the story of one of the Weeks' men who, at the end of the Civil War, walked home to south Georgia, ragged, tired, and whipped. "I just want food," he said to his family. "Pour clabber in a hog trough and I'll eat it. I'm just so glad to be home."

In Hazel's family, another Civil War veteran did not fare as well. He had fought in the war and, knowing it was lost, but before the formal surrender, he left the troops to walk home. He was captured before reaching home and was imprisoned in Savannah, where he died. Other members of the Weeks family went on to care for and support the family members he had left behind.

Taking care of each other was a Weeks trait that was exemplified over and over. Alvin Weeks, Freda's new husband, had been a recipient of that generosity and trait himself.

Alvin was the son of Ed Weeks who died in 1937 at the age of forty-three of Typhus fever; he died just two weeks after his ten-year-old daughter also died of Typhus. Ed Weeks left a wife and six sons behind. Alvin and his brother Chesley were almost old enough to be out on their own, but the others were not.

Alvin's uncle Jess – his father's older brother – took on the responsibility of the family.

Jess was a good businessman and very resourceful. Eventually he became a store keeper in Ellenton with a renown credit collection system. If customers charged goods and didn't pay he put them on the list. On public display at the candy counter was the SOB list, naming each person who owed Jess money and the amount owed. The only way to get off the list was to pay the bill.

Looking for a way to make some money to support his brother's family, in February, 1938, Jess called the owner of a 267-acre area of woodland in the Reed Bingham area. He was willing to pay the man $4,500 for the timber rights. He would cut the timber and sell it, giving the profit to his brother's family.

The owner told Jess, who had not mentioned his price, that he would not consider selling the timber rights – but he would sell him the entire farm for $4,000. It was a deal.

BURNED - THE TRUE STORY OF THE SHEILA BRYAN MURDER CASE

It was to this "family farm" at Reed Bingham that Alvin Weeks brought Freda, his new bride. For over a decade they lived in the old wood house with the tin roof located there on the family land. The roof leaked and the winter wind blew threw the cracks of the house.

They were poor people who made a life for themselves by farming the land.

Alvin was a sharecropper who would try to wring a living wage from the tired South Georgia dirt. Sharecroppers were the poorest of the poor in south Georgia, just a notch above what had been slave labor.

Sharecropping in the south was an outgrowth of the Civil War and had emerged as an economic solution to slave labor in the 1860s. After the war, Northerners, ex-slaves and ex-slave masters had engaged in a struggle over the future of the South's labor system, eventually leading to a compromise solution called sharecropping.

The plantations, or farms, were subdivided into rental units and leased out to the sharecroppers. Under the sharecropper system, the cost of doing business – and profits – was shared between the land owner and the laborers on the land.

So it was that Freda Weeks began her life as a sharecropper's wife. It was a hard life in which money was scarce and the long, hot days were filled with back-breaking work and endless chores.

Sharecroppers in the south usually had large families; family members were all laborers in the fields; the more children, the more hands to tend the soil. Freda Weeks had toiled in the fields alongside her husband. She hoed the long rows and cropped the tobacco. Soon enough, she added to the farm laborers.

On January 21, 1945, Freda Weeks gave birth to their first child, a beautiful baby boy named after her husband: Zelmar Alvin Weeks, Jr. The family called her husband Bill and his namesake they called Jeff. Freda was a good mother and proud as any mother could be of her first offspring. Tending to the baby kept her out of the fields some, and she didn't mind.

A little over three years later, Freda and Bill had their second child, another boy, who they named Edward Dwight Weeks. He was born on August 12, 1948, and the family called him Eddie. His nickname was "Mutt."

As the small, dilapidated farmhouse began to fill with children, Freda Weeks found precious little time to spend with her sewing. She liked to sew and quilt and she spent as much time as she could on her sewing projects. She was a simple woman with simple pleasures.

She took on extra jobs to earn money. She raised chickens and sold the eggs at market. More time had to be spent cooking and she found ways to stretch the grocery money, mostly living off the produce from the land.

Another three years passed before Freda and Bill added to their family again. Their third son, Donald Lee Weeks, was born on June 11, 1951. This child was known as Donnie by the Weeks family.

The proud mother of three fine boys, Freda weeks' family picture was not complete without a daughter. And so, as she had hoped, two years after her youngest son was born, she gave birth to her first and only daughter: Sheila Kay Weeks.

Through the years and all of the children, the family had stayed in the old house on the family farm. But just prior to Sheila's birth, they had moved to another farmhouse near Ellenton. It was another old, unpainted wood house with a tin roof, and quite small. Freda was a strong and determined woman who always did what ever needed doing – whether it was moving or hoeing. She would make do.

She didn't have much materially in her life, but she had her family and she tended to them with care. She continued to work the fields, raise the chickens, coming to the house to wash and cook, making sure her family's needs were met, before returning to her outside labor.

In 1955, when Sheila was two years old, the family moved again, as was the way with sharecroppers. None of the moves much improved the family's lifestyle.

Tragedy struck early and hard for Freda Weeks – and once it came it never left. Her oldest son, Jeff, was only eleven years old when he went out to play and never came back.

Jeff had gone off with friends to the local swimming hole. The three youths were swimming in a cattle watering hole on the C.A. Hardy farm near Omega; the hole was estimated to be twelve to fifteen feet deep. Little Jeff went into the deep water and drowned. His fifteen-year-old friend, Homer Randall Kerr, tried to save him and drowned also. Kerr's younger brother, Donald, witnessed the drownings.

The story made local headlines. Freda Weeks' family came out of obscurity for the first time.

Somehow, her family says, Freda survived her young son's death and went on with her life. Farm chores never waited for melancholy very long. But Freda missed the happy, growing child who had been her oldest son. The sky never seemed as blue after the day little Jeff drowned.

Tragedy struck again with the death of her husband on February 1, 1969; Bill was just 53 years old. No one can say exactly what happened to Zelmar Alvin Weeks, Senior. His body was found out in the road with a gunshot wound in his chest and a note in his pocket. Family members say it was a suicide; no foul play was suspected.

The story made local headlines, and once again Freda Weeks' family moved from the shadows of obscurity.

Freda was left in a sharecropper's house with their daughter Sheila still at home. Sheila was just sixteen years old and not out of high school yet. They were desperately poor, and Freda took odd jobs, including baby-sitting, to make ends meet. Any hopes she had ever had of a brighter future were gone.

It is hard to comprehend what happened to Freda Weeks just two years later: both of her remaining sons – ages twenty and twenty-two – were killed on the same day in a terrible accident – as Freda Weeks watched from the porch swing of her farmhouse.

It was late on a Saturday afternoon and Eddie had been hauling watermelons. He had been working as a truck driver after he had returned from Vietnam and been discharged from the service. Both Donnie and Eddie were assisting Johnny Fletcher, who was operating a crane truck.

Fletcher was inside the truck, operating the wench. They were attempting to lift the trailer loaded with watermelons onto the bed of the truck when the boom on the crane truck touched a power line. Both Donnie and Eddie were in direct contact with the truck.

Freda Weeks saw Eddie get hit by the voltage; he was killed instantly. Donnie, who had been out of Freda Weeks' sight on the other side of the truck, died before he reached the hospital.

Both of Freda Weeks' sons were electrocuted on July 3, 1971, and once again she found her family in the local headlines.

The once proud mother of four children, Freda Weeks had lost all of her sons in tragic accidents and her husband to suicide. Her only remaining child was her baby daughter, Sheila, the apple of her eye.

Sheila was eighteen years old and had just finished high school when her two brothers were electrocuted. She married Karlas Bryan that November, some four months after the family tragedy, leaving Freda Weeks completely alone for the first time in her life.

Alone and heartbroken, Freda Weeks had to muster all her strength to find a reason to go on. Some days it was hard just to find a reason to get up in the morning. But Freda was a strong woman, not just physically strong, but mentally and emotionally strong, and in time, she found a way to put the bad memories to the back of her mind.

Only one good thing had come from it all. For the first time in her life, Freda Weeks owned her own home. There had been a small insurance policy on the boys and Freda had taken the insurance money and bought herself a mobile home. No one could have been prouder than Freda Weeks of that new trailer.

Twenty-five years would pass before her own death. Many of the years she would live alone, tending her garden, visiting with family and friends. Some of those years, Sheila and Karlas would live with her.

As she moved through her senior years, and with failing health, Freda depended on her daughter to look after her. She had no one else. No longer able to drive, and some ten years before she died, Freda Weeks moved her beloved mobile home onto her daughter's property in Omega. There she would spend her remaining days.

Perhaps she had expected to die quietly in her bed one fateful day. But the tragedy that had plagued her family for so long was to reach out and include her one more time; if the investigators were right, she died a horrible death, alone, on a desolate highway.

She deserved better.

Eight miles east of Norman Park, in a small community named Cool Springs, Freda Mae Cable Weeks rests peacefully, surrounded by her family in the cemetery at Weeks Chapel United Methodist Church. It is a small, country church cemetery, not unlike hundreds of others dotting the south Georgia landscape.

The Weeks people had started the church – the first organized Methodist church in Colquitt County – in 1854. Many years later, in 1918, they opened the cemetery.

The Weeks family has deep roots in this community. Many of the streets and businesses are named after Weeks' family members and the graves at Weeks Chapel Cemetery are filled with their loved ones who have lived, worked, and died on this land.

Freda Weeks and her family are buried in Row 3.

The five of them are united together again. Each of the five has died a tragic death: one by drowning, one by gunshot, two by electrocution, one by burning. Only Freda Weeks lived into old age, all the others had lives cut short.

The courtroom in Moultrie seems a long way from this place. No sound is heard here, save for the quiet whisper of the summer wind in the trees.

What would Freda Weeks want to have happen in the courtroom in Moultrie? Mothers are the bastion of unconditional love, after all.

It was a question begging an answer.

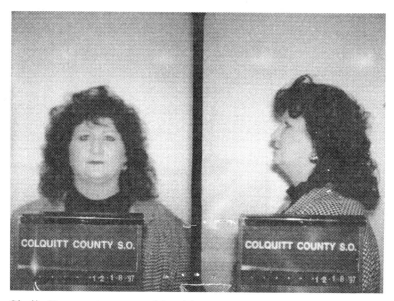

Sheila Bryan at arrest and booking *(Courtesy of the Colquitt County Sheriff's Office)*

BRYAN, SHEILA

Sheila Bryan at Pulaski State Prison *(Courtsey of Georgia Department of Corrections)*

Freda Weeks in 1983 *(Evidence file photo)*

John Heinen, agent with the Georgia Bureau of Investigation
(Courtsey of John Heinen)

Medical Examiner Dr. Anthoy Clark and Coroner Rodney Bryan
at GBI crime lab *(Courtesy of Dr. Clark and Rodney Bryan)*

Donald Davis, criminal investigator with the Colquitt County
Sheriff's Office *(Author's photograph)*

Ronnie Dobbins, arson investigator *(Courtesy of Ronnie Dobbins)*

Charlie Stines, Assistant District Attorney *(Courtesy of Charlie Stines)*

Livingston Bridge Road at accident site. Car entered ditch to the right of the guard rail. *(Author's photograph)*

Livingston Bridge Road noting the width of the shoulder at the accident site *(Author's photograph)*

Open gas tank and missing fuel cap as found the day of the accident. Note burn pattern above the open gas tank. *(Evidence file photo)*

Driver's side view of Mercury Cougar during investigation. Note the electric key pad on the door. *(Evidence file photo)*

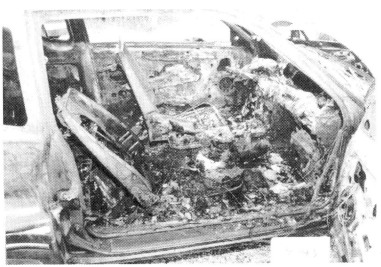

Inside view of burned Mercury Cougar on the day of inspection. Note the reclined position of the passenger seat. *(Evidence file photo)*

Burned remains of Freda Weeks as found by investigators. *(Evidence file photo)*

Burn pattern at driver's side door threshold. *(Evidence file photo)*

Part Two :
Trial

"May Justice triumph over Law."
- Oliver Wendell Holmes

CHAPTER THIRTY

Monday, August 31, 1998

Colquitt County's courthouse, like most of the courthouses in south Georgia, sits strategically placed in the middle of the town square. The large, white building looms over the downtown business area in Moultrie. But, like most of south Georgia's old courthouses, many built at the turn of the century, the antiquated structure was badly in need of renovation. Work was in progress on the old courthouse when Sheila Bryan's case came to trial.

In August, 1998, all of the county's trials were being held at the Justice Center, located at the CCSO headquarters on the by-pass road. A large complex, dominated by police patrol cars, concertina wire, uniformed inmates, and all the usual hustle and bustle inherent with law enforcement, the Justice Center lacked the grandeur – and dignity – usually associated with a major trial held in a conventional courthouse setting. The courtroom was on the second floor of the center – directly above Donald Davis' office at the criminal investigations unit. The jail was conveniently located right next door.

The courtroom itself was utilitarian and nothing to brag about. Its most striking feature was its smallness. It was so small – only about 25'X50' – that it was almost claustrophobic when fully occupied.

The arrangement did not leave a lot of room for the prosecution and defense tables. The two tables were squeezed into the center area in front of the witness stand. With no room for the tables to be placed side-by-side, they were situated one in front of the other – prosecution table at the front, defense table directly behind it.

It was an uncomfortable arrangement for everyone involved. John Heinen, who would sit with Charlie Stines at the prosecution table, would be seated directly in front of Sheila Bryan, who would occupy the seat between her two attorneys. Many of the people attending court would not be sure of Heinen's role in the Bryan case, and, because his name was always followed by the letters SAP – for Special Agent Principal – many made the assumption he was a Special Assistant Prosecutor, a minor point that would amuse Heinen when he learned of it.

Beyond the smallness of the courtroom, it had another less than endearing quality: it was cold. There was no thermostat in the courtroom, and the temperature was set by the thermostat located in the CCSO offices below. The courtroom was always too cold in the summer and too hot in the winter.

The morning of August 31 was unseasonably cool for south Georgia, with temperatures eventually reaching the lower 70s, with cloudy skies, thanks to Hurricane Bonnie, which had passed by and blown ashore in North Carolina over the week-end.

By 10 a.m., the small courtroom had filled, and Judge Horkan rapped his gavel to begin case number 97-CR-494. Most of the fifty-four spectator seats were filled by Sheila's supporters from Omega, prospective jurors, and the local press.

While the Bryan case was getting heavy coverage in Colquitt County by the *Moultrie Observer*, the story had been initially usurped in Tift County by the *Tifton Gazette*'s coverage of another major story involving arson. In a fire in late July, Tifton's Prince Chevrolet car dealership suffered more than one million dollars in damages; the fire destroyed the personnel offices, showroom, accounting department and service department. Just before the Bryan trial began, the car dealership fire had been ruled arson. Ronnie Dobbins had been called in on the case, and in that instance, he had gotten lucky: a canine unit found traces of accelerants in the area where the fire had started.

By noon, the twelve jurors and two alternates had been selected and court recessed for lunch.

Court reconvened at 2 p.m., and having invoked the sequestration rule for witnesses, the jury was seated, given their oath, and Charlie Stines rose to give his opening statement.

Reminiscent of actress Betty Davis when she said, "Buckle up, you're in for a bumpy ride," Stines began his opening statement to the jury by telling them, "I guess the best thing I can tell you to do is fasten your seat belts and get ready for a long ride. Today we're trying the case of the State of Georgia versus Sheila Bryan."

Stines did not plan to make a long opening statement; he just wanted to outline the case and give the jurors the lay of the land before witnesses took the stand. He laid out his case and told the jurors, "Ladies and gentlemen, she could have unlocked that door. But she sat there and let Mama burn to death."

In closing, Stines told the jurors, "It's going to be an interesting case, and it's going to be a hard case."

When Charlie Stines sat down, Heinen's ears picked up. He had known everything Stines had to say; what he was interested in learning was what the defense was going to say. It would be the first time he would hear the details of their defense.

Moore took the podium. He had planned a lengthy opening statement in defense of his client.

"We're going to prove to you that this case was an accident, pure and simple," he began. "You are going to see from the evidence that Sheila Bryan could not have committed these acts. You are going to see that there is no plausible or rational way that Sheila Bryan could be viewed as a killer in this case, much less a perpetrator of this horrible, horrible tragedy. Ladies and gentlemen, the evidence in this case will clearly show you that a victim is on trial here."

Moore said the defense would show the jurors that the fire had started under the front seat from a short in the electric seat motor.

Moore told the jury that they would hear about Sheila's life in the course of the trial. "She tragically lost all three siblings and her father," he said. "She met Karlas in Tifton and married him twenty-seven years ago. They've had a good marriage. Sheila has worked almost all her life, and recently as a data processing employee, and also a secretary at her church."

Moore went on to talk about the family's relationship with Freda Weeks.

"You will hear testimony of how the entire Bryan family wanted Granny Weeks, as she was affectionately referred to, to move into Omega from the country so that they could take care of her. Her home was, in fact, moved and placed on the Bryan property. You will also learn when she moved to Omega, this was one happy family. Ladies and gentlemen, there is not one skeleton in Sheila Bryan's closet. You will hear how she was a Girl Scout mom, how she was a leader in her church, how she taught and still teaches two Sunday School classes, works with Latin-American kids, how she's a leader in the school, the Omega school."

"Karlas is a paint contractor," Moore said. "He has provided well for the family, and he's a good father and a good husband. The Bryan family is as solid as any family you could have. And the evidence will show you that."

Then Moore said, "Sheila will testify, to the best of her ability."

Moore had Heinen's and Stines' full attention now. Until this moment, they had not known that Sheila would take the stand in her own defense; most defendants did not.

Moore talked about the accident, and went on to say, "At any rate, the vehicle came to rest. Sheila by now is in a virtual state of shock. Sheila looked over at her mother and her mother appeared okay. But she did not respond to Sheila."

Heinen and Stines looked at each other and then quickly looked down at their note pads for fear the jury would see the amazed reaction they felt, but could not show. *Sheila was changing her story again*, they both thought. *Incredible.*

Moore said that what happened after that was a blur to Sheila.

Moore then addressed the state's motive in the case. "You will see that Karlas Bryan, her husband, had insurance on this vehicle," he told the jurors. "The property damage paid a very little amount. And the coverage was what was recommended. And you'll see the reason that the coverage was increased was because of the acquisition of this lake property and the fact that they had property in addition to what they had when they initially took this policy out. You'll also see that if this were a motive, which it's certainly not, because nothing has ever been done to collect on this policy, but if it were a motive, there would have been a much higher face amount to the policy."

Moore had saved his strongest words for last, and for the person he held responsible for this injustice to Sheila Bryan and her family.

"Ladies and gentlemen," he said, "the evidence will show you that ten days after this accident, Ralph Newell examined this car, a Ford product, and came to the conclusion that the fire was incendiary in origin. After this, the law enforcement community generally was convinced that Mrs. Weeks was murdered, or something was afoul, so they had her body exhumed by a search warrant and put this family through the additional trauma of having her mother's body autopsied."

He said, "You will see from the evidence that Mr. Newell is a servant of law enforcement because of his background, and a servant to Ford Motor Company because of his pocketbook. We will show you that he has been paid literally hundreds of thousands of dollars by the Ford Motor Company. He is a real pro. And you may be inclined to believe him, but reserve your opinions until he has been cross-examined."

In closing, Moore told the jury that "Sheila Bryan earnestly looks forward to your discovering the truth in this case, and ending this nightmare."

CHAPTER THIRTY-ONE

Monday, August 31, 1998

Without so much as skipping a beat after Moore sat down from his opening statement, Stines straightened his tie, cleared his throat, and called his first witness for the prosecution. He figured he might as well get the worst of it behind him. He called Dr. Anthony Clark.

Getting to the heart of the matter, Stines asked Clark if Freda Weeks died from the fire, or from another cause.

"That's where the question lies," Clark said. Stines held his breath. He could not be totally certain of what might come next. "I think it's a combination of those two factors, of heart disease and of thermal injuries," Clark said.

"Did you inspect inside the mouth and throat area?" Stines asked.

"In the throat I found a small amount of soot within the larynx or voice box," he said.

Stines asked him where else he had found soot.

"I also found a little bit of soot down the airway, what we call the trachea, that goes down to the lungs into the bronchi, mostly on the left side. Again, it was very little. There was some heating effect of the mucosa lining of the airway, which you see when hot gases or thermal injuries are involved," Clark said.

"What does this soot indicate to you, although it might not absolutely prove it?" Stines asked, knowing he was now going head-on into deep water.

"The small amount of soot tells me a couple of things," Clark said. "One, it could be solely due to what we call a post-mortem artifact. The fact that the individual was dead and that there was extensive burning of the body, a little bit of soot will go in the airway. Two, the person was alive and breathed a little bit of smoke in, but dies before they could breath very much in. Three, that the person breathed in a lot of hot gases instead of very much soot. Not much soot had been developed at that point. And a lot of hot gases will kill somebody very rapidly, quicker than the soot would – and there would be only a small amount of soot in the airways. These are the three possibilities I see."

Stines asked Clark if any of the three possibilities he had named was more likely than the other.

"Not really," Clark said. He testified that he felt that it was more probable that Freda Weeks had held hot gases, and didn't stay alive very long.

Saliba began cross-examination of Clark after the two photographs of Freda Weeks' burned body were passed among the jurors.

Saliba zeroed in on Clark's first theory, that Freda Weeks had been dead before the fire started.

"It would be impossible to tell whether she'd been dead one minute or thirty minutes; would it not?" Saliba asked the witness. Clark said that was correct.

"Okay. So you cannot testify with any certainty to this jury that she was not dead prior to the fire, can you?" Saliba asked. Clark said that he could not.

Saliba then moved to his favorite part of Clark's autopsy report.

"Have you ever made the statement that the cause of death was undetermined?" he asked. Clark said that he had stated that the manner of death was undetermined.

"Are you familiar with the word 'homicide'?" Saliba asked.

Heinen thought he heard a snicker; maybe it was his imagination.

Clark gave the definition: the death of an individual by the hands of another individual.

"You chose not to put 'homicide,' did you not?" he asked. Clark said that was true.

Clark was excused from the witness stand, and Stines and Heinen were relieved to have it over. They hoped that the jurors would see the testimony about the manner of death as just so much quibbling over a word on a piece of paper.

Dr. Pamela Gouth and Dr. Michael Whittle, who had examined Sheila in the emergency room the day of the accident, were the next witnesses. Having gotten the medical testimony out of the way, Stines was ready to begin testimony about the fire. He called Jamie Hinson.

Hinson told about getting the call and going to the fire with his father and putting out the fire. On cross-examination, Moore asked Hinson if he had any idea of how many gallons of water he put on the fire, and Hinson said he had no idea.

He was excused, and Stines called CCSO Deputy Randy Stephens to the stand. Stines had known Stephens for a long time. He knew him to be a man of integrity who had spent eighteen years in the Navy.

Stephens testified about the tracks of the car along the shoulder of the road and the photographs were entered into evidence.

During cross-examination, Saliba showed Stephens a picture of the roadway and asked him, "Do you see this mark right here?"

Stephens said he did.

Thus began testimony which would run through out the trial about a mysterious black mark on the road, which the defense would contend was a skid mark made by Sheila on the day of the accident as she attempted to brake the car to avoid going over the embankment.

When Stephens was excused, the Court took a ten-minute recess. The recess hardly gave Stines long enough to catch his breath, and when court reconvened, he called Chris Gay to the stand.

After having Gay explain his arrival at the scene of the wreck and enter into evidence the photographs he had taken that day, Stines moved to one of the main points he wanted to elicit from Chris Gay: that Sheila Bryan had given Chris Gay her driver's license and insurance card.

"Were they burned?" Stines asked Gay.

"No, sir," Gay answered.

Stines then had Gay testify about Sheila's statement to him of what had happened that day and then Stines moved to Gay's inspection of the scene. When shown a photograph of the mysterious black mark in the road, Gay testified that it was not a skid mark, but an acceleration mark, and that in his opinion it did not have anything to do with the accident.

Saliba took Gay to task about the black mark on the road, saying Gay should have included it in his report as evidence in the case. Gay disagreed.

"And you think you have the right to decide what's evidence and what's not evidence?" Saliba asked.

"Yes, sir, I do," Gay answered.

On redirect, Stines had Gay testify that the mark on the road was twenty to thirty feet from where the car went off the road, at a point where the car was traveling on the grass, not the road.

It was late afternoon now, and Stines was starting to feel some fatigue, but no matter; he still had several witnesses to get on the stand before the day was out. They would be "quick" witnesses, thankfully, but the next one he would call, although short in length, Stines knew was long on importance to his case. He called Bobby Underwood.

Stines moved rapidly through the preliminaries, having Underwood testify to his occupation as an insurance agent for Georgia Farm Bureau.

Through Stines' questioning, Underwood testified that in October 1994 and October 1995 Karlas Bryan had not increased the car liability insurance, although Underwood had recommended it be increased, but had come into the office in May of 1996 and increased it to $100,000.

On cross-examination, Moore had Underwood clarify that it was Karlas Bryan, not Sheila Bryan, who had asked for the policy increase.

Bobby Underwood was excused and Stines called wrecker drivers William David Hickey and William Davis to the witness stand to tell the jurors about the removal of the car from the scene of the accident.

Stines had gotten nine witnesses to the stand on the first day after the jury had been selected and left the courtroom tired, and satisfied that the case was hanging together.

But he did not go home after his first day of the Sheila Bryan trial. Stines went to his office at the Governmental Building to work on the next day's testimony.

When he got to the office, Assistant DA, Scott Gunn, gave Stines a telephone message. It was from an elderly woman who sang in the choir at Omega Baptist Church. She had some information she wanted to give Stines.

The woman told Stines that Sheila had been fired as church secretary for stealing money from the church and that the incident had just about split the church in two. The woman said that he should talk to Gene Hiers, the pastor at Omega Baptist Church at the time the incident happened, and she gave Stines the man's telephone number.

Stines thought about it before he picked up the telephone to call the former pastor. Stines had his case all lined up and he didn't like surprises. Still, Stines knew that Sheila was going to use Omega Baptist Church – her membership there and her friends there – as her defense. As Moore had said in his opening statements, Sheila was going to be portrayed as a victim, as a woman who could not possibly have done what she was accused of – and her church connection was a large part of that picture. Stines picked up the phone.

Gene Hiers told Stines it was true what the woman had said: Sheila had taken $1,100 from the church. After much discussion, Hiers agreed to come to Moultrie to testify in the trial without a subpoena. Stines did the paperwork to notify the Court and the defense that he was adding a rebuttal witness to his list.

The defense would not appreciate the surprise witness.

CHAPTER THIRTY-TWO

Tuesday, September 1, 1998

Court resumed at 9 a.m., and Stines called Walter Young to the stand. Stines had Young explain that he was the chief of police in Omega.

"On August 18th, 1996, were you acquainted with the defendant's mother, Mrs. Freda Weeks?" Stines asked.

"Yes, sir. I'd met her a couple of times."

"And how did you meet her?"

"Well, I knew her, you know, by her living there. But I had got a call around there. Two women had called and said she was laying out beside the road disoriented. And we called somebody around there to check her, and we helped her get up and get back in the house. And then the second time, she had fell off the porch, I believe, into the flower bed."

"The time that you met her at the ditch, how did she appear that time?"

"Well, she was laying out there beside the road. And we asked her was anything wrong, and she, you know, she wanted to get up. We were scared to let her get up because we didn't know if she had something broke or what. So we called, you know, to get somebody there and come around and check her. Then, like I said, we got her up after we established she was all right and she walked, we walked her back into the house."

On cross-examination, Moore had Young testify that both of the episodes had occurred during a time of day when Sheila was at work.

"And you've never had any problem with Sheila or her family, have you?" Moore asked.

"No, sir," Young said.

"You have no reason to believe she would ever harm her mother in any way?"

"No, sir."

"And you know her?"

"Yes, sir."

Stines was not happy with chief of police Walter Young when he stood back up to do redirect.

"Chief Young, you don't know the first thing about the evidence in this case of your own knowledge, do you?" Stines asked.

"No, sir," Young said.

"That's all," Stines said in his most disgusted voice, and sat down.

Moore came back on re-cross with a stunning question.

"You don't think Sheila Bryan killed her mother, do you?" he asked.

Stines immediately objected and Horkan sustained it. But it didn't matter. Moore had made his point.

It had not been an auspicious start for the day for the prosecution, but Stines had no time to cry over spilt milk. He called his first expert witness to the stand: William James Sullivan, known as Jamie Sullivan. Sullivan was an expert in the area of collision investigation and forensic mapping of automobile collision scenes. He had been with the Georgia State Patrol for fifteen years and was on the Special Collision Reconstruction Team (SCRT).

Sullivan testified that he had gone to the scene at Livingston Bridge Road on July 9, 1998, to do a scene analysis and to make a forensic map. Stines had Sullivan explain his map.

Sullivan testified that the shoulder of the road was more than six feet wide at its narrowest point and at its widest point was more than ten feet wide. In other words, there was plenty of room on the shoulder of the road for the car to travel without running off the embankment.

On cross-examination, Saliba moved to the subject of traffic accident investigation in general and brought out an investigation manual by Lynn Fricky, which is an authoritative source used in accident investigation training. He had Sullivan read a paragraph. When Sullivan would not agree with the statement from the book, with a gesture of disgust, Saliba took the book away from Sullivan.

Stines watched as Sullivan – in a gesture of quiet defiance – reached into his briefcase and pulled out his own copy of Fricky. It would prove to be Stines' favorite moment in the trial.

The state called Doug Eldridge to the stand. Eldridge was a sales representative with Robert Hutson Ford, Lincoln, Mercury in Moultrie, who testified that the car doors on the Mercury Cougar did not lock automatically when the door was closed and that the doors could be unlocked by grabbing the door handle and pulling it. Moore had Eldridge say that there had been two recalls on the Mercury Cougar; one in 1987 regarding the fuel line and one in 1992 regarding the fuel coupling.

Stines called Danny Weeks to the stand.

Stines had Danny testify that he was related to Sheila on his father's side of the family. He began questioning Danny about encountering Sheila at the bridge on Livingston Bridge Road, seeing the smoke, running to get the bucket of water, and returning to the car.

"At the time you got back to the vehicle, to what extent was the car burning?" Stines asked.

"Well, it was going good," Danny said. "I mean it was really burning then. The whole front of the windshield, the dash area up there was burning."

Stines asked Danny what Sheila had told him about trying to get her mother out of the car.

"Well, she said that the doors automatically locked and, and the keys was in there and she couldn't get the doors opened and it was done getting hot. I couldn't get down to the door myself."

"Could you get close enough even to reach the doors, even touch the doors?"

"No, sir. I didn't try to get that close."

"And tell the jury why you didn't."

"Because she had told me that she had filled it up with gas, and that car was straight up like that, and I didn't know where gas was leaking or not. And if it was, it could have exploded and we'd all have went."

On cross-examination, Moore had Danny repeat the entire episode again – running across the bridge, running to get the bucket of water, running back to the car.

"What kind of condition were you in at that time?" Moore asked.

"Scared," Danny said.

After a fifteen-minute mid-morning recess, coroner Rodney Bryan took the stand. Stines had Bryan go through his arrival at the accident scene and his attempt to have an autopsy done – and why it was not done.

Stines was about to become very frustrated with Rodney Bryan. He had examined difficult witnesses before, but Rodney Bryan would soon end up in a class all by himself.

It was the very first time that Rodney Bryan had testified as the coroner of Colquitt County, and he was nervous.

When Stines began questioning Bryan about the statement he took from Sheila at the accident scene, the trouble began.

"Did she tell you how the accident happened?" Stines asked.

"Briefly, yes, sir," Bryan said.

"What did she tell you about a curve?"

"I don't remember about a curve."

"Did she tell you anything about a guardrail?"

"She told me how the wreck occurred."

"How was that?"

"That her and her mother was going down the road talking, just riding, and she ran off the shoulder of the road or the edge of the road."

"What did she tell you happened when she approached that guardrail?"

"That the car went into the ditch."

"Do you recall talking to me about this last week?"

"Yes, sir."

"What did you tell me about dodging – do you recall what you told me about her dodging a guardrail?"

"I understood that she ran off the edge of the road, that's when she saw the guardrail and went into the ditch."

Stines gave up.

Moore had Rodney Bryan testify that he had not known of any inconsistencies in the statements Sheila gave the day of the accident or on the day he visited her home.

Both Stines and Heinen sat amazed at Bryan's testimony. By this time they were convinced they never should have let the man get near the witness stand. But hindsight did them no good.

Bryan was turned back to Stines, who had no redirect. Stines and Heinen thought the best thing to do with Coroner Rodney Bryan was not only to get him off the stand, but to get him out of the building. There would be words spoken about Bryan's testimony, but not there, and not then.

Donald Davis, who would be the next witness called, of course knew nothing of the testimony that had preceded him. Much later, when he learned what Bryan had said on the stand, Davis would write Bryan off as a mental midget – and their friendly relationship would come to an end. For Davis, Bryan's testimony had been the last straw.

Unaware of the previous disastrous testimony, confident in his ability to testify, and happy to at last be getting a chance to have some input into the case, Investigator Donald Davis went to the stand.

After the preliminaries, Stines had Davis testify about arriving at the scene, about the fire already having been put out, and about the car sitting in the ditch at a ninety-degree angle to the road. Then Stines moved to Davis' interviews with Sheila Bryan and put into the record her statements to Davis the day of the accident and nine days later.

Pleased with Davis, and having regained his composure after Rodney Bryan, Stines turned Davis over for cross- examination, confident Davis could hold his own.

Moore went to the subject of Davis' second interview with Sheila. Moore asked Davis if, since the interview had been done at Rodney Bryan's request, would he [Davis] rely on what Coroner Bryan said about the second interview? Davis was not going to fall into that one. Davis said he relied on the notes he had taken himself.

Davis was off the stand. He felt pretty good about his testimony. And, after having lived through Rodney Bryan's testimony, Stines and Heinen felt very good about it.

CHAPTER THIRTY-THREE

Tuesday, September 1, 1998

Stines was ready to begin the most important part of the case: proving it was arson. He called Gerald Psalmond, Colquitt County fire coordinator, to the stand.

After testifying that he had arrived at the scene about a quarter to one, and that the car was sitting in a ditch perpendicular to the highway with no collision damage, Psalmond testified that the driver's side floorboard, in front of the front seat, was the area of worst damage and deepest burning.

After entering photos into evidence, Stines moved to the subject of the missing gas cap and open filler door, and Psalmond testified to his inspection of the gas tank area and the search for the missing gas cap. He told the jury how he had determined that the gas cap was missing at the time of the fire.

Psalmond testified that it appeared to him that an accelerant had been used on the driver's side floorboard and he stated that he did not know the result of the lab test for the accelerants.

"In your experience, is it common for an accelerant to be used but not be detected?" Stines asked.

"It happens all the time," Psalmond said.

Moore was ready to give Psalmond a hard time. In an article written by reporter Charles Shiver, which appeared in the *Moultrie Observer* the day after the accident, Psalmond had been quoted saying the fire might have been electrical. Psalmond did not recall having given that information and said, "I don't know why I would have said that."

When Psalmond testified that he had not known the results of the tests for the accelerant and had not bothered to find out the results, Moore asked, incredulously, "Sir, this lady is on trial for her life. Do you know that?"

"Yes, sir," Psalmond said.

Stines had no redirect. He thought it was best to let a sleeping dog lie.

The court took its noon recess.

Stines felt like he had been through a wringer. He had lived through Walter Young's marshmallow testimony, only to have Rodney Bryan do his backtracking, and then had gone headlong into the Psalmond fiasco. He had a headache and could only imagine what the rest of the afternoon might bring.

"Get me a deli sandwich," he told Heinen. "I'm going to rest a minute."

After lunch, Brian Hargett, with the GBI crime lab in Columbus, took the stand.

A one-gallon can and two quart-size cans were entered into evidence. The cans contained burned foam padding and a section of a floor mat. Hargett explained that he had been requested to test the materials for the presence of ignitable liquids and said that the tests for accelerants had come back negative.

"Does that preclude the fact that there may have been ignitable liquids used?" Stines asked his witness.

"No. That's just to say that in these samples submitted to me, there were no liquids in these samples. There's some possibility that another type of liquid, an acetone or ethyl alcohol, a real volatile substance, would not be detected by my testing."

Stines called Ronnie Dobbins to the stand. Dobbins would be on the stand for several hours, up until time for the mid-afternoon break and beyond.

Putting Ronnie Dobbins on the stand before Ralph Newell was a trial strategy Stines and Heinen had discussed at some length. There was nothing pretentious about Ronnie Dobbins; he presented as "one of the good-old-boys." Although the material he would cover would be almost identical to Newell's, it was the *way* Dobbins would present the information that was almost as important as the information itself.

If Newell was "the bad guy," at least according to the defense team, they would have a hard time re-making Dobbins into anything other than what he was: a hard-working arson investigator with the State Fire Marshal's Office. And his testimony would be just as solid as Dobbins was built. And best of all, Ford Motor company had never paid Ronnie Dobbins one thin dime.

Dobbins began his testimony about the inspection of the Mercury Cougar, using a diagram as a visual aid along with the numerous photographs of the burned Mercury Cougar.

Dobbins testified to the trunk being cleaned out, with only a spare tire left in the trunk.

"My trunk in my personal car ain't that clean," he said. "And I thought that was odd."

He talked about each area of the car and explained why it had been eliminated as the cause of the fire. Then he talked about the discovery of the wooden claw hammer.

"I thought it was kind of unusual to have a wooden claw hammer in the back seat of a car," Dobbins said.

Dobbins' home-boy approach to his testimony tickled Heinen, and he knew it must be irritating the defense team.

When explaining how he had determined that the driver's side door was unlocked, Stines asked Dobbins why the door could not be readily opened after the fire.

"Just the searing heat," Dobbins said. "With the door handles burning off, you have no way of actually opening the doors."

"And did you notice any unusual burning patterns around the door?" Stines asked.

"Yes, sir. Once we opened the door there was a section of the rubber near the front of the door at the base where the threshold is, was a burn pattern going across it."

"And what did that show you?"

"That would indicate that prior to the fire the door was opened, and it shows that some type of ignitable liquid had been placed in the floorboard of the car and was ignited, therefore burning the rubber seal, and then the door was slammed shut."

Heinen sneaked a peek at the jurors. They were as stone faced as he was. But Heinen knew that the testimony and photographs of the burned door sill was devastating for the defense. Dobbins' words hung in the courtroom like a heavy blanket thrown over the defense camp.

"What did you notice about the carpet and padding?" Stines asked.

"Had very irregular burn patterns on it indicating that some type of ignitable liquid had been placed on it, because carpets normally are self-extinguishable, very hard to ignite," Dobbins said.

Dobbins was then asked if he had examined the wiring in the electric seats and he said that he had.

Immensely pleased with Dobbins, Stines was ready to finish with his witness.

"Mr. Dobbins, based on your training and your experience, and based on the examination you performed on this 1987 Mercury Cougar, do you have an opinion as to the origin of the fire?" Dobbins said it was an incendiary fire which began in the floorboard of the vehicle.

Stines was finished with Dobbins. But Dobbins had a long way to go with Saliba before he would leave the witness stand.

Saliba asked Dobbins if he had removed any switches, motors, circuits, wires, or any other electrical components from the car, and Dobbins said that he had not.

"So you did not test anything except by observation?" Saliba asked.

"That's correct," Dobbins agreed.

Saliba then asked Dobbins, "And you're aware there's no evidence in this case of any flammable accelerant, right?"

"There is, observation-wise, in the floorboard," Dobbins said.

Saliba went on to question Dobbins about the fuel load of the Mercury Cougar. Dobbins agreed that the Cougar probably had four or five hundred pounds of the fuel load in the car.

"And so there's plenty of fuel inside the car after the ignition source began, a good bit of fuel in there to burn?" Saliba asked Dobbins.

"Yes, sir," Dobbins agreed. "But that's the reason they put flame retardant material on the upholstery and in the carpet, to retard the fire growth."

Dobbins agreed with Saliba that plastic materials were in the car, and that plastic materials can burn with a heat release rate similar to those of ignitable hydrocarbon liquids – the same heat intensity as an accelerant. However, Dobbins disagreed in part.

"Most of the plastics that you burn in a vehicle have to have a fire directly to it. If you take the fire away, it's gonna go out," he said.

"Okay," Saliba said, ready to make his point, "So certainly power seats can start a fire?" he asked.

"Might could," Dobbins said.

"Well, does this say it can?" Saliba asked, pointing to the 921 (arson investigation) text.

Dobbins talked about the discrepancies in the book and the fact that he did not agree with everything said in the manual.

Saliba was frustrated with Dobbins.

"And you think power seats cannot start a fire?" he asked in his most incredulous tone.

"It's well fused against that type of fire loss," Dobbins said.

When Dobbins would not agree with a statement from the 921 text, Saliba got angry.

"Do you think that you can come into this court and testify under oath as to the cause of this fire without doing any physical tests?" Saliba asked.

"Well, the physical tests was that we took samples and they came back negative, but that doesn't eliminate the possibility an accelerant was present in the floor," Dobbins said.

"Well, now that's interesting. The samples came back negative. Wouldn't that cause you to maybe doubt that it was incendiary, instead of coming to this jury and saying, 'Well, it could be'?"

"No, sir, 'cause the burn pattern in the floorboard don't change."

"Did that cause you to think at all, have second thoughts, when the test came back negative, sir?"

"No, sir, because there's a lot of accelerants out there that are water-based, and once the fire fighting efforts to put water on it, you know, if it's water soluble, it washed away."

"And then you got back a substantial bit of information saying there was no incendiary chemicals found, didn't you?"

"Yes, sir, but most of my cases do come back with an accelerant not present."

"And that didn't slow you down one bit with your conviction, did it, sir?"

"No, sir."

"And even though the lab did not confirm anything about any chemicals being there that would burn?"

"That's correct."

"That didn't change your opinion one bit?"

"No, sir."

"So you would have kept right on the same path in spite of evidence against your position?"

"Yes, sir."

"Is that fair investigating?"

"It is when I see burn patterns like I did in the floorboard."

"That's all Your Honor."

Stines and Heinen were proud of Dobbins. He had held his own under a tough cross-examination by Saliba and had not given any ground with his opinion about the cause of the fire. In truth, he had been like a yard dog with his first bone.

On re-direct, Stines had Dobbins testify that in all the fires he had investigated he had never seen a fire that was started by an electric seat motor.

Stines then had Dobbins talk about the fact that there was evidence of a fast burning fire.

"We've got about a five-minute response time from the fire fighters putting out this fire. And we've got too much fire in a short period of time," Dobbins said.

"Based on your training and your experience, do you have an opinion as to about how long this fire burned?"

"Twelve to fifteen minutes."

"That's from the time it actually started?"

"Yes, sir."

Dobbins was at long last excused from the witness stand. Neither Heinen nor Stines felt that Saliba had been able to make much headway with Dobbins. He had been an outstanding witness for the prosecution.

Without any pause, Stines called Ralph Newell to the stand. Stines and Heinen had saved their strongest witness for last – and they both knew that Newell would either make or break their case.

CHAPTER THIRTY-FOUR

Tuesday, September 1, 1998

After a brief, late afternoon recess, the state's star witness took the stand in his mis-matched sports jacket and slacks. With his lap stacked with files and notes, and his hands folded on top of the pile of paper, Ralph Newell's unassuming appearance gave no hint of the formidable witness he would prove to be.

Stines took Newell slowly through the preliminaries: he was a fire investigator who owned his private company since July 1982; he had been in fire investigation work for twenty-nine years. Newell stated that he had first become interested in fire investigation when he trained in explosives and incendiary devices while in the Army, preparing to go to Vietnam.

"And what happened in Vietnam?" Stines queried, wanting to bring out Newell's military record.

"There was a war," Newell answered, straight-faced.

There was a wave of laughter in the courtroom. Stines didn't mind. That was part of the charm of Ralph Newell. It was late in the day, the jurors were tired, and Ralph Newell knew how to work a jury.

Under Stines' questioning, Newell went on to say that he had investigated nearly five thousand fires and "just over fifty percent of them were automotive fires." Stines had Newell review his lengthy list of credentials.

Stines asked Newell if he ever testified on behalf of automotive companies, and Newell said that he did so quite often.

"Which ones?" Stines asked.

"Ford, GM, Honda, Toyota, Suzuki, Nissan."

"Are you on their payroll?"

"I'm on nobody's payroll."

Stines was ready to begin questioning Newell about the automotive fire on Livingston Bridge Road, and he asked Newell to step down from the stand and explain photographs already put into evidence by Ronnie Dobbins.

The relocation of the witness was more than a transition from one place to another. Once Newell began testimony about the Mercury Cougar, he transitioned into a learned professor. Everything in his tone of voice, manner, and gesture changed. He was *the* authority on automotive fires.

Looking at the photographs, Newell explained to the jurors, as he would to the students he taught, about each piece of the car he had inspected and why he had included or excluded it as the cause of the fire.

Saliba interrupted Newell's testimony to request that Newell return to the witness stand when he was not using a photograph for demonstration. From that point on, Newell was constantly back and forth between the witness stand and the display of photographs.

Newell went on to testify that the carpet and upholstery had to meet Federal Motor Vehicle Safety Standards. He said the standard for the carpet, which was a tufted nylon called Forepart, had a degradation temperature of 420 to 480 degrees. It was self-extinguishing and could only burn one inch laterally in four minutes. Newell said the seat cushions were polyurethane foam, and the degradation temperature for them was 400 to 500 degrees. The foam was also self-extinguishing, and the standard for the foam was one-point-five inches, laterally, in four minutes.

Newell told the jury that the standard meant that if you set the carpet on fire, the fire was not allowed to move more than one inch in four minutes – or it would not meet government standards.

Stines turned Newell's attention to a photograph of the fuel filler area.

"Here in Georgia, we call it where you put the gas in. That's where the gas cap is. This particular car has a locking fuel door," he said.

Newell went on to explain all of the reasons he knew the gas cap had not been in place at the start of the fire. He said that when you have a locking fuel door, such as was on the Mercury Cougar, the door is locked with a metal latch that does not blow off in a fire.

Stines showed Newell a photograph showing a view through the windshield of the car into the front passenger area. Newell said he had looked at the metal seats to see if he could come up with an indication of which direction the fire had moved inside the vehicle.

"And what I saw on the driver's seat, toward the front and on the back, was this blood-red oxidation and dark blue color, versus a metallic color on the passenger's seat, with less oxidation on the passenger's seat. That's telling me the fire originated over near the driver's seat and moved crossways toward the passenger's seat."

They next reviewed what Newell referred to as an important photograph of the door threshold on the *passenger* side of the car.

"This is rubber and plastic all the way across this bottom," he said. "It sits on what we commonly refer to as the rocker panel. There are no burn patterns on that rubber or plastic threshold. It's in excellent condition."

Newell said it was important because it was not what he found on the door threshold on the driver's side of the car.

They were moving to one of the most damaging pieces of evidence for the defense: the burn patterns on the driver's side door threshold.

"What I'm looking at is several things here," Newell said of the photograph. "Number one is, on the threshold, across the rubber seal, is what we call a pour pattern. That is a burn pattern that is caused by some type of flammable or combustible liquid. The burn pattern itself says that it had to get there before the door was closed and before the fire, or the exact same time the fire was ignited, because once the door is closed, as you saw on the other side, it didn't have anything. There's a seal there that's airtight and water tight. So whatever created this pattern had to be put there before this door was closed. Also, that same pattern lines up with the burn pattern on top of the car, the burn patterns across the front of the seat, burn patterns into the dash, and burn patterns all across the console."

Newell said that in his opinion the accelerant used was a liquid. Stines asked him to explain why he thought it was a liquid as opposed to some other form of accelerant.

"Well," Newell said. "We cleaned the floorboards. We cleaned all the debris out of this car. What we found was burn patterns in the carpet that were irregular and weaving-type burn patterns that – some went all the way through the bottom layer of padding. Now, we had a floor mat, we had carpet, and then we had padding, all of which are fire retardant and self-extinguishing. These patterns went all the way through, through to the bottom layer and right down near the metal, irregular, leading from the door across and up on the console towards the passenger seat. None of the other part of the car had any of these patterns, yet the range of the car – both sides of this car – are made of the same material. And that's very inconsistent with an accidental car fire and that type of burning."

Under Stines' questioning, Newell went on to say that there were no sources of ignition under the carpet in front of the driver's seat.

"Even dripping plastic from the dash assembly, from a dashboard, when it drips, it doesn't continue to burn," Newell said. "When it hits flat on the carpet, it goes out, and it seals itself into the carpet. And we found some of that. And it wasn't the same burn pattern."

"Absent an accelerant, what would have happened if heat had been applied to this carpet?" Stines asked.

"You've got a lot of smoke, but that's about it," Newell said.

"And what would it take to keep this carpet from self- extinguishing?"

"A continuing fire from some fuel source that's not self-extinguishing."

Following a review of the ashtray, they reviewed the key lock assembly. "Now, the key lock assembly," Newell explained, "is where you stick the key. On a Ford, that is not the ignition switch, believe it or not. The ignition switch on a Ford is about eight inches, mounted on the steering column and is operated by activating rods. This key lock assembly is where the key would go."

Newell said that there was no key found in the key portal.

"I personally examined every square inch of that floorboard under the driver's side, on the driver's side of that car where this was located, and looked at all of the debris looking for keys," he said.

"Did you find any other keys, such as house keys, other keys to other automobiles, anything like that?" Stines asked.

"I didn't find a key, a key ring, or anything there except what you see in that photograph, and that's the key lock assembly," Newell said. Newell said that he knew there was no key in the car at the time of the fire. He also said that in order to remove the key, the car had to be in Park, according to government standards.

Newell next reviewed several photographs of the wiring harness and wiring system located in the instrument panel.

"I examined the wiring throughout the dash assembly area," he said, "from the fuse box across to the opposite side where the electronic, what we call the EEC module, which is the inner brain, is located. Examining for malfunction, shorting, arcing, or anything that could cause a fire."

Newell stated that his examination revealed that the insulation on the wiring was still present; in fact, the tape wrapping put on at the factory was still there. "And so that tells me this is not an under the dash fire caused by wiring or the wiring harness," he said.

Newell said that there was over six miles of wire in a Mercury Cougar. He said he found one wire that had an indication of electrical activity on it. It was located in an area where the AC and heat control and the rear window defroster controls are located.

State's Exhibit 60 was the terrycloth towel found in the car. "This is the terrycloth towel remains that I located; it was draped across from the driver's seat, across the console, onto the passenger's seat," Newell said.

"How completely was it consumed?" Stines asked.

"About eighty percent of it," Newell said

All this time, Newell had been running back and forth between the witness stand and the display of photographs. "I'll quit making you run back and forth shortly, I hope," Stines told Newell.

"I don't believe that," Newell said as he stood to return to the display of photographs one more time. There were more chuckles in the courtroom.

Newell discussed two photographs he had taken of the dome light in the Cougar, which had been found in the floorboard.

Newell said, "This is located in the rear floorboard, behind the driver's seat. What was interesting to me, when I looked at it, was that it was stuck to the carpet and had melted down into the carpet. That told me this light came down very quickly in this fire, and it was very hot when it came down, and that there was basically no fire in that rear floorboard right behind this driver's seat when this light came down. The fire got to the light before the fire got to the rear, to the rear of this seat, and the carpeting behind it."

"Is that consistent with the origination of a fire underneath the driver's seat in any way?" Stines asked.

"Absolutely not," Newell said.

"Now, Mr. Newell, how did the carpet burn in the back floorboard different from that in the front floorboard?" Stines asked.

"The carpeting in the back floorboard simply charred from heat exposure," he said. "It baked is basically what it did. And it cooked down into a solid pad. Whereas the carpeting in the front floorboard was burnt out irregularly, all the way down to the base and bottom pad."

Newell went on to discuss the subject of electrical malfunctions and said that he had found no significant electrical malfunctions in the car. He said that his review of the electric windows and door locks had turned up nothing.

Then Newell discussed the electric seats. He testified that the seats have impendence proof motors. He said, "That means they're the type of motors that if you interrupt them, or stop them, or they get hung up on something, they'll sit there and hum, but they won't do anything else."

Newell said that he had examined the seat motors and found nothing unusual. He had found no shorting or arcing.

Asked how many times he had seen a seat motor cause a fire, Newell said, "Never."

Newell said that he had eliminated the electric seats, switches, circuit breakers, and fusible links as a source of the fire.

"Based on your training and experience, do you have an opinion as to whether or not this fire started in this particular car underneath the driver's seat?" Stines asked.

"The fire did not start under the driver's seat. The fire started in the front of the driver's seat and on the driver's seat and on the rocker panel cover at the door."

"Now, was this a quick fire or a slow burning fire?"

"In it's inception it was a pretty quick fire. That was verified by the dome light that came down and melted into the carpet before there was any damage to the carpet."

"Based on your training and experience, do you have an opinion as to the nature of this fire?"

"This fire is what we classify as incendiary in origin. The definition of incendiary is very simple; it's an intentionally caused fire."

"Can you rule out all accidental causes of this fire?"

"I did."

When Stines finished his direct examination of Ralph Newell there was only about thirty minutes left before court recessed for the day.

During that thirty minutes, Saliba cross-examined Newell and went down many roads leading nowhere. Through his questioning on the subject of the burned threshold at the driver's side door, some of the most damning evidence in the case, Saliba contended that the burned area was simply deterioration caused by wear and tear of getting in and out of a ten-year-old car.

Stines and Heinen breathed a sigh of relief. They didn't think Saliba had been able to touch Newell's damning testimony.

CHAPTER THIRTY-FIVE

Wednesday, September 2, 1998

Court convened at 9:40 a.m., and Judge Horkan instructed the jury in the procedure for a scene view. Jurors would be taken to Livingston Bridge Road on a bus furnished by the Board of Education; the court bailiff would accompany them. The purpose of going to the scene was to help them understand the evidence that had been presented in the courtroom, but the scene view was not to be considered as evidence in the case.

With that said, the jurors were loaded into the school bus and dispatched to Livingston Bridge Road.

When court recessed for lunch, Stines stayed briefly to talk with Heinen. They had done all they could do with their case-in-chief. After lunch, the state would rest its case.

Stines didn't tarry in the courtroom. He had a lunch date. He was due at the going-away party being thrown for him by the staff at the Governmental Building across town.

There were just some things that David Miller had no control over. Stines would enjoy his lunch and the fellowship of his colleagues, and breathe a short sigh of relief to be half-way through the Sheila Bryan case. It would not be long before he, like Newell, would be seeing Moultrie in his rear-view mirror.

A little after 1 p.m., court reconvened and the State officially rested its case, having entered sixty-four items into evidence, mostly photographs of the burned Mercury Cougar. The defense began its case-in-chief by calling a number of character witnesses. They would move quickly through the character witness testimony.

Helen Patrick, Cynthia Camp, and Paul Whittington, took the stand to say that Sheila had a good reputation in the Omega community and was known to be truthful and non-violent. Each cross-examination by Stines was the same: they had to admit they did not know what had happened on Livingston Bridge Road and they would not know which story to believe if Sheila had given several conflicting stories. With Cynthia Camp, Stines had Camp admit that prior to the car wreck Sheila had not attended church very regularly.

Moore called Kay Weeks to the stand. She related to the jury what had happened on Livingston Bridge Road that Sunday morning.

On cross-examination, Stines asked Weeks if she had ever seen the burning vehicle, and Weeks said that she had not. Stines asked Weeks, "In fact, by the time you all got there, it was too late to make any rescue attempts or anything, wasn't it?"

"I didn't go down there. I don't know. Danny said that they couldn't get close enough to the car to, to get her out, or they couldn't get her out. It was too late," she said.

"That would indicate by the time Danny Weeks was there, then the fire was going pretty good and heavy, wouldn't it?"

"I don't know. I guess. I don't know."

Kermit Bryan, Karlas' brother, was the next witness for the defense. Moore asked Bryan to tell the jury what he had observed over the years about the relationship between Sheila and her mother. Bryan described a loving, caring relationship. He said that he did not know of any problems in their relationship and had never heard them exchange cross words.

On cross-examination, Stines had Kermit Bryan say that Freda Weeks had become forgetful and feeble and would wander off from home.

Right before ending his cross-examination, Stines said, "One other thing. Your brother Karlas is a house painter, isn't he?"

"Yes, sir," Bryan said.

"And they deal with a lot of flammable materials, don't they?"

"If you paint houses."

Sheila's neighbor, Mary Woodall, was the next character witness for the defense. She described the loving relationship between Sheila and her mother and Sheila's hysterical state at home after the accident.

On cross-examination by Stines, Woodall was able to get in her opinion that Sheila was not guilty.

"That one kinda got away from you, huh?" Heinen whispered to Stines when he returned to the prosecution table.

"Guess so," Stines chuckled.

When Saliba called Michael Bresnock as the next witness, Stines whispered back to Heinen, "This one won't get away." And Heinen believed him, because he knew that Stines had done his homework.

Saliba began the direct examination of Michael Bresnock with questions regarding his background in order to qualify him as an expert witness. Stines had already notified the Court that the state did not recognize Bresnock as an expert in the area of automotive fires, although Stines considered Bresnock "an excellent mechanic." Bresnock said that he was a cause and origin consultant from Marietta, Georgia and had worked for Chevrolet Motor Division from 1969 to 1975.

Under Saliba's questioning, Bresnock told the jury he had examined the Mercury Cougar in March or April of 1998, and that, in all, he had examined the car three times.

The wiring to the electric seats had been removed from the car and sent to the GBI crime lab in Atlanta. In August, Bresnock had gone to the crime lab and examined the seat motor parts using the lab's high-powered microscopes. In particular, he examined the power seat switches for both front seats, the motors, electrical wiring, fuse box, and wire fragments.

Saliba then had Bresnock explain to the jury that when copper is subjected to an electrical short, beads, or globules, form at the end of the wire, and that it required a temperature of nineteen hundred eighty-one degrees to melt copper and form the beads.

Bresnock testified that the circuit breaker that serviced the power seats was in two pieces when he found it, and he showed the pieces to the jury.

Stines interrupted Bresnock's testimony to ask that Bresnock return to the witness stand when not involved in demonstration. Turn-about was fair play.

Bresnock testified, from the witness stand, that the circuit breaker that serviced the electric seats had failed: the contact section of the breaker had separated from the main body. He said that in order to determine what had caused the breaker to detach, he had looked at it under the microscope.

Bresnock said, "This type of failure is consistent with too much electrical current passing through this attachment and through the contact point, causing it to overheat and separate."

When Bresnock was showing the jury the copper beading on the passenger side power switch, something extraordinary happened in the courtroom: a juror interrupted the testimony to ask, "What's that a picture of?"

The testimony had been at times complicated and confusing, enough so, evidently, that the juror had been frustrated to the point of speaking out.

Saliba clarified the subject for the juror, and the testimony continued.

Bresnock said that it was his opinion that the fire was caused by the damage he saw.

Bresnock said that he estimated the hottest temperature that was reached in the vehicle was fifteen hundred degrees.

He said that he had found two fusible links in the car that were blown, one of which was to the electric seat motors.

He concluded with his opinion that the fire was initiated from electrical failure.

Stines rose to cross-examine the defense's expert witness. He moved quickly to the major point he wanted to make with Bresnock. Stines pointed out that if the fusible link was blown there was no way for current to go through the circuit breaker. And that Bresnock could not say that the circuit breaker opened and failed at the same time.

"So you can't have it both ways, can you, Mr. Bresnock?"

"No, you can't."

Stines then went through portions of the state's case that Bresnock did agree with: the driver's side window was down; the door was unlocked; the car was sitting at a steep angle; the gas cap was not on the car at the time of the fire; and the key was not in the car. Bresnock also agreed that the fire had not been started by the ignition switch.

Stines had Bresnock admit that when he had inspected the car, he was not aware that the carpet, with the burn patterns, had been removed.

Stines changed subjects to the time it would take the car to burn. Bresnock said that he thought the fire had burned for forty minutes and that it would have taken the fire "at least two minutes and possibly five minutes to get started."

Stines had begun to review with Bresnock all of the reports he had been given by the prosecution for review, when the testimony was interrupted by the court clerk, informing the court of a "bad storm" that was nearing Moultrie. It was actually a hurricane named Earl that was barreling down on the town. Agreeing that they would leave within thirty minutes, the testimony resumed.

Stines reviewed with Bresnock that he had seen reports by Newell, Psalmond, and Dobbins.

"But you didn't do a written report, did you?" Stines asked.

"No, sir, I did not," Bresnock said.

"And is it typical of you to do an investigation like this that you've got a hundred hours into, $10,000, have been working on for months, and not even make a written report?"

Saliba rose to object and asked for a bench conference. Judge Horkan said to the lawyers that he didn't think Stines had asked anything objectionable.

"But I guess we do need to go ahead and find out how far you intend to go," Horkan said.

"I intend to sit down," Stines said.

"Well, we certainly won't object if you sit down," Saliba said.

It was the end of another long day and the weather outside the courtroom was deteriorating quickly. The rain had come and the nearby town of Cairo had begun to be evacuated. Because the hurricane was predicted to pass over Moultrie around nine the next morning, Judge Horkan asked jurors and attorneys to call the sheriff's office to determine what time the trial would be resumed.

Thursday promised to be an exciting day: a hurricane and the testimony of Sheila Bryan.

CHAPTER THIRTY-SIX

Thursday, September 3, 1998

Hurricane Earl, so large it nearly filled the Gulf of Mexico, packed 100 mile per hour winds. It had been headed due north and was expected to make landfall in Texas or Louisiana when court recessed on Wednesday afternoon. But Earl took a sudden and unexpected turn east, and headed straight for Florida and Georgia.

Late Wednesday night, as Earl rumbled across Georgia, it lost much of its punch, but still dumped six inches of rain and blew down trees and power lines, leaving thousands of homes in south Georgia without electricity.

Because of the storm, court was delayed on Thursday morning, not starting until nearly 11 a.m.

Moore called Charles Shiver, the managing editor of the *Adel News Tribune*. Shiver testified that on August 18, 1996, he was employed by the *Moultrie Observer*, and that he interviewed Chief Gerald Psalmond after the accident.

Moore had Shiver read from the article in which he quoted Gerald Psalmond: "'The fire's cause has not yet been determined', Psalmond said. 'It looked like it might have been electrical and started on the inside of the car.'"

Moore turned his witness over to Stines, who had known Charles Shiver a long time; Stines had been Shiver's eighth-grade social studies teacher.

On cross-examination, Shiver said that Psalmond's comment about the fire being electrical was a suspicion, or simply conjecture at the time, and that he *had* said that the cause was undetermined.

Pastor John Spivey was the next person to take the stand for the defense. A balding, bespectacled fellow, Pastor Spivey was usually as jovial as he was round. But on this day, it was a stone-faced, unsmiling Spivey who took the stand.

Spivey said that he had been a pastor for almost forty years, and that he was presently the pastor of Omega Baptist Church. He said that he had been pastor at the church for a little over three years.

Moore questioned Spivey about Sheila's church attendance, and Spivey said that Sheila had been "very active the last couple of years," and prior to that time she had "some" involvement in the church. He told the jury that he was responsible for bringing Sheila back into the church after her mother died.

On cross-examination Stines brought out that Spivey had once agreed to testify as a character witness for a convicted child molester and that Sheila's return to the church had caused a division in the church. Stines also brought out that after Sheila resigned as church secretary the church had adopted a policy that a church member could not be secretary and that the church secretary could no longer count money alone.

Evelyn Swain and Susan Harris were the defense's next character witnesses. They testified to the good relationship Sheila had with her mother.

The judge told Moore to call his next witness, and Moore said, "Your Honor, we call Sheila Bryan."

When a defendant in a murder case takes the witness stand, it is always high drama, and all other testimony fades into the background. All the attorneys – both prosecution and defense – realize that once the defendant steps to the witness stand, the entire case will rest on the credibility of the defendant.

The process was simple: If the jury believed Sheila Bryan, she would walk out of the courtroom a free woman.

But putting a defendant on the stand, especially in a murder case, was always risky business and had to be given careful thought by both the defendant and the defense attorneys. The risk was in the cross-examination that the defendant would be exposed to.

Unlike her husband, Karlas, in his murder trial, where he was allowed to take the stand and give a long, unsworn statement without being cross-examined, Sheila would have to face a "thorough and sifting" cross-examination by Charlie Stines.

And Stines was sitting on ready. He had planned for the possibility of Sheila giving testimony months before. Although murder defendants rarely did testify, Stines had such an aversion to surprises that he always prepared for the possibility.

The decision to take the stand had been Sheila's decision alone and went against the judgment of her defense attorneys.

Presentation of the defendant was important. The jury would watch the defendant like they had no other witness. And they would not just listen keenly to her words. They would watch her demeanor, and take note of every gesture, every smile, every tear.

Heinen had been keeping a beady eye on Sheila during the entire trial. He had watched as she came to court every day in her Sunday School dresses and had emitted muffled sobs and dabbed at her eyes as she sat between her two attorneys.

It had shocked Heinen how much weight she had gained since the wreck on Livingston Bridge Road. She had become a whale of a woman. Heinen decided that Sheila must be one of those women who dealt with anxiety and depression by eating.

No one sitting in the courtroom was more interested in Sheila's testimony than John Heinen. He had tried time and again, month after month, going through lawyer after lawyer, to speak with Sheila to get her side of the story. All to no avail. And now, there she was, on the witness stand, ready to "tell all."

Heinen would not miss a word. And when Sheila said something that perked his interest, he would elbow Stines. Not that he needed to. Stines, too, would be hanging on every word.

With his game plan in place, Saliba began the questioning of the defendant. The courtroom was quiet, all eyes and ears now upon the woman on trial for killing her mother.

If it were a poker game, Sheila had just bet all her chips.

Moving slowly, gently along, Saliba had Sheila testify that she had worked as a secretary, bookkeeper, store manager, and a data entry clerk, and that most of her life she had taken care of children.

Wanting to highlight that Sheila was a mother, Saliba had her talk at some length about her two daughters, Karla and Karrie. Sheila said that Karla attended Tift County High School and was in the tenth grade. She went on to talk about the wonderful relationship her daughters had with her mother, saying they spent time together and enjoyed activities together.

Saliba had Sheila testify that she grew up in the surrounding area of Omega and had lived there all her life, moving to the Omega area when she was around two.

Returning to the subject of work, Saliba had Sheila talk about working as a substitute teacher at the elementary and junior high schools. Then he moved into more detail about her work as a church secretary.

Sheila testified that she had worked as the secretary for Omega Baptist Church for a little over seven years, and she denied that she had ever taken any money from the church. She admitted that she had a disagreement with Reverend Hiers. Saliba asked Sheila to tell the jury how she and Reverend Hiers had disagreed over insurance.

Sheila said, "I had – he was going over the budget and he said, he made a statement that the insurance, my insurance, was too high. And I explained to him that that was my insurance through an increase in the insurance in lieu of a raise that had been given to me by the previous pastor, Jim Mullins."

Sheila went on to say that the raise, which was not in money, had happened because she had told Mullins that she wanted to raise her medical insurance to cover the children, and Mullins had given her the raise in medical coverage, in lieu of a salary increase. Then, when Mullins left, and Hiers came, Sheila said he did not approve of her receiving the insurance coverage that the prior pastor had given her.

"And what did Pastor Hiers do about it?" Saliba asked.

Sheila said, "He brought me before the deacons and I explained it to them."

Sheila denied ever having wrongfully taken anything from the church and, "out of the goodness of my heart," agreed to repay the medical premiums.

Changing subjects, Saliba then had Sheila talk about their finances at the time Freda Weeks died.

Sheila said her husband was a paint contractor and that they were not having any financial problems, that they were having no problem in paying their mortgage on their home. She testified that they were not in debt, and their house payments were current, as were all of their bills.

Asked who handled the family finances, Sheila said that Karlas handled the family money, and she "took care of the household expenses like groceries and a few other things."

She said they had good credit and that there were no financial problems that she was aware of. Satisfied that he had put some distance between Sheila and any financial problems or the insurance policy on the car, Saliba moved on after having Sheila say she had her own income and had been working as a data entry clerk for Firestone Manufacturing.

She said that she was aware that there was a Georgia Farm Bureau policy covering the '87 Cougar. Sheila testified that the property damage on the car was paid by Georgia Farm Bureau, and that no other claim had been filed.

It was time for Saliba to begin painting the picture of this all-American, middle-class family.

Reminiscent of "show and tell," Saliba then had Sheila go into a long recitation of the Bryan "home life," in which photos of Freda Weeks' home and Sheila's home were shown to the jury and entered into evidence. Sheila would explain each photo, adding information, such as, "and Karlas built about a forty-foot porch across the front of it [her mother's mobile home] for her, so she could sit out there and watch the kids play in the back yard." Regarding picture number 19 of the homes, Sheila made further reference to Karlas and the porch, saying, "This is an overall view of my mother's home. Karlas built the porch and the rail for her."

Sheila went on to say that her mother lived by herself in the mobile home next to her house, and that the home was kept in good condition. Evidently not satisfied that the jury had clearly understood that Karlas had built the porch on Freda Weeks' house, Saliba again asked Sheila, "Had a porch been attached to that home, ma'am?" And Sheila, taking the cue from Saliba, answered, "Yes, sir. Karlas had built it on there for her."

Sheila said that her mother's mobile home was paid for, and that Freda Weeks had been living next door to her for about six-and-a-half years in August of 1996. She had moved next door to Sheila in January 1991.

Sheila said that before moving next door, her mother had lived out in the country about three-and-a-half miles from her. Sheila claimed that Freda Weeks had made the decision to move from out in the country to town and next door to Sheila.

Sheila testified at some length about the trouble they had gone to, moving her mother onto the property. They had hired a house mover, not a mobile home mover. Karlas had gotten a backhoe and dug up all of her plants and shrubs and moved them to the new place next to Sheila.

Sheila then testified about the family activities they shared: going to the lake, cooking out, going for walks, going for rides, looking for wildflowers and berries, sharing meals together.

Then Saliba moved into some of the family history and Sheila talked about her father being a sharecropper and the deaths of her other family members.

"I was three when little Jeff died," she said. "I was fifteen when Daddy died, and I was about eighteen when the boys both got electrocuted."

Saliba then returned to "show and tell" and had Sheila talk about more family pictures: the family at Christmas, trips to north Georgia and Tennessee, and her mother playing with the children.

Saliba had Sheila talk about the lake lot they had purchased. Sheila said that the lot was paid for. Saliba had her talk about their plans to build a house and Sheila described the house they had intended to build.

"It wasn't going to be a big house," she said, "more or less a retirement home, because the girls were growing up so quick. So it was just gonna be a small house, not a big house."

Sheila said they planned to pay to build the house by using the equity from the sale of their present home, or rent out both their home and her mother's home. Her mother was going to move to the lake with them. She showed the jury an artist's sketch of the house she had planned to build and the basic floor plans. Sheila had written the word "Mom" on one of the rooms of the new house, saying that it was a bedroom close to hers, in case her mother had needed her.

Next, Saliba went into the state of Freda Weeks' health. Sheila testified that her mother was able to take care of herself, and that even at age eighty-two, she did not require any kind of special care. She said that her mother was pretty self-sufficient.

Sheila said that her mother did all of her own grocery shopping; she was picky about what she bought. She explained that her mother controlled her own finances.

Saliba then had Sheila testify to some of the problems Freda Weeks had as she had aged.

"She would forget where she put stuff," Sheila said. Sheila said that up until her mother's death, her health had been pretty stable. She said that she had suggested to her mother that she use a cane, but that her mother would not consider it. Sheila said that her mother had a regular doctor and would "go when she wanted to."

She said that her mother weighed about one hundred forty-six pounds at the time of her death and said that her mother had never been a burden to her in any way.

After a lengthy time of Sheila on the stand, having painted the picture of the family he wanted to portray, Saliba slowly moved towards the day of the accident.

"Did she [Freda Weeks] spend the night there [at Sheila's house] Saturday, August 17, 1996?" Saliba asked.

"Yes, sir," Sheila answered.

"At that time, what condition did you believe your mother's health to be in?"

"She had a real bad sore throat and she, she had a lot of drainage, and she was congested real bad. And she, uh, she, you know, she was just coughing a lot and all. And she spent the night with us."

Continuing to set the scene for the day of the accident, Saliba inquired, "At that time and, say, early August of '96, did your family have any major problems?"

Sheila answered, "We were excited about we were gonna – everything was going fine. We didn't have any real problems or anything, and we were gonna build a house and we were excited about that."

"Now, do you specifically remember that day of August 18, 1996?"

"Yes, sir."

"Were there any plans for that day in your family?"

"Yes, sir."

"Share with the jury what the plans were."

"We were gonna go to the lake and the kids were gonna jet ski. And Mama and I were gonna go to the cemetery because I didn't get to take her the day before. And we were gonna meet them at the lake afterwards."

"Okay. What time did the children and Karlas leave, approximately?"

"9:30, I guess, somewhere – 9:30."

"And were you and your mom, tell me whether or not ya'll were to meet Karlas and the children at the lake that day?"

"Yes, sir, we were going to."

"Now, Sheila, tell me whether or not you invited anyone to ride with you and your mother?"

"Yes, sir, I did."

"Who?"

"A friend of mine named Peggy Dean."

Sheila said that she and Peggy Dean had been in school together and when she was younger she had helped Peggy's grandparents pick tobacco. Peggy had returned to the Omega area after having been gone for some time, and Sheila had spoken with her earlier in the week and made plans to see her. Sheila testified that on the morning of August 18, she had called Peggy Dean to ask her if she wanted to ride out to the cemetery, and then go to the lake. She said that Peggy had not answered, so she had left a message on Peggy Dean's answering machine.

Saliba asked, "Sheila, did you obtain gas that morning?"

"Yes, sir, I did," she said.

"Did you fill your car up?"

"Yes, sir."

"Where?"

"At the Suwannee Swifty store at the end of Maple Street."

"Do you ever leave your gas tank top off?"

"Oh, yes, sir."

"How many times have you done that?"

"Well, I don't know. Several times."

"Have you ever had a carton of milk on top of your car?"

"Yes, sir."

"What happened to that?"

"It fell off and busted."

"Did you drive off with it on top?"

"Yes, sir."

Saliba then had Sheila testify about Weeks' Chapel Cemetery and its significance to her family. Sheila said it was where her father and brothers were buried, and she said that it had been important to her mother to keep the graves clean and flowers put on their graves.

Sheila explained that she had attended the Chapel when she was small, and that back then the church would only meet every other Sunday. Sheila testified that she and her mother were going to Weeks' Chapel the morning of August 18, 1996, but when she had passed by Liela Methodist Church, she realized that "they were having church on regular Sundays now."

So, she said, she turned around. She said she thought it would be "improper" to go to the church cemetery with church going on, "because the plot was right there and it would disturb the church activities. I mean, if somebody looked out there and saw us, it just wouldn't look right."

So, she said, she and her mother decided they would just ride around and look at where they used to live. They turned around again, and went back past Liela Church, and turned off and went toward Kinard Bridge Road, where her mother and father used to take the family swimming, and where Sheila was baptized. They continued to ride around, and eventually cut back towards Omega, and went down Troy Cox Road and over to what is called County Line Road, which is another place they had lived, "where the boys got killed in the front yard."

Sheila said they had been enjoying their ride, and at some point they had turned onto Livingston Bridge Road. She said that her mother had lived in that area for some fifty years and knew most everyone in that community who had been there for any length of time.

She said they had turned off Ellenton-Omega Road on to Livingston Bridge Road, and they were going to go down and visit "an old home place of a friend of hers."

Sheila said that her mother has asked to go there, that she had not been there in a while. Sheila said her mother's friend's house had been torn down, but her friend had moved back and built a home there, and "she was real proud for her."

Moving ever closer to the time of the accident, Sheila talked about the curve on Livingston Bridge Road before you approach the bridge over Ty Ty Creek. She said that she knew the people who lived in the house just before the curve, Ed and Rhonda Powell. She had known them since she was in grade school.

Sheila testified that on the other side of the bridge she also had friends, "named Vickie and Tony Garrick, who lived in that house." She said she had known Vickie since she was in high school, and that she had spent the night at that house many times. Sheila said that there was maybe about a mile and a half between her friends' houses, with the bridge in the middle. Sheila testified that the bridge was in "plain sight of Vickie Garrick's driveway."

Finally, Saliba was ready for Sheila to talk about the accident.

CHAPTER THIRTY-SEVEN

Thursday, September 3, 1996

"Now, in your own words, Sheila," Saliba said, "tell the jury what happened as you approached the bridge."

The courtroom fell totally silent. It was the testimony everyone had waited so long to hear. Saliba, with his slow, prodding questions, would walk Sheila through the accident, step-by-step.

Stines and Heinen sat on the edge of their seats.

"I glanced away, and I lost control of the car," she said.

"Is that consistent with all the other times you've related this story?"

"Pretty much, yes, sir."

"Okay. What happened to the car when you lost control?"

"It run off and, uh, I, and I jammed on brakes, and it come to the edge of the embankment."

"All right. Sheila, I'm gonna show you what we're going to call Plaintiff's Exhibit 1. Does that show, ma'am, the area that you lost control and ran off the road?"

"Yes, sir."

"Is there a mark on the road?"

"Yes, sir."

"Is that mark consistent with the path you took?"

"Yes, sir."

"Now, were you going at a slow rate of speed or a fast rate of speed?"

"Slow."

"And what happened to the car ma'am?"

"I – After I slammed on brakes and I got it, it come to rest on the edge of the embankment."

"And?"

"Teetering a little bit."

"And what did you do at that point?"

"Well, for a few minutes we just sat there. And, uh, I opened the car door. I looked over there, and Mama was just sitting there. She was wide-eyed and I said, I told her, I said, 'I'm going – I'll be right back.' And I opened the car door, and when I opened the car door, I still had my seat belt on and, and my arm got – the car tilted and started down, and the door closed on my arm."

"Were you able to get out of the car at that time?"

"No, sir."

"What happened to the car once you tried to step out? What happened to the car?"

"It, it went down the embankment."

"All right. Was it at an angle, Sheila?"

"No. No, sir."

"Was the back higher than the front or vice versa?"

"It might have been just a little."

"Now, were you still in the car at that time?"

"Yes, sir."

Heinen and Stines sat amazed, scribbling notes on their legal pads. They both thought they had never heard such a cock-and-bull story in all their lives. Heinen was beginning to think that maybe Donald Davis had been right: the woman did have balls to get on the stand and tell such a story.

"Tell us what happened to your arm during all these events," Saliba continued.

"Well, I had jerked it. Somehow I had gotten my arm back inside. I don't – And the door, going down the hill, the door must have gotten slammed shut. And I tried to get – would you ask that again? I have -."

"Do you have a clear memory of all these events?"

"No, sir."

"Do you remember some of them?"

"Yes, sir."

"Are some hazy for you, ma'am?"

"Very."

"You were inside the car when you went down the embankment?"

"I was inside the car."

"What's the first thing you remember when you got to the bottom of the embankment?"

"Well, I, I was dazed but I looked over and I checked on Mama to see if – she was leaning forward this way, and her head was caught in the shoulder, you know, the shoulder harness. And I checked to see if she had any blood on her head where she might have hit the, the window or anything. And, uh, and she hadn't. And -."

"Did you see any damage to your mom?"

"No, sir."

"Did you check your mom?"

"Yes, sir. I couldn't get a response out of her. I listened to her heart and everything too. I just couldn't hear, I mean, I couldn't get any response from her."

Assistant District Attorney Charlie Stines couldn't have been more pleased and wouldn't have interrupted this story for the world. It was more than he had ever hoped for.

Saliba continued, "Tell me whether or not your mother was positioned at an awkward angle?"

"Yes, sir."

"What did you do at that time?"

"I reached across the seat and let it back so that she'd be more comfortable."

"Now, did you recline the back of the seat? Is that what you mean?"

"Yes, sir. You have to reach across, you have to reach across, and there's a button that reclines the back of the seat."

"Tell the jury specifically where you had to reach in order to recline your mother's seat back."

"I had to reach across her, between her door and, which it was located right on the edge of her seat next to the door."

"Now, what was located on the edge of her seat?"

"A little, a little button that you, – rocker button that you mash."

"Okay. Did you have to lean over the console to do that?"

"Yes, sir."

"And did you lean over your mother to do that?"

"Yes, sir."

"Did you, in fact, recline the seat?"

"Yes, sir."

"Could you get a response from your mom at this time?"

"No."

"Did you nevertheless talk to her and try to reassure her?"

"Yes, sir, I did."

"Now, were you able to get out of the car at that point, Sheila?"

"I tried to open the door, but it was hard to open, and I had to bump it real hard to get it to open."

"Did you put your weight against it?"

"Yes, sir."

"And were you able to open the door?"

"Yes, sir."

"All right. At that point, was the car still running or was it not running?"

"No, sir. It was running."

"Did that concern you?"

"Yes, sir."

"What, if anything, did you do about the car running?"

"Well, I tried to get, get the car turned off, and I couldn't get it, get it turned off."

"Would the key turn?"

"No, sir. I couldn't get it to turn. I couldn't get it to do anything."

"All right. Well, go ahead then and tell us what you did."

"I, I got out of the car and I went – pulled the hood latch. And then I opened the hood of the car, and I thought about doing the battery, trying to get the battery cables off. That might make it stop. And then I got back in the car and I, I tried to turn it off, and I couldn't – I couldn't get the battery cables off. And I tried the ignition switch again, and I couldn't get it. And I moved the gear shift and, uh, and I got it turned off then."

"Now, let's go back to the cables. Did you have any tools in trying to remove the battery cables?"

"No, sir."

"How'd you do it?"

"I just did it with my bare hands, but I couldn't get 'em to move. They, they were too tight."

"Did you put any tool on that, on that battery at all?"

"No, sir."

"And were you able to remove the battery cables with your hands?"

"No, sir."

"Now, at some point did you discover that you might need to put the car in Park?"

"Yes, sir. When I was back in there. I was moving the gear shift."

"And did you do that?"

"Yes, sir."

"And at that point were you able to turn the car off?"

"Yes, sir."

"Sheila, what happened to the keys?"

"I took the keys out, and, and they dropped, and I – they just dropped out of my – slipped out of my hand and fell down."

"Do you know where those keys are?"

"No, sir, I do not."

Like so many parts of her story, Sheila never did the obvious. When she dropped the keys, why didn't she bend over and pick them up? It was a common sense thing to do and Saliba was aware that most of the jurors had to be wondering the same thing. For that reason, Saliba went into an explanation of why Sheila had not picked up the keys.

"Now, what was your state of mind at this time?"

"I was frantic. I – my arm was hurting. I was worried about Mama. And I just – I was in a daze. I, I, I have what's called anxiety attacks, and if anybody's had anxiety attacks, they know. They feel like you're having a heart attack."

"Were you scared?"

"Very."

"What, if anything, did you do to try to take your mom out of the car?"

"Well, when I got out, I got out, and I was gonna go for help, and I fell against the door, and it closed. And I went around, and when I got on her side, I realized that the, the window was up. And, uh, I tried to open her door, and I couldn't get it open. And then I went around to the other side, and I couldn't get it open."

"Did you try to open both doors, Sheila?"

"Yes, sir."

"And were you able to, ma'am?"

"No, sir."

"At the time, what did you think was wrong?"

"I thought that the doors was locked, that I had hit the automatic lock, because I've done that so many times before."

"Do you know why the doors wouldn't open yourself? Have you found out later on?"

"Yes, sir."

"Okay. Why?"

"The doors were jammed."

"Okay. Now, at this point, were you in any way aware of any danger of fire in the car to your mother?"

"No, sir."

"What did you do at that point?"

"I went, I went – there was lots of briars and stuff, and I went, I was looking for a place on the ditch bank to go up the embankment. And I finally got up, and I started toward Ed and Rhonda's, and I realized that their house was further away than, than Tony and Vickie. So I turned around and went back down that way."

"Did you find any help?"

"Yes, sir."

"In what form did help come?"

"Danny Weeks and his wife."

"At the time you went up the bank, did you have knowledge that the car was on fire at that time?"

"No, sir."

"Now, Sheila, what did Danny Weeks – when you stopped Danny Weeks – what did he do, ma'am?"

"He run back down there toward the car with me."

Saliba was coming to a critical question. It was one he knew the prosecution would ask, and he planned to take the bite out of it by asking it first.

"Did you ever actually go back to the car?"

"To the car, no, sir."

"Were you afraid?"

"Yes, sir."

"Did you or did you not do everything you could to obtain help?"

"Yes, sir."

"Now, at what point did you first realize that there may be some smoke or fire or whatever in the car?"

"It was after I had gone across the bridge, and I had gone across the bridge and toward Vickie's lane. I went down it and I come back up because I thought I heard a car. And I didn't. The car didn't come. Because there's such an echo chamber in that area there. And I turned around and I went back and then, toward her house again and -."

"Did you see the car at that point?"

"Yes, sir."

"Okay. Now tell me, though, at what point did you realize the car may be on fire?"

"Before, right before I saw Danny and them."

"What did that do to your emotional condition?"

"It scared me real bad because I didn't – I knew I couldn't get back in the car."

"Now, Sheila, I'm gonna ask you, ma'am, did you do anything at all to cause the death of your mother?"

"No, sir, I did not. I loved my mother and I respected her, too."

Finished with Sheila's account of the accident, Saliba had to lay some groundwork for the cross-examination by Charlie Stines that would soon be forthcoming. Saliba was well aware that when it was Stines' turn to ask Sheila questions, he was going to hone in on her "prior inconsistent statements" to law enforcement officers Bryan, Gay, and Davis. Saliba wanted to leave Sheila with a little wiggle room.

"What was your physical condition at this time?"

"I was, I was, I was throwing up. I was, I was hurting. I was scared. And everything was like, it was, like it was in a tunnel."

"Did you talk with anyone while you were there at the scene?"

"Yes, sir."

"Did you talk with any law enforcement officials?"

"Yes, sir."

"Was it painful to talk to them?"

"Yes, sir."

"Did you or did you not do all you could to help them, however?"

"Yes, sir, I did."

"And, again, is your memory of this particular point in time clear or cloudy, ma'am?"

"It's very cloudy. I was real numb."

"How many times were you questioned by various people?"

"One, one, one would come in and he'd ask questions, and then another one would come – and he'd go out, and another one would come in and he'd ask questions, and he'd go out and, and then another one would come in and he'd ask questions. And then they started it all over again. It just, it just, like it was going on forever."

"Now, how long were you at the scene before you were able to leave the scene?"

"I've been told it was about two hours."

"How long did it seem?"

"Forever. Eternity."

"Tell the jury whether or not you were hurting during this accident?"

"Yes, sir."

"And how were you hurt?"

"My arm. When the door closed on my arm, it crushed it some, and it caused it to snatch my back."

"What were the next couple of days like for you?"

"Well, they were the worst three days I've ever had."

"On what day was your mom buried?"

"On a Wednesday."

"Did you at some point learn about your mother being exhumed?"

"Yes, sir."

"How'd you learn of that?"

"He pulled up in my driveway and told me."

"Who did?"

"Heinen. Officer Heinen."

"All right. And did you know he was coming?"

"I – they were – I was told that he was coming to see me."

"Were you there for him to see?"

"Yes, sir."

"Did you know what news he was going to have for you?"

"Not really."

"And once he told you what was gonna happen to your mother, what effect did that have on you?"

"Sir, I consider an exhumation a desecration of the grave."

"Did that cause you emotional pain?"

Crying, Sheila nodded her head affirmatively.

"What's it like without your mother?"

"You feel like a part of you – I just feel like a part – I have a hole in my heart and she just – it's, it's not filled up."

"Did you love your mother?"

"Very much."

"Did you do anything intentionally to cause your mother harm at all?"

"No, sir."

"Are you guilty of what you're charged with?"

"No, sir, I'm not."

Saliba said, "She's with the Court, Your Honor."

Court was recessed for lunch. Assistant District Attorney Charlie Stines would have a little over an hour to prepare for the cross-examination of Sheila Bryan. He and Heinen had a lot to talk about. They would do more talking than eating.

CHAPTER THIRTY-EIGHT

Thursday, September 2, 1998

The prosecution's cross-examination of Sheila Bryan began after the lunch recess at 2:10 p.m.

Stines intended to set the tone for the cross-examination early. He would let Sheila, and the jurors, know that he had no intentions of handling the defendant with kid gloves; it was not going to be pretty.

"Good afternoon, Mrs. Bryan," Stines began. They were the most cordial words she would hear from Stines for most of the rest of the afternoon.

"Hello," she returned the greeting.

With the civilities over, Stines was ready to dig in.

"Now, you have cried a good deal up here on the stand, haven't you?" he queried.

"Yes, sir," Sheila said, unaware where Stines was going.

"Kind of dry crying, no real tears – "

"No, sir. They were genuine."

"What I'm saying, they weren't wet? They were dry?"

"Sir, they were wet tears."

Sheila's voice had an edge to it, and Stines liked that. He wanted the jury to see the "other Sheila." Not the respectful, meek, crying Sheila, but the Sheila who had killed her mother.

"Now, you admit that when you were driving, and you ended up down at the bottom of the embankment, your mother was alive; wasn't she?" Stines asked, getting to the heart of the matter, feeling no need to pussy-foot around.

"Sir, she must have been unconscious because I could not get her to respond," Sheila answered.

"Do you remember talking to law enforcement officers and telling them as you went down the bank she said 'Sheila'? Do you remember telling the law enforcement officers that?"

"Sir, she went – she said 'Sheila' when I run off the road the first time."

Stines paused and gave Sheila an incredulous look. He was ready to begin going over every sentence she had spoken to law enforcement, word by word.

"But when you talked to Coroner Rodney Bryan, you told him you lost control going around the curve, didn't you?"

"Um, I don't recall saying going around a curve."

"You came around the curve and lost control of the car then, how's that? Is that correct?"

"After I got around the curve, yes, sir."

"And you told him you got up there and tried to dodge a guard rail, didn't you?"

"There was a guard rail when I, when I come to rest on the edge of the embankment."

"Well, you remember – you heard Rodney Bryan testify to that part, didn't you?"

"Yes, sir."

"And Rodney wrote down notes at the time, didn't he?"

"I, I – yes, sir, I guess he did."

"And you're not going to deny that you told him that, are you?"

"No, sir. But you have to understand what kind of condition I was in at that time that these statements were given."

This was the wiggle room Saliba had provided Sheila before he had turned her over for cross-examination. Sheila would retreat to this defense many times during the course of the afternoon.

Stines said, "But I also understand that you talked to Trooper Chris Gay, didn't you?"

"Yes, sir," she said.

"He came up and you produced your driver's license and insurance for him, didn't you?"

"No, sir, I did not."

"You didn't?"

"No, sir, I did not. How could I do that when I didn't have them?"

"Well, you heard him testify that you did, didn't you?"

"Yes, sir. And I did not understand where that come from."

"And he had your numbers for them, didn't he?"

"Yes, sir."

"Um, I guess he made them up and he made them up correctly, didn't he?"

"No, sir. I told them to him."

"Told him your insurance policy number?"

"No, sir, I did not tell him that."

"What is your insurance policy number?"

"I have no earthly idea."

"So Trooper Gay is wrong in saying that you presented that stuff to him, is that correct?"

"Yes, sir, it is."

"And you told Trooper Gay that you were not paying attention and you ran off the road, is that correct?"

"That's correct."

"You told him you were going real slow."

"Slow, but not real slow."

"And you told him nothing appeared to be wrong with your mother and that she was not injured?"

"After we went down the embankment at the end? When are you talking about?"

"Well, you told him at the time you went down, there was nothing wrong with your mother and she was not injured, didn't you?"

"At the bottom of the embankment?"

"Right."

"Yes, sir. I was referring – "

"You got out of the car – "

"I was referring to no bleeding or anything."

Stines had made his point and he had been ready to move on, but Sheila had felt the need to explain further. She had caught on very quickly that it was not in her best interest to agree with Stines and she would repeatedly use the tactic of feigning confusion to give herself more thinking time, to figure how to get out of the box Stines would repeatedly put her in.

"Okay," Stines said. "And you said you crawled up the hill in order to get help?"

"Yes, sir."

"Now, you'll agree that you were about thirty-one feet off the hill, weren't you?"

"Yes, sir."

"How far would you say thirty-one feet is?"

"Sir, I'm not good at distance."

"Do you think this room is more than thirty-one feet long?"

"No."

"Well, Mrs. Bryan, get down and let's time you and see how long it takes you to walk at normal speed to the end, down over there."

Sheila clearly did not want to leave the witness stand and she had no idea where Stines was going with this one.

"Sir, you have to realize I was climbing up a steep embankment through briars," she said.

"But that wasn't what I asked you," Stines said. "I asked you just to come down, and see how long it takes you to walk down through there. Let's time it. Tell me when you want to start."

Sheila stepped down and walked toward the back of the courtroom.

"It took you about thirteen seconds, didn't it?"

"I have no idea."

"And it's harder to climb up a bank than it is to walk up through here, isn't it?"

"Yes, sir."

Sheila returned to the witness stand.

"But it doesn't take anything like two minutes to walk up that bank, would it?"

"Two minutes?"

"Yes. There's no way in the world it'd take two minutes to walk up that bank, is there?"

"Well, it depends on if you're going straight up it or if you were looking for a place to get up."

"Well, you would admit there was a trail where your car had turned down through there, wouldn't you?"

"A trail for the tire tracks, sir?"

"Yes."

"Yes, sir."

"The car had rolled off there, hadn't it?"

"Sir?"

Stines would prove to be willing to repeat questions as many times as necessary to get Sheila to answer them.

"The car had rolled down through there, hadn't it?" he repeated.

"Yes, sir."

"It was in drive when you went down the bank, wasn't it?"

"Yes, sir."

"And you were on your brakes all the way down, weren't you?"

"I assume I was, yes, sir."

"And you went very, very slowly?"

"No, not really."

"And you went fast down that bank?"

"Fast?"

"As you went down that bank, you came to rest – "

"I rode pretty hard. At the bottom of it I remember it being a big jolt, if that's what you're saying. Is that what you mean?"

"Well, I'm just saying it was--"

"It was not slow, if that's what you mean, if that's what you're saying."

Stines stopped to give Sheila another of his incredulous looks. Although she had just a short time before testified on direct examination and on cross-examination that she had been going "slow", now she had denied it. Perhaps now, totally wary of Stines, she had felt it had not been a good idea to agree to "slow" if Stines had wanted her to say "slow." Whatever the reason, she had reversed course, again.

"Now you told Trooper Gay that you went down there and crawled up the hill, didn't you?"

"Yes, sir."

"And you told him you walked toward the house on the other side of the bridge?"

"Yes, sir. But I also told him that I had went up the ditch bank trying to find a place to get up because there was so many briars and stuff."

"You remember real well what you told him now, don't you?"

"No, not real well. I just remember going up and down the ditch bank."

"You said when you got halfway across the bridge you looked back and saw smoke coming from the vehicle, is that correct?"

"Do what now?"

"When you were halfway across the bridge, you looked back and saw smoke coming from the vehicle?"

"No, sir. Not when I was halfway across the bridge."

"That's what you told Trooper Gay on that day though? Were you confused when you talked to him?"

"Yes, sir."

"But you wouldn't deny that's what you told him, would you?"

"I have no way of knowing, sir. I mean, I – if that's what he said I said. But I was very confused that day."

"Then you saw a man coming from the other direction. It turned out to be your cousin, is that correct?"

"That's correct."

"You told Trooper Gay that. You told him that the man ran to the other side and got a bucket of water, is that correct? You told Trooper Gay that didn't you?"

"Yeah. We went down to the car first. I went toward the car."

Stines quickly switched topics on Sheila.

"You don't deny that there were tire tracks, not just tire tracks, but *your* tire tracks, were in the grass for a considerable distance prior to running off the embankment itself, do you?"

"Do what now?"

"You admit that you drove all four wheels off the pavement for a considerable distance before running off, don't you?"

"No, sir."

"How do you account for the tire tracks from your car to go down there and make that turn off the road?"

"Sir, I don't know. There was a lot of vehicles down there on both sides."

Sheila was starting to lose her patience with Stines. Her voice had taken on a hard edge and her body language was not friendly. Stines continued on his set course.

"But you realize that Trooper Gay and Randy Stephens came out there and tracked your car along the roadway, don't you, for at least sixty feet prior to turning off?"

"Sir, I don't know that that was my car. I doubt it was."

"But you don't remember that well, do you?"

"No, sir."

"And you told someone you tried to steer back onto the road, didn't you?"

"Yeah. Immediately."

"But there was nothing in your tire tracks to show that, was there?"

"Which tire tracks are you talking about?"

"The tire tracks running along in the grass showing you were trying to steer back onto the pavement?"

"Sir, I don't know about those tire tracks."

"Well, now, you've had a considerable length of time to go over all of this material, haven't you?"

"Yes, sir."

"And you know what you told everybody, don't you, basically?"

"Basically."

"And you saw the pictures, didn't you?"

"I saw the pictures of the tire tracks, yes, sir."

"Um-hum. And when you talked to Donald Davis on that day, you told him a little bit different from what you told Chris Gay or Rodney Bryan, didn't you?"

"I talked to him, yes, sir, that day. But you have to realize I was throwing up and I was in pain and I was in a very bad state that day. I had lost my mother, sir."

Familiar with the statements she had made to Donald Davis, Sheila knew she was boxed in again, and she knew now that Stines would take her through those statements sentence by sentence. So she had retreated to her "state of mind" defense. Stines knew he had her on the run.

"Would you expect anybody, regardless of what the circumstances, who'd lost their mother to be upset?"

"Yes, sir, I would expect them to be upset."

"In fact, even if someone had killed someone, it'd probably upset them a great deal, wouldn't it?"

Stines' point had not been missed by Sheila Bryan. Her voice gave way to her rising anger.

"Sir, that would probably be the individual."

"But don't you think most people would be pretty upset if they'd killed someone?"

"If they were a very cruel person, they probably wouldn't be too upset."

"Of course, you're not a very cruel person though, are you?"

"No, sir, by no means."

With the battle lines clearly drawn, Stines continued along his set course without so much as skipping a beat.

"Now, you told Donald you and your mother were riding around. You were riding around talking and you looked off?"

"Yes, sir."

Stines began reading from Donald Davis' report.

"'The next thing I knew I had run off the road in the ditch?'"

"Um-hum (affirmative)."

"You didn't say anything about stopping up there and opening the door and getting out, did you?"

"No, sir. I didn't get out at the top."

"You didn't get out at the top?"

"No, sir. I said I opened the car door of the vehicle and it closed back on my arm."

"Well, where was your arm?"

"It was out the door."

"When you stopped at the top of the embankment?"

"At the top of the embankment. I was unsteady and I had opened the door. I was gonna get out. And the door – and the car shifted and the door come to on my arm."

"You didn't tell Rodney or Donald Davis any of that, did you? Or Chris Gay?"

"Sir, you have to remember I was not going into complete detail when I – at that time. You have to realize what state I was in and I could not recall all the little tiny details."

"And you said, 'When the car stopped I tried to turn the motor off but it wouldn't stop.'"

"That's correct."

"You said you, 'Got out and tried to raise the hood so I could take the battery cable off but I couldn't.'"

"No. I said I raised the hood and tried to get the battery cable off and I couldn't get the battery cables off 'cause all I had was my bare hands."

"You said, 'I got out of the car and tried to raise the hood so I could take the battery cable off, but I couldn't.' You couldn't take the battery cable off, is that true?"

"That's correct."

"Now, you told Donald Davis that, didn't you?"

"Yes, sir, I guess so if he wrote it down."

"You said, 'Mama was sitting in the car?'"

"Yeah. She was reclined. By then I had reclined her back."

"You didn't tell anything about reclining her though, did you?"

"Sir, again, you have to understand I was not going into complete detail. I was not even thinking in complete detail."

"But you did tell him, 'She was okay, so I climbed back up the ditch bank?'"

"That she was okay?"

"Yes."

"I could not tell. As far as no bleeding or anything like that was what I was referring to."

"It says, 'When I got to the top I looked back down at the car and it was smoking.' Is that correct?"

246

"No, sir, that is not correct."

"That's what you told him on that day though, wasn't it?"

"Then, then it must have been taken out of context."

"And said, 'Then I started down the road to get some help.'"

"Again, sir, he must have taken that out of context."

"Well, are you denying saying that?"

"No, sir, I'm not denying it, but it may have not been in that order. I don't know. I was very upset that day and I was being badgered actually."

Stines stopped and looked at Sheila Bryan.

"You're pretty upset today and think you're being badgered now, don't you?"

"Yes, sir, I really do, with all due respect, sir."

"And it says, 'I started down the road to get some help?'"

"Yes, sir."

Stines stopped and took another long look at Sheila Bryan. He paused. Then he went to make his point.

"After you'd already seen the car smoke? You were gonna walk off and leave your mother while she's – while the car's smoking – "

"No, sir. No, sir. I did not see the car smoking when I got to the top. Again, I – he must have taken that out of context."

"'When I got across the bridge, I stopped a car.' Do you agree with that?"

"When I was across the bridge a car came, yes."

"'It was my cousin.' Do you agree with that?"

"Yes, sir. But, but at the time I did not know who it was."

"'And I told him that I'd run off the road and needed some help?'"

"I told – yes."

"'When we got back to the car it was smoking real bad and it was on fire?'"

"I did not see any fire. It was smoking real bad."

"You said, 'We tried to get Mama out but the car was on fire and we couldn't.' Is that correct?"

"Yes, sir."

"'My mother was okay when I left her in the car?'"

"Again, I was referring to that she didn't have any physical damage appearing."

"It says, 'I don't know what happened.'"

Saliba was on his feet for the first objection of the cross-examination. He objected to Stines saying, "It says." Saliba said that Stines should show Sheila the statement and then ask her if she had said it.

It truly had not been much of an objection from Saliba, especially that far along in the cross-examination when Stines had been using the same tactic almost since the beginning.

But it had given Sheila a little break. It was becoming apparent that she was about at the end of her rope with Stines. She had been on the stand a long time, and she was wearing down. Stines knew it, and so did Saliba.

Stines said he had no problem with Saliba's objection.

"In fact," he said, being the poster boy for affability, "I'll give Mrs. Bryan all the chance she needs to read the next things I'm going to question her about. Tell me when you're through with it, Mrs. Bryan."

"All of this or just one page at a time?" she asked.

"Go through all of it and then I'll take it back."

"Well, I don't have my glasses with me, sir."

"Well, would you like to use mine? But I don't know that they'll help."

"I don't know what your prescription is."

"I don't either."

"Well, you should, they're yours."

After Sheila snapped at Stines, Saliba was back on his feet, asking the court if he could get his client's glasses. It was a distraction from Sheila's hostility, if nothing else. While they wrangled over Sheila's glasses and the paperwork, Sheila had a chance to get her second wind.

Stines thought Sheila's anger made her look haughty and unattractive on the stand. She was not the sympathetic figure she had been on direct examination, and Stines planned to do everything he could to keep it that way.

Heinen would have smiled if he had not thought it would have been inappropriate.

CHAPTER THIRTY-NINE

Thursday, September 2, 1998

Stines was on an adrenaline rush. He felt no fatigue and was ready to cross-examine Sheila into the next century if need be to get his points across to the jury.

He picked up right where he had left off.

"Now, you do recall talking again with Donald Davis on the 27th, don't you?" he asked.

"When he came to my home?"

"Right."

"Yes, sir."

"And you've been able to read this statement, haven't you?"

"Yes, sir, but it's muddled because I'm so confused and nervous right now."

"And what you told Donald, Mr. Davis, on that day, was that you and your mother, Freda Weeks, were riding around looking at places you used to live?"

"Yes, sir."

"Did you say that?"

"Yes, sir."

"'We were just riding down the road talking and I looked off.' Did you say that?"

"Yes, sir."

"'The next thing I knew we were in the ditch.' Did you say that?"

"Probably, yes, sir."

"'I heard my mother say my name, 'Sheila,' when we were going down the ditch bank.'"

"I don't recall saying that, because she said 'Sheila' when we went off the road to begin with. She's the one that probably saw that we were going off the road."

"'When we stopped at the bottom of the ditch, I couldn't get the car to switch off.' Did you say that?"

"Yes, sir."

"'I got out and tried to get the battery cable off so the car would stop.' Did you say that?"

"That's correct."

"'I couldn't get the battery cable off, so I went back to the car and tried again to shut off the car.'"

"Yes, sir."

"Did you say that?"

"Yes, sir. I went back to the car."

"'Mama was sitting in the car with a dazed look on her face.'"

"No, sir. She had the dazed look on her face when we were up on the edge of the embankment."

"Did she still have it on her when she was down there at the bottom?"

"No, sir."

"She didn't. 'She was wearing her seatbelt.'"

"Yes, sir."

"'I think I got the car turned off.'"

"Yeah."

"Now, you remember how you got it turned off, don't you?"

"Yeah."

"How'd you do that?"

"Moved the gear shift."

"'I told Mama I was going to get help and I said I would be right back.'"

"Yes."

"You told her that?"

"I told her at the top, yes sir, and at the bottom, but there was no response from her."

"'I shut the driver's side door.' Did you say that?"

"Yes, sir."

"And after you said that then you said it was locked?"

"Well, I didn't know that it was locked until after I had gone back around. You have to realize that my mother had just been buried not long before this, and it was hard to go back and relive this."

"You said you went around on the passenger's side of the car and couldn't get the door open?"

"Yes, sir, that's correct."

"You told her you were going to get help?"

"I told her – no, I did not say that, I don't think."

"'I climbed the ditch bank to go for help.'"

"I did climb the ditch bank."

"'I knew that there was a woman that I knew that lived just up the road.'"

"Yes, sir."

"'The car was not smoking when I got to the road.'"

"No, sir."

"It was not smoking?"

"No sir, it was not smoking when I got to the top of the road."

"'I made it across the bridge and a car was coming.'"

"Yes, sir."

"'I waved them down and they stopped.'"

"But I had already gone towards Vickie's house. I was completely across the bridge, at her driveway."

"'I didn't know that in the car was my cousin, Danny Weeks.'"

"Yes, sir."

"'I told him I needed help. My Mama was in the car in the ditch and I couldn't get her out.'"

"Yes, sir."

"'When we got back to the car it was smoking.'"

"Sir, it was smoking when Danny pulled up."

"'I didn't see any fire.'"

"No sir, I didn't see any fire."

Stines and Sheila both knew what was coming next, and it was another box for Sheila. Danny Weeks had already testified, and what Danny Weeks had said on the witness stand did not match what Sheila had told Donald Davis.

"'Danny made me sit down on the road, and he went to get some water to put on the car.'"

"I went back towards [the car] with him, and he made me sit down – it's really vague right there. I just – I don't know. I don't know what, really, what I done there, because it's still real hazy. I just – I can't – I'm muddled. I can't remember."

"'When we got back the car was on fire.'"

"Again, I never seen the fire. All I saw was smoke."

"'He made me stay about half way down to the bridge.'"

"I had gone towards the car with him and he made me turn around and go back."

Stines paused. He wanted to be sure the jury had time to think about what Sheila had said, which was contradictory to what Danny Weeks had said on the stand.

"'I didn't hear anything that sounded like an explosion.'"

"No, sir."

Stines had finally come to the end of the statements Sheila had given to Rodney Bryan, Chris Gay, and Donald Davis. But he had other issues he also wanted to question Sheila about. He began with the gas.

"Did you pay for your gasoline with a credit card or with cash?"

"With cash."

"And you know that your gas cap was never found anywhere, don't you?"

"Yes, sir."

"Were you afraid when the car was burning that the gasoline tank might explode when you saw all the smoke and everything?"

"Yes, sir."

"You think that's pretty common, what people commonly think about gas tanks?"

"I, I would think so, yeah."

"You don't know if they do, or they don't, though, do you?"

"No, sir, I have no knowledge of them. I've just seen them on TV."

"But on that day, you thought they did, didn't you?"

"Well, yes sir, where there's fire and gas."

"And you knew it was full?"

"Yes, sir."

Stines thought he had made his point, and he switched topics.

"Now, the fact is that probably at the very, very longest, it would take forty-five seconds to come up that bank. Would you agree with that?"

"No, not really, sir."

"Come thirty-one feet up a bank, you don't think you could do that in forty-five seconds?"

"Sir, you have to realize I was, I was very tired, and I was having an anxiety attack."

"But you also knew your mother was in that car, didn't you?"

"Yes, sir. But she was not in any danger at that time. The only thing I was concerned with was, you know, the fact that I couldn't get a response, but there was no, nothing there to make me have to go."

Stines paused to let Sheila's statement hit home with the jury.

"Well, why did you tell them all that she was okay and didn't mention anything about her not responding?"

"Sir, again, you have to remember what kind of state I was in."

"Isn't it true that you're just trying to make this jury think that she was dead before this happened?"

"Sir, I hope with all my heart that she was."

"And, you pretty well know she wasn't, don't you?"

"No, sir, I do not know that."

Stines switched subjects again. He had already decided exactly how he was going to handle the next subject before he had ever started the questioning. It wouldn't take long.

"You did have a terrycloth towel over her, is that correct?"

"A terrycloth towel over her?"

"Over her."

"There was a terrycloth towel in my car, yes, sir."

"And it was extended over across some part of her body, at least on her lap, didn't it?"

"I don't remember, but it could have been."

Stines had gotten exactly what he wanted, so he moved on.

"And your mother was incontinent at that time, wasn't she?"

"Was what?"

"She didn't have control of her bladder?"

"Sir, the only reason she had on that undergarment that you keep referring to is because she had a weak bladder, and when you go off somewhere, you can't readily find a bathroom. Around home, she did not wear one of those. That's the only reason she had it on that day."

"But she was wearing it that day, though?"

"Yes, sir."

"And you've testified, and you've heard a lot of testimony, that your mother was affected considerably by the aging process?"

"Somewhat."

"And she was eighty-two."

"Yes, sir."

"And not really a big woman, was she?"

"Well, sir, I consider a hundred and fifty pounds fairly good size."

"She was short, though, wasn't she?"

"Yes, sir."

"And all that was left of her was seventy-eight pounds, is that correct?"

"Yes, sir."

Stines switched subjects again. At least when he had been questioning her about her prior statements to law enforcement, Sheila had known where they were headed. Now she had no idea.

"And, now, this car had a keyless entry system, didn't it?"

"Yes, sir, it did."

"And you drove that car regularly, didn't you?"

"Yes, sir, I did."

"You knew how to open it with that keyless pad, didn't you?"

"No, sir, I did not. Ever since I acquired that car, I've never used that because we did not have the, uh, the combination to open it."

"Well, you know you can program that combination, don't you?"

"You can program it?"

"Right."

"Sir, I never bothered to have it programmed."

"And the car had been in the family since it was new, hadn't it?"

"Yes, sir."

"Been your mother-in-law's car, in fact, hadn't it?

"Yes, sir."

"Pretty nice Cougar, wasn't it?"

"Yes, sir."

"Had lots of electrical equipment on it, leather seats?"

"Yes, sir."

"Pretty blue paint?"

"Fully loaded, yes, sir."

"Pretty hubcaps?"

"Yes, sir."

"None of them came off going down that hill, did they?"

"No, sir, not that I know of."

"So you'd have to say you were going down that hill real slowly, weren't you?"

"Do what now?"

"You ran off that hill very slowly, didn't you?"

"Well, define slow, sir."

"If I had to define it, would you accept no more than ten miles an hour?"

"I, I couldn't give you a guesstimate on that. Sir, I wasn't even concentrating on how, how fast or how slow we were going down. All I know is we were going down."

"And you know this was a Mercury Cougar, weighed just a little under thirty-one hundred pounds curb weight, don't you?"

"I'd have – I don't know. I'll have to take your –"

"Total full, it might be a hundred and fifty pounds of gasoline and four hundred pounds of you and your mother. You're talking probably no more than thirty-five or thirty-six hundred pounds in that car, fully loaded, would you?"

"Okay. Yes, sir. I guess so."

"And it's not a real heavy car, and it's not a real tiny car either, is it? Sort of a medium car?"

"To me it's a heavy car."

"Nevertheless, you're talking about thirty-six hundred pounds going down that embankment. You'd agree that the car was not bent up in any way, wouldn't you, as a result of going down the embankment?"

"Would I agree?"

"Right."

"No, sir, I wouldn't agree to that. I don't know."

"Where would you say it was bent?"

"I would say around the door."

"Which door?"

"The driver's door."

"You think the driver's door was bent up? Well, if you would, Mrs. Bryan, step over here with me to the jury. [Sheila stepped down] You agree that's how it came to rest, don't you?"

"Yes, sir."

"Now, show us where the driver's door is bent up. And hold it where the jury can see it."

"It looks like the door is ajar up here [indicating]. See, where it's out of line at the top? It probably happened when it was, when it came down the embankment."

"Show the jury where you say it was bent."

"It looks like it's ajar right here where I come down the embankment. It must have caught on the side because it was –"

"Mrs. Bryan, let me show you [exhibit] fifteen. That's a larger picture of the same thing, isn't it?"

"Um-hum [affirmative]."

"Show me where it's bent there?"

"Now, in this one, it doesn't look quite as bad, so I guess it might be because the car is straightened back out and the pressure is off of it."

Charlie Stines was coming into the home stretch. He could see the finish line. In the final phase of his cross-examination there were some things he wanted Sheila to answer for and he wanted her to answer for them on the stand, under oath.

CHAPTER FORTY

Thursday, September 3, 1998

Sheila returned to the stand and Stines continued with his cross-examination.

"You've certainly driven Ford vehicles a good deal, haven't you?" Stines asked.

"Ford? Well, no sir, not really."

"Well, you agree that this Mercury is a Ford vehicle?

"Yes, sir."

"But you're aware the Ford products you drive, that to open the door, even with the door locked, front doors, and [the Cougar] only had front doors didn't it?"

"Yes, sir."

"That all you have to do is just pull on the handle and it opens, doesn't it?"

"Yes, sir, if they're in good working condition."

"Now, it was a hot day, wasn't it?

"Extremely, yes, sir."

"About ninety degrees?"

"I don't know."

"Very little wind that day, was there?"

"I have no idea."

"And it was not raining in any way, was it?"

"No, sir."

"The road wasn't slick, was it?"

"No, sir. Only from the heat I guess."

"But you turned your engine off before you left, hadn't you?"

"Yes, sir."

"And you left your mother down there with only about six inches of ventilation by one window, didn't you? You only had one window down, didn't you?"

"Yes, sir."

"And it was only down about six inches?"

"Three or four, I guess. I don't know."

"You left your mother buckled in that car on a hot day like that for you to go out and walk to a house, is that right?"

"Walk to the house?"

"Well, how were you going to get to a house?"

"Well, you go a little quicker than a walk."

"So then you were coming up that bank as fast as you could then, weren't you? You were going a little faster than a walk coming up that bank, across that bridge, weren't you?"

"Yes, sir. But you have to remember I had done gone up the ditch bank trying to find a way to get up because the briars were like very high going up that ditch bank, and I was trying to find a place to get up."

"And your mother is sitting down there in the car and you're considering all this about where the fewest briars are, is that correct?"

"Well, sir, it, it was – I was trying to get up the ditch bank."

"But that bank is not so steep that you can't just walk up it?"

"Yes, sir, it is."

"It's kind of hard but it's – "

"Yes, sir, it is because I fell back down a couple of times trying to get back up it."

"Oh, but you didn't tell any of the officers that, did you?"

"Sir, you have to remember what condition I was in when I was giving these statements. And you also have to remember they were coming in and out and I was throwing up. I had no medical attention. I had to ask for some water to drink because I was throwing up."

"You weren't throwing up a few minutes ago though when your own attorney was questioning you, were you?"

"No, sir."

"You didn't tell him anything about falling down the bank two or three times, did you?"

"But I did."

"When did you decide that?"

"Sir, I had done that. It's not when I decided. It's what happened."

"You've had two years to think about this, haven't you?"

"Yes, sir, but I try to think as little as possible because I do not want to relive it."

"And you've had access to any of the statements you made, haven't you?"

"Yes, sir."

"And come up with any kind of story you wanted to if you wanted to come up with one, couldn't you?"

"Yes, sir, but I was telling you the truth."

"Were you telling Donald Davis the truth?"

"Yes, sir, as I thought at the time. And like I said, he must have taken some of that stuff out of context."

"Were you telling Chris Gay the truth?"

"Yes, sir, as I could recall it at the time."

"Were you telling Rodney Bryan the truth?"

"As I could recall it."

"Now, their mother hadn't just been burned up in a car, had they?"

"No, sir. I hope not."

"And they weren't throwing up or anything, were they?"

"No, sir."

"And they were pretty coherent, weren't they?"

"I assume they were."

"And they were able to write down and make notes and prepare statements of what you said, weren't they?"

"Yes, sir."

"And you admit there are very significant differences between what you told each of them on all of these different occasions back then?"

"Yes, sir, and, again, you have to remember what kind of state I was in."

"But you do admit that your story you're telling today has a whole lot more detail even though you were much closer in time to it then, don't you?"

"Sir, when you are close to a tragedy, you don't recall stuff. You may not even recall stuff years later. And if anybody's ever been in a tragic situation, they would understand that."

"And you had all the time in the world to go tell them what had happened since then, haven't you?"

"Yes, sir."

"You haven't done that, have you?"

"No, sir."

"You could have, couldn't you?"

"Well, when someone comes to you and tells you that they're gonna exhume your mother, what do you automatically do?"

"They came as a courtesy, didn't they?"

"I would hope so, yes, sir."

"And without going into anything that Karlas said or anything, Karlas was pretty well lit that night, wasn't he, or that day?"

"No, sir, not that I know of."

"But you would not have wanted them to exhume your mother and not have told you, would you?"

"If they had done that it would have caused a lot less grief on my part, but I accept it was a courtesy on their part, sir."

"And after that you knew that an investigation was proceeding, didn't you?"

"Yes, sir."

"And without going into for what reasons or whatever, you went through at least three, at least two law firms, didn't you?"

"Two law firms?"

"Yes."

Saliba asked for a bench conference. He objected to the relevance of the questions about the law firms. After some arguing back and forth, Judge Horkan instructed the jury to disregard the testimony about the law firms.

"Now, Mrs. Bryan, you admit that when you start timing two minutes, it seems like a long, long time, doesn't it? You sit there and watch the clock for two minutes and it seems like a long, long time, doesn't it?"

"Yes, sir, if you're just sitting there looking at it, it does."

"And you'd agree that it only took you about thirteen seconds to walk the length of this courtroom, wouldn't you?"

"Yes, sir."

"And you'd agree that even if a fire like this had happened, that it would have taken a pretty good length of time for it to reach that kind of intensity, wouldn't it?"

"I don't know."

"And you had all the time in the world to get your mother out of that car, didn't you?"

"If I could have gotten the doors open."

"Well, there'd been no real problem getting that driver's door open at least, would it? We know that. It was unlocked, wasn't it?"

"The driver's door was unlocked?"

"Right. Unlocked."

"Sir, I tried to get the door open and I could not get it open."

"There was no malfunction of that door whatsoever was there, Mrs. Bryan?"

"I have no idea."

"And you'd taken the key out; didn't you?"

"Out of the ignition? Yes, sir."

"But you never told Trooper Gay, Donald Davis, Rodney Bryan anything about losing your keys; did you?"

"Sir, I don't, I don't know if I did or not. Again, you have to understand what I, what I was going through at that time."

"And you have never mentioned this key until today, have you?"

"Yes, sir, I have."

"You never told law enforcement anything whatsoever about dropping your key? Have you?"

"I'm not sure about that."

"You never told them anything about opening the door and the door shutting on your arm? When you talked to trooper Gay, you didn't mention the first thing about losing your key, did you?"

"Sir, I don't, I don't recall whether I did or not. I don't know if he chose to write it down or not."

"And you talked to Donald Davis twice and you didn't tell him about losing your key, did you?"

"Again, I don't know if I told him that and he just chose not to write it down or not."

"And when you talked to Rodney Bryan, you didn't tell him anything about losing your keys, did you?"

"The same applies, sir."

"Now, the facts are that you did run along the road for a considerable distance before coming to a stop up there on top of the hill near the guard rail? That's a fact, isn't it?"

"The fact. No, sir, I don't know that that's a fact. You're saying that I run –"

"Off the road – "

"On the grass for a long – "

"Right."

"No, sir, I don't know that that's a fact."

"At a slow speed? You were at a slow speed, weren't you?"

"A slow speed?"

"At a very slow speed?"

"No, I wouldn't say very slow, no, sir."

"And you agree that there were no skid marks or anything like that where your car left the pavement, don't you?"

"Yes, sir, there was a skid mark."

"Not from your car though, was there?"

"Yes, sir. I would say that that was the skid mark from my car."

"You would agree that the skid mark was considerably west of where your car ran off the road, wouldn't you?"

"No, sir."

"And you agree there were no tire tracks to show where you traveled to steer the car back onto the road? You'd agree with that, wouldn't you?"

"Again, are you saying that I run along the edge of the road? Is that what you're implying?"

"That's what I am asking. I'm asking if you're denying it?"

"Am I denying what?"

"Running along the edge of the road?"

"Sir, I don't recall running – you're saying that I run along the edge of the road for a considerable amount of distance?"

"At least sixty feet."

"No, sir."

"So Randy Stephens and Chris Gay were absolutely wrong about that? Do you contend some other car made those tire tracks that ran along the side of the road and then sharply turned off down the bank?"

"Did some other car?"

"Yes."

"There were some other cars up on that side of the road. I don't know if they got mixed up in with mine or what happened."

"How many other cars ran off the bank that day that you're aware of?"

"That's not what I said, sir."

"No, but that was my question. I said, how many other cars ran off the bank that afternoon that you're aware of?"

"None other than mine that I'm aware of."

"And, Mrs. Bryan, this was at the Ty Ty Creek Bridge, wasn't it, right there near Jernigan's?"

"All I know is it's the Livingston Bridge Road."

"How long do you contend that fire lasted?"

"Sir, I have no idea."

"But you agree it didn't even burn the trunk of the car, don't you?"

"Yes, sir."

"And you agree the only thing in your car at the time was a change purse, a claw hammer, and a spare tire and jack?"

"A wallet was in there, yes, sir."

"Change purse, right?"

"It was a wallet."

"I show you State's Exhibit 67."

"Okay."

"Is that it?"

"Yes, sir."

"And what is that?"

"It's showing some coins, but it's a small wallet. You notice that's a small wallet. It is not a change purse. It's not a wallet this size. It's a half size wallet that carries money and other stuff in it. So it's not just a change purse."

"There was a claw hammer in there as well, is that correct?"

"Yes, sir, there was."

"You knew that claw hammer was in there, didn't you?"

"Yes, sir, I did."

"And the window was down?"

"Yes, sir."

"And you could have reached in through that window, and if need be broken out the window and got your mother out, couldn't you?"

"Sir, if you'll look at the embankment, this car, I'm five foot-two inches tall. There's no way for me to reach through that window."

"It's also down there next to Ty Ty Creek too, isn't it? A lot of trash around there, isn't there?"

"Trash?"

"Rocks, sticks, things of that nature?"

"Yes, sir."

"Been probably no problem whatsoever to have gotten the window broken out with some of the stuff lying around there, would it?"

"No, sir. If there was some impending danger I would have done that."

"And so by all the testimony, it'd have taken this car probably at least five minutes to even to have caught afire?"

"I have no idea, sir."

"And you would agree there was plenty of time to go back and rescue Mrs. Weeks, wasn't there?"

"Plenty of time, sir?"

"Yes, ma'am."

"From when, what time, sir?"

"From the very time that you went out there and wrecked the car."

"I did not wreck the car, sir. I had an accident."

"And you had more than enough time to go and get your mother out, didn't you?"

"I had more than enough time?"

"Right."

"Sir, I went up – after I first saw the smoke? Is that what you're saying?"

"Yes."

"By the time I got – I ran back towards the, toward the car and then I heard the car. I run back the other way and I saw the car coming. And then we run back down there."

"You've told a lot of things today that are considerably inconsistent with what's written down from these law enforcement officers, haven't you?"

"Yes, sir, but, again, you have to understand what state of mind I was in at the time that was taken."

"And wouldn't you agree the jury also has to consider that you've had two years to think about this and to get your story together?"

"Yes, sir, but I have not."

"That's all."

Stines sat down and Saliba stood up to begin re-direct examination of the defendant.

"Do you agree that the state has had two years to fabricate a case?" Saliba asked.

"Oh, absolutely, sir."

"Now, when you talked with any of these officers at the scene, Sheila, did, did they tape record you?"

"No, sir, they did not."

"If they had tape recorded you, would we have a record of what you said?"

"Yes, sir, you would."

"So whose fault is it that we don't have an accurate record of what you said?"

"It's theirs, sir."

"Have you heard all the officers in this case say that you cooperated with them to the best of your ability?"

"Yes, sir."

"Sheila, you were on the scene about how long, ma'am?"

"Two hours."

"Were there or were there not numerous vehicles up and down both sides of that road?"

"Yes, sir, there were."

"She's with The Court."

Saliba sat down and Stines stood up to begin a very short re-cross-examination.

"Mrs. Bryan, I'm going to show you what's been marked for identification purposes as State's 68. I warn you that it's burned and black," Stines said.

"Yes, sir."

"Is that your mother's change purse?"

"No, sir. It's my change purse."

"Your change purse."

Sheila, who had totally missed Stines' point of the question, continued, "And it's not really a change purse. If you'll notice there's also money in it, in the other compartment of it, so it's not qualified as a change purse. It's a small wallet."

"That's all," Stines said.

After several hours of exhausting testimony, Sheila Bryan left the witness stand. Stines and Heinen thought Sheila had been her own worst enemy on the stand. But it didn't matter what they thought, only what the jury thought, and the jury, of course, gave no indication of how they felt about Sheila's testimony.

CHAPTER FORTY-ONE

Thursday, September 3, 1998

Testimony following the defendant is always anti-climactic, and A.M. (Sonny) Dampier, one of the defense's expert witnesses, drew that unlucky card. Fifty-five-year-old Dampier was a retired Georgia state patrol officer. He had worked for the GSP for thirty-two years and had experience in accident investigation. The point of his testimony was to tell the jury that the mysterious mark on the road was a yaw mark, which is made by a tire that is sliding sideways.

Under Saliba's questioning, Dampier also testified that he had seen Sheila's Mercury Cougar, and that the doors had to be opened by inserting a large screwdriver between the front of the door and the rear of the fender because the doors opened outside of the fenders – and the door had to be pushed inward for the door to open around it. He said the damage could have been caused by the accident.

Stines and Heinen were always a little amazed, if not amused, at what nonsense the defense could come up with. Stines would get his chance to address the purportedly damaged door when he brought Newell back on rebuttal, but for now, he had other concerns.

In his cross-examination, Stines established that Dampier had not reconstructed the accident. He had Dampier testify that he thought a car moving at a very slow rate of speed could leave a mark in the road fifteen feet long – which was the length of the purported skid mark.

The attorneys were headed to the finish line. All of the expert testimony was in. All that remained were a few more character witnesses and then the rebuttal testimony. Hopes were high that the testimony would be completed that day and the jury would begin its deliberations on Friday. If all went well, they could anticipate a verdict by the end of the week.

The defense would dispatch several more character witnesses to the stand in short order: Lisa Whittington, Ernest Weeks, and Mary Ann Bryan, Sheila's former sister-in-law.

Peggy Dean was an important witness for the defense, and she was the next to take the stand. Dean worked for an investment brokerage, A.G. Edwards and Sons, and lived in Ocilla. She had gone to high school with Sheila and they remained best friends.

After having Dean also testify that Sheila had a good relationship with her mother, Moore then asked Dean to talk about the day of the accident.

"I had to leave that Sunday morning," Dean said. "I was going looking for a place to move my mobile home. And I had come home that afternoon, and Sheila had left a message on my recorder. Sheila had called me that morning and asked me if I wanted to go for a ride with her and her mom. But I wasn't at home, and I got the message when I got home that afternoon."

"And do you recall what time that message was left for you?"

"I believe it was sometime in the morning because – I don't know exactly what time it was – because my answering machine would [not] leave a time and a date. I don't know what time it was. I know it was very early sometime."

Stines had been impressed with Dean's testimony. He thought she had been honest and sincere. In fact, he thought she was the best witness the defense had put on the stand. But he had a job to do, and he set about doing it.

Stines asked Dean again about the time of the message, an important point.

"I don't know what time it came, "Dean said. "I know it was early, probably around nine o'clock or something. And they'd go for a ride in the morning, when it was cool, because that was in August, and it was hot."

Stines excused the witness after having her acknowledge that she didn't know anything about what had happened on Livingston Bridge Road.

Karla Bryan, Sheila's oldest daughter, was the next witness to the stand. She was fifteen years old and attended Tift County High School.

Under Moore's questioning, Karla said that she saw her grandmother almost every day, and that her mother saw her grandmother once or twice a day. She said that her grandmother was in good health before she died.

Karla told the jury that on a typical Saturday or Sunday, they would go to the lake property in Tifton to go fishing, or cook out, or go jet skiing. She said that if her granny felt like coming, she would.

Moore then moved to the night before the accident.

"And did you stay in your bedroom that night?" Moore asked his youngest witness.

"No, sir," Karla said. "I was in the den watching a movie, and I had fallen asleep. And then I'd gotten up and went and got in my sister's room with her."

"And who stayed in your room?"

"My grandmother."

"Okay. And do you recall what time you got up the next morning?"

"Maybe five-thirty or six."

"Okay. And tell us what happened after you got up."

"I went and got in my sister's room."

"Then you slept later?"

"Yes, sir."

"And did you see your granny the next morning?"

"Yes, sir, I did."

"Tell the jury how that came about."

"I had gone in there and, and I was saying, 'Hey, how are you?' you know. And we talked a little bit. And I got what I needed, and left the room. And they had told me that we were going to the lake, and I said, 'Well, okay.' So I went and told my, I said, 'Well, Granny, we're gonna go to the lake.' And she said, 'Well, okay, Baby. Bye. I love you.'"

"And that was the last thing she said to you?"

"Yes, sir."

"And later, did you go to the lake with your dad and sister?"

"Yes, sir, I did."

"And were you supposed to see your mother after that?"

Karla said that her mother was to take her to Tift County High School to pick up her softball uniform around two in the afternoon.

"And when did you find out about the accident?"

"A sheriff's car came and told my dad that there had been an accident and he, in turn, told me."

Stines was no fool, and he knew there would be no cross-examination other than to have Karla say that she had not been at the accident scene. Short and sweet.

The defense called their last witness in their case-in-chief to the stand: Pat Newsome. A resident of Tifton, Newsome had, for seven years, been the principal of Omega School, which serves pre-K through seventh grade.

"Do you know Sheila Bryan?" Moore asked.

"Yes, I am proud to say that I do," Newsome answered.

Stines and Heinen had already gotten the drift that Mrs. Newsome was a strong witness. Evidently the defense had planned to finish with their strong suit.

When asked by Moore to describe the type of work Sheila did at the school, Newsome went into a long explanation. Too long, Stines thought.

After putting twenty-nine exhibits into evidence, the defense rested its case.

The prosecution would start their rebuttal case off with a bang: Stines called Gene Hiers to the stand.

Hiers told the jurors that he was a retired Baptist minister who once lived in Omega, and that while there, he had been pastor of Omega Baptist Church and Sheila worked there part-time. He said that he had resigned from the church in December of 1989.

"What were the circumstances leading to her leaving?" Stines asked his reluctant witness.

"It started, I guess, when a business in Tifton called and wanted to know about their money that had not been sent to them, for a bill that the church owed them. And I went and found a folder that had bills and all in it," Hiers said.

"And as a result of the other things that you found out, did you recommend a certain action?"

"I believe I gave the information to the chairman of the deacons."

"And what was done as a result of that?"

"They had a meeting and dealt with it."

"What was the resolution of the controversy?"

"I think that because of the things that were found, that she [Sheila] was given the opportunity to either resign or be terminated."

"Was there an agreement to pay certain money, perhaps relating to insurance, back to the church?"

"That's what I understood."

"How many payments were made on that to the best of your knowledge?"

"I was not aware of but one or two. I don't know. There may have been others. But that's all I was aware of."

"And after that, Sheila resigned. Did she continue to be an active member of the church, come pretty often, or did she more or less drop out?"

"I think she came some, but not on a regular basis."

Moore stood for cross-examination of this surprise rebuttal witness. Moore got to his point quickly.

"Did you ever, sir, tell Mr. Stines, or anybody from his office, that Sheila Bryan misappropriated funds from the church?"

"The only thing that I know about was the insurance premiums."

"Isn't it true that when you came on board, that you and Sheila had a personality conflict?"

"I'm not aware of any personality conflict we had."

"Why'd you leave, sir, Omega Baptist Church?"

"I left because of some accusations against me, and I did not want to deal with those, from a secretary."

"And those accusations were about improper advances toward a secretary, isn't that true, sir?"

"Yes, sir."

"Isn't it true, sir, that you were asked to leave because of improper advances towards the church secretary?"

"I was not asked to leave. I left on my own."

"And isn't it further true that you, in fact, prior to that, made some improper advances toward the defendant, Sheila Bryan?"

"No, sir."

"That's not true?"

"That's not true."

"And you never told Mr. Stines or anybody in his office that she stole anything from Omega Baptist Church, did you, sir?"

"No."

"Or that she misappropriated anything?"

"The only thing I knew about was the insurance. And as far as I knew, the insurance had not been approved by the church."

"So the implication is there, sir, that Sheila did something on her own, or she and the minister did something on their own, without approval from the board, is that correct?"

"As far as I know."

"And the deal was to have Sheila repay the $1,000, or whatever of increased insurance benefits that she and the former minister had agreed upon. Isn't that correct?"

"Yes, sir. That is what I understood. That she was to repay that."

Stines rose for a touchy cross-examination, but he didn't get far. You could feel the tension in the courtroom and tempers were hot.

"Mr. Hiers," Stines began, "I hate to ask you this, but after that, Sheila Bryan was terminated, was there a rule change about who could be secretary and who could count money?"

Moore was on his feet, and he was mad. He asked to approach the Bench. In heated whispers, the attorneys exchanged words. "You are trying to get this case mistried!" Moore spat at Stines. The attorneys went off the record, sending the jury out for a break and adjourning to the judge's chambers.

Out of sight and sound of the jury and courtroom spectators, the lawyers continued their legal arguing. Judge Horkan ended the legal bickering by telling the lawyers that if the defense wanted to make a motion for a mistrial he would grant it. Moore discussed the subject of a mistrial with Sheila. Like the decision to take the stand, the decision to end the trial right then and there would also rest with the defendant. Sheila, feeling confident in how the trial was going, decided to forgo the mistrial and continue. When the jury returned, Hiers was excused from the stand without further adieu.

Although Hiers was gone, the atmosphere had not much improved. When Stines called Ralph Newell back to the stand, Saliba immediately went on the record to complain that he had just been handed four pages of material, and that he had not had a chance to review the document. Saliba asked for a recess to review the material. His words were curt and his tone was one of anger.

The court took another ten-minute recess. It was an opportunity for tempers to cool.

When court reconvened, Newell took the stand. Stines asked Newell about the condition of the left front door that he had examined shortly after the accident. Stines asked if there was any collision damage to the door, and Newell said that there wasn't any.

"What did you have to do to open the door?" Stines asked.

"Reached in, run my hand up in the locking device, flipped the correct lever, swung the door open," he said.

"How much body damage was there to prevent that door from coming open?"

"None," Newell said, "until we picked it up with the wrecker." Newell explained that the wrecker had dropped the car after it had been lifted into the air the day of the inspection.

With those words, the state rested its rebuttal case, and Newell was excused from the witness stand. He didn't know how the case had gotten so contentious; he just knew he would be glad to have Moultrie in his rear-view mirror.

Moore called Gibbs Patrick to the stand. Patrick had lived in Omega all his life and had been a member of Omega Baptist Church for sixty years. He testified "there was a little personality conflict between them [Sheila and Hiers]." He said he thought the problem was Sheila was working in an establishment that sold alcoholic beverages, and the deacons didn't think the secretary of the church should have been working there.

Stines had no cross-examination, and Moore called his last witness, Cynthia Camp.

Camp said that she was the church treasurer in the 1980s at Omega Baptist Church, but that she was not the treasurer when Sheila was the secretary. She told the jurors that Hiers resignation had been a joint decision between the church and the reverend.

The defense rested its case.

"The evidence is in, the case is closed, and the witnesses are excused," Horkan said.

They had come to the end of a long day, and everyone was about spent. But now they had to get their second wind and deliver one of the most important parts of the case: closing arguments.

While opening statements in a murder trial tend to be well organized and laid out, closing arguments tend to be like buckshot. By this time in the trial, attorneys are tired and have a thousand facts pertinent to the case rolling around in their heads. From those myriad facts, which have been presented during the course of the trial, they must pull out the most salient points to argue for their side of the case. As soon as the last witness has spoken, they must be ready to rise to their feet and deliver an argument that is designed to be, if not eloquent, at least poignant. And while it might not always follow an organized sequence, it is usually passionate – the attorneys for both sides arguing with all of their fervor for their side of the case. And so it was in the Sheila Bryan case.

All the words had been spoken, all the evidence presented. The next morning, Judge Frank Horkan would charge the jury and put the case in their hands. While the jury deliberated, everyone else could only wait.

CHAPTER FORTY-TWO

Friday, September 4, 1998

"Teetering," Donald Davis said to the staff at the CCSO. "I've been teetering on the brink of doing that paperwork."

He was driving the staff crazy. He was working the word "teetering" into every conversation, and when he wasn't using the word in a sentence, he was talking about it.

"I like that word 'teetering,'" he said. "It reminds me of twittering. Like the birds twittering this morning. Maybe the birds have been twittering and teetering. You never know. They could have been teetering on the power line while they were twittering."

Word had gotten to Davis about what Sheila had said on the witness stand, and somehow he had gotten hung up on her "teetering" on the edge of the embankment. He thought it was the most ridiculous thing he had ever heard in his life.

"Picture this," he said to anyone who would listen. "She runs off the road, according to her, and the car stops – teetering on the edge of the embankment. And she has her 82-year-old mother sitting there with a dazed look on her face. And what does Sheila do? What would you do?"

No one ever answered the hypothetical question. No one wanted to encourage Davis to continue a discussion about teetering.

"Any normal person," he said, ignoring everyone's lack of interest, "would put the car in reverse and back off the edge of the embankment. But she doesn't do that. She never does what a normal person would do. When she drops her keys, she doesn't reach over and pick them up. Well, never mind all that. So she doesn't put the car in reverse and back up. Well, you say, another thing a normal person might do would be to, at that point, put the car in park.

"But she doesn't do that either. Here she is, according to her, teetering on the edge of this steep embankment with her mother beside her, and she doesn't back up and she doesn't put the car in park. What she does do, according to her, is she opens the car door to get out. The car is teetering. Her mother is dazed. The car is in drive. She still has her seat belt on. And she opens the car door to get out. Why does she want to get out you ask?"

The staff just looked at Davis. They could have cared less about why Sheila would want to get out. And if they had cared enough to answer, they figured it was a trick question.

"I'll tell you why," Donald continued unabated. "For no damn good reason that's why. There was no reason for her to get out. None whatsoever. All she had to do was back up off the embankment. Problem solved. But anyway, she says, she goes to get out of the car, and that is when the car door slams shut on her left arm, and she goes down the embankment. So obviously the car was still in drive. She even said the car was in drive. Does this story make any sense at all to anyone?"

No one ever answered. They took the break in the one-sided conversation as an opportunity to return to their work.

Davis considered it his work to try and figure out this latest turn of events in the Sheila Bryan case. It had stumped him all that day about why Sheila would have gotten on the witness stand and changed her story – again – and then, not only changed it, but had come up with this ridiculous teetering business. After some time spent in his thinking room, he thought he had it figured out.

She knew the evidence in the case. She knew he had gone and gotten the medical records from Colquitt Regional Medical Center. She knew that the evidence of the injury to her left arm was going to come into the court record. The problem for Sheila was, Davis figured, she had no explanation for how she had hurt her arm.

He had gone back over her various stories told at the time of the wreck. Not one of the versions accounted for an injury. She must have figured she was going to have to explain that injury when she took the stand. So she had made up this whole ridiculous teetering story to account for the injury to her left arm. Davis thought it was a stupid story, but, nevertheless, it accounted for the injury. As far as he was concerned, all Sheila had done with the teetering story was dig herself a deeper hole.

How did she really injure her arm? he wondered. He figured he would never know the answer to that one.

Then there was the business of Peggy Dean. *Nice touch*, Davis thought.

Stines had told Davis that he thought Peggy Dean was Sheila's best character witness. Stines had said he thought Dean was honest in what she said about getting the call from Sheila on her answering machine. But Stines and Heinen also thought that Sheila knew that Peggy Dean was not going to be home when she called her. So the call had been Sheila's alibi.

Davis decided Sheila's testimony about leaning over and reclining her mother's seat was another ridiculous story. He found a lot of things wrong with that picture. The most obvious thing was that Sheila was five-foot-two inches tall, and the toggle switch to recline the seat was between the passenger door and the seat. That would have been a long stretch. Davis thought it would be an impossible stretch. Her shortness had been a problem when Stines asked her why she didn't reach her hand in the car and unlock the door – but it had been no problem at all to reach all the way across the console and her mother's seat and get to the toggle switch on the bottom right hand side of the passenger seat.

The reclined seat was just another of many contradictions in her story, as far as Davis was concerned. She was so worried about her mother's comfort that she had leaned across the seat and reclined it. But she had been totally unconcerned about the heat. Didn't leave the air on or the door open. Just closed her up in that boiling hot car, but had her comfortably reclined. It didn't make any sense to Davis.

Who goes to the lake at nine-thirty on Sunday morning? Davis wondered. That was another ridiculous story. Davis had been to the "lake lot." He knew this was a suburb where Sunday mornings were a quiet time. People around that lake were either sleeping late or heading off to Sunday School. Nobody was out there boating at nine-thirty on a Sunday morning. But that is what Sheila said Karlas and the girls were doing. And Karla was a teenage girl. Davis had one of those himself. He knew what it was like to try and get a teenager anywhere on a weekend morning.

On the stand, Sheila had portrayed the house they were going to build as a "little" retirement place. And the house plans had been introduced into evidence by the defense. Davis had taken a good look at the house plans.

House plan BG9853 from *Country House Plans*, was for a "Quaint Traditional." It was a 2,090 square foot home, which sported four bedrooms and three baths. The exterior of the home was board-and-batten siding and cedar shingles. There was a great-room, with fireplace, front and back porch, large master bedroom with two walk-in closets, laundry room, formal dining room, breakfast nook with a bay window, and a large kitchen with an island bar.

"Wooooooooooweeeeeeee!!" Davis said when he saw the plans for the first time. One look at the plans, and Davis knew he had been right on target: This was no little retirement home; this was a dream home.

Sheila had drawn on the house plans, writing "Karla" in the bedroom off the kitchen/laundry room area, "Karrie" in the front bedroom, and "Mom" in the middle bedroom, next to the master bedroom. She had also drawn in some furniture – a sofa and several chairs around the fireplace in the great-room, and a dining table with *four* chairs in the breakfast area, as well as *four* bar stools at the kitchen breakfast bar.

Davis doubted the jurors knew the "little retirement home" was just as big as the house they were living in and cost about twice as much. *Yeah, it was a retirement home*, Davis thought. Because it was going to be the most expensive home they had ever owned, and they would never have been able to afford another one – unless they decided to have another wreck. And it was never pointed out that the lot alone for the little retirement home cost more than their home in Omega did – at least what they had originally paid for it.

The more Davis thought about it, the more he thought it had been stupid of Sheila to introduce those house plans and refer to it as a little retirement home. *How many of those jurors would look at those plans and think this was anything other than somebody's dream home?* he wondered.

Davis knew for a fact that Sheila had lied on the stand about the Liela Church business. Sheila had said that she had gone past Liela Church and saw they were having services and realized they would probably be having services at Weeks Chapel as well, and had then decided to just drive around. Heinen had sent Davis to check it out. Davis had learned that Liela Church had not had services that Sunday. Another lie.

Davis thought a lot about Sheila saying Freda Weeks had spent the night at her house that Saturday night. Sheila had said that her mother had a bad cold. The autopsy had not found any evidence of that. But, according to Sheila, her mother had been sick enough to stay at her house rather than in her own bed that night. Figuring he knew old people, and especially old people who were country people who had a mind of their own like Freda Weeks, Davis decided that Freda Weeks would have had to be pretty darn sick to stay at Sheila's rather than in her own bed a few yards away.

But, miraculously, according to Sheila, Freda Weeks' health had not been an issue early the next morning. *Had Freda Weeks had some kind of miracle*

BURNED - THE TRUE STORY OF THE SHEILA BRYAN MURDER CASE

cure that night? Davis wondered. Because, according to Sheila, by Sunday morning everyone was up and dressed and headed to the lake or off to drive around the countryside. There was no mention of Freda Weeks being sick on Sunday morning.

Davis wished that Stines had asked Sheila about the claw hammer and the beach towel. Not that Davis thought Sheila would tell the truth; he just wanted to see what her ridiculous explanations would be. He was sure she had some.

But what galled Davis more than anything was Sheila's defense attorneys painting the Bryans as the perfect all-American family with no skeletons in their closet. Davis figured Karlas was a big skeleton all unto himself. And it was not wasted on Davis that all those fine folks in Omega, Georgia, had taken the stand to say how great Sheila was, even her own daughter. But not Karlas. No, the ever-loving husband had kept his butt off the stand. Davis wondered what the jury would make of that.

Davis started praying for common sense. He prayed the jury would use a little common sense and see through some of Sheila's ridiculous stories. But you just never knew about juries.

When word got to GSP Trooper Chris Gay about what Sheila had said on the witness stand, all he could do was laugh. The same woman who had sent him the 'thank you' card had said that she was badgered at the accident scene. *My, how stories can change over time,* he thought. If he had known that Sheila was going to come up with the badgering business, he could have taken Stines the 'thank you' card to impeach her. But he had found out too late.

But what had amazed Gay was that Sheila had said that she had not given him the driver's license and the insurance card. Beginning to doubt his own sanity and memory, Gay went to the computer and pulled up information on Sheila Bryan. He saw where she had gotten a speeding ticket after her arrest. He then checked to see if she had ever had her driver's license reissued. Nope, it had never been reissued. So when she had gotten stopped for speeding, she had produced her driver's license – the very same license she had produced for him.

Gay wondered if she had ever had more keys made after she had lost them the day of the wreck. Somehow he doubted it. He figured she didn't need to make more keys any more than she needed to have her license reissued.

In Omega, it was hotter than a firecracker on the fourth of July, and Omega Baptist Church remained the epicenter of distress. Some of the church members had been infuriated that *their* church had been the heart of Sheila's defense. Two of the church's pastors – one present and one past – had taken the stand to testify, not to mention all of the church leaders who had marched themselves to the stand. And all the dirty laundry had been aired. Heated conversations had been taking place on the church steps after prayer meeting. Some members directed their anger at Pastor John Spivey – once affectionately referred to as Brother John – and thought that he should leave and take his support of Sheila Bryan with him. For Spivey, side-stepping the Sheila Bryan issue or joking it away was no longer an option. The only consolation was that it was soon going to be over. The verdict would come in and that would be the end of it. Alpha and omega.

Behind closed doors, the jury had deliberated all day Friday. After electing Sonja Willett foreman, the jury took an initial vote: ten for guilty on all counts and two undecided. One of the elderly women jurors just could not believe that anybody could do that to her mother. The juror kept repeating, "It's hard to believe." A younger woman juror who had voted undecided could not get past Sheila's children and what it would do to them, even though the juror felt in her heart that Sheila was guilty. The woman had cried the entire time that Sheila's daughter, Karla, had testified, and she just could not bring herself to "destroy that child's life."

Two of the men on the jury had excellent backgrounds in cars and electronics and they went to the blackboard and drew out the information on the electric seat motor and connections, making it simple so everyone could understand. After a great deal of study, everyone eliminated the electric seat motor as the cause of the fire.

No one on the jury believed Sheila's testimony. "She hung herself, big time," one juror said. "She should have stayed off the stand." The jurors had found her to be "haughty" and "arrogant." But the last straw with Sheila was when she had snapped at Charlie Stines. They felt she had shown her true colors.

When they went over Sheila's story, although they did not believe most of what she said, they agreed to give her the benefit of the doubt about the beach towel over Mrs. Weeks, the claw hammer and the missing gas cap.

She had changed her story too many times and they thought her story about teetering on the edge of the embankment was ridiculous. It had insulted their intelligence.

278

The house plan Sheila had submitted to the jury was the cause of some discussion. As fate would have it, one of the jurors was in the process of building a home. She had looked through hundreds of house plans and finally gotten it down to two plans. One of the two she was considering was the same one Sheila had chosen! It was no little retirement home. The juror knew that it would cost almost $200,000 to build. "How could a house painter and a data clerk afford that?" she asked the others.

The jurors spent hours scrutinizing the photographs and going over the details of the accident. The missing key was a big problem. The car sitting at a ninety degree angle to the road was a bigger problem. But as they looked at all the evidence, it was some of Ralph Newell's testimony about the burn patterns that tipped the scale.

The passenger side of the vehicle had been more badly burned than the driver's side. The driver's side threshold had the gooey burn pattern, but the passenger side had no such burn pattern. Yet, as Ralph Newell had said, both sides of the car were made of the same material. The jurors decided that some kind of paint thinner had been used as an accelerant.

When they voted again it was unanimous for guilty on all counts. They decided to go to lunch, pray about it, and take one more vote before announcing their verdict.

It wasn't until late afternoon that the bailiff reported that the jury had reached a verdict. After everyone had reassembled in the courtroom, Judge Horkan read the long-awaited verdict: guilty on all three counts. Sobs and hysteria broke out in the small courtroom. Some of Sheila's supporters sat stunned, unable to move. Some of her supporters, so confident in a not-guilty verdict, had gone about their daily business and not even come to court that day. Sheila sobbed quietly as her attorneys consoled her.

The verdict form, which was signed by Sonja Willett, foreperson, had "Guilty" printed in large letters after each of the three counts: malice murder, felony murder, and arson in the first degree. Horkan would have to correct the verdict, setting aside the verdict of guilty on count two, felony murder.

Sheila Bryan and her attorneys stood for sentencing. In somber, measured tones, Judge Horkan sentenced Sheila on count one, malice murder, to life in prison. On count three, arson in the first degree, he sentenced Sheila to twenty years.

Heinen and Stines felt like a huge weight had been lifted off them. They quickly gathered their belongings to leave the courtroom. Amidst unkind remarks by Sheila's supporters, the two of them said their good-byes. It was

Stines' last day in Moultrie, and he was headed to finish cleaning out his office. Heinen had other cases waiting. They shook hands, saying they might meet again.

It was not a long walk for Sheila to the jail; it was just next door to the courtroom. Like a boomerang, she had come back to Donald Davis.

Davis had sat in the back of the small courtroom when the verdict was read. As Horkan said the words "Guilty, Guilty, Guilty," Davis' face broke out in a wide grin. *This is for you Freda, this is for you*, he said to himself. *Rest in peace. Some small justice has finally come.*

Davis would wait a while before he tippy-toed over to the jail to get a look at Sheila behind bars, a sight that had eluded him for too many long months. The woman always amazed him, and she amazed him now. She sat playing Solitaire like she had not a care in the world. *This woman is made of steel.* It was over, and he was through with it, or so he thought at the time.

Soon thereafter, Sheila was transferred to Pulaski State Prison to begin serving her life-plus-twenty-years sentence. Pulaski State Prison, located in Hawkinsville, Georgia, was a maximum security facility housing adult female felons. The prison complex consisted of six buildings with forty-eight double rooms to house up to ninety-six inmates per building. The facility supported a Correctional Industries garment plant.

"That should work out well," Davis said on learning of Sheila's new home. "She always liked to sew."

CHAPTER FORTY-THREE

October 2, 1998

Within a month of the verdict, Bill Moore and George Saliba filed a motion for a new trial.

Among the reasons cited in their motion was "prosecutorial misconduct." According to Sheila's attorneys, Stines had misrepresented to the Court what Gene Hiers would say on the witness stand. Sheila's attorneys said that Stines had acted "in bad faith," which had resulted in a miscarriage of justice for Sheila. They called Stines' conduct at trial "reprehensible and contrary to the notions of justice."

Additionally, Moore and Saliba stated that the Court had committed error when the insurance testimony was not restricted. They said that there was a car liability policy in place, not a life insurance policy, in which Sheila had no interest and did not pursue, that Sheila did not own the policy, and that there was no named beneficiary to the policy. The attorneys said that the state had not proven a nexus, or connection, between Sheila and the policy, and that the jury was left to infer that she would have benefited from the insurance.

Further, in the motion, Moore and Saliba complained that the State had destroyed the evidence containing the burn patterns (the floor mats), which prevented them from conducting a scientific examination of the mats. And moreover, the State had picked up and dropped the car, which had made it impossible for them to show that the damage to the car door had occurred during the accident.

Finally, Moore and Saliba said that Dr. Anthony Clark had ruled that the manner of death was undetermined. They noted that one of the jurors, M.D. Wilson, Jr., believed that Freda Weeks was dead prior to the fire. In an affidavit attached to the motion, Wilson stated that he felt just going down the embankment itself would have been enough to frighten Mrs. Weeks to death.

On November 10, 1998, a hearing was held at the Governmental Building in Moultrie on the motion for a new trial. Sheila was transported from prison to attend the hearing and Stines drove up from Valdosta. The accusations of prosecutorial misconduct would produce a heated hearing. Stines would say that he did not appreciate being called a liar and a cheat, and that he regretted ever getting the phone call about Gene Hiers.

On November 20, 1998, Judge Frank Horkan denied Moore and Saliba's request for a new trial. In late December, the appeal was taken to the Georgia Supreme Court. It would take seven months before the Supreme Court ruled on the appeal.

Banished to Valdosta after his victory in the Bryan case, Stines had continued to try cases and had won another difficult murder case, but Miller's criticism of Stines being too close to law enforcement persisted while he was in Valdosta.

On June 14, 1999, the Georgia Supreme Court handed down its ruling in the Bryan case.

The high court concluded that a rational trier of fact could have found Bryan guilty of the crimes charged, but the legal problem came, it said, with the insurance testimony, finding the connection "tenuous at best." The Court stated that all prior cases reviewed involved life insurance, whereas this was automobile liability insurance and, it said, the only way the policy could have benefitted the defendant would be through a claim made by her mother's estate against her for negligence in the automobile accident. Even if the estate prevailed, its debts would have to be paid prior to any distribution to beneficiaries under a will, or to heirs at law, if there was a will. Although the state is generally entitled to present evidence of motive, it cannot introduce evidence of an automobile liability policy that has only an indirect, contingent relationship to the crime.

Beyond that, the Supreme Court said that the State had failed to present any evidence that Bryan knew about the increased coverage. Her husband was the policyholder and the only family member who had dealt with the insurance agent. The fact that Sheila Bryan knew the car was insured was not relevant.

The guilty verdict in the case was reversed, with all justices concurring. According to the high court, Judge Frank Horkan had erred in his decision to allow evidence of the insurance policy increase.

David Miller went on record saying that he would take Sheila back to trial.

When the newspapers announced that Sheila had won a new trial, a collective groan could be heard from Omega. Just when they thought they had put it all behind them, it was going to start all over again. Whether they believed in her guilt or innocence, or just plain didn't care one way or another, no one wanted to discuss Sheila Bryan any more. As they say in the South, they had had a bellyful of Sheila Bryan.

"Well, sonofabitch," Donald Davis said when the news of the new trial reached his ears.

At Omega Baptist Church, Pastor John Spivey was not having a good time. The division in the church had now grown into a continental divide. And Spivey was beginning to wonder if the church was going to survive a second trial.

It would take five weeks before the paperwork wended its way through the penal system, and Sheila was released on a $30,000 bond signed by Ed Scarbor, an Omega sweet potato farmer. While her family and supporters waited for Sheila's release, they were busy tying the entire town of Omega in yellow ribbons and placing "Welcome Home" signs in strategic locations. On July 19, 1999, after three hundred and nineteen days of incarceration, Sheila was released from prison and returned home to Omega and Omega Baptist Church. Church attendance plummeted.

By September, Charlie Stines was starting to feel like a Ping-Pong ball. After a year in Valdosta – longer than Sheila had spent in prison – Miller returned Stines to his office in Moultrie. Like Sheila, he was glad to be back home.

Blame had to be placed for her conviction, and Sheila and her supporters firmly placed the blame on Bill Moore and George Saliba, the two attorneys who had fought so hard for her at her first trial, and afterwards, who had gotten her a new trial and release from prison in record-breaking time.

Moore and Saliba had met with Sheila in preparation for "round two," but, considering the fact that their firm had lost thousands of dollars and man hours on her defense – not to mention the wear and tear of a long trial – the two lawyers had quoted a $25,000 retainer figure to Sheila for the second trial. Sheila attempted to have the attorneys take less than the $25,000, but their terms were steadfast. Moore and Saliba felt that they had done the appeal basically for nothing, and they were not about to go into a second trial without some fees being paid.

On September 24, 1999, Moore and Saliba officially withdrew from the case. Court records listed the cause of the withdrawal as Sheila's inability to pay the attorneys for a second trial. However, five days after Moore and Saliba's withdrawal from the case, Converse Bright went on record as Sheila's new attorney for the second trial. Fifty-nine-year-old Bright was a veteran criminal defense attorney from Valdosta who was known around the local courthouses as being very well prepared at trial; he won more than he lost. Bright required a $20,000 retainer to take the case. Four members of Sheila's support groups put up the money; $5,000 each.

By October 1999, pre-trial motions were being filed in the case by Bright and Stines. But for Stines, all was not well in Moultrie.

Soon enough, the criticism from Miller had begun all over again. A drug agent made the remark to Stines that the voters needed a new district attorney because Miller was not sufficiently pro-prosecution. Stines told the drug agent that he hoped no one ran against Miller, because he wanted to keep his job. Word of what Stines had said reached Miller in Valdosta and, according to Stines, Miller went ballistic.

The next major skirmish came in a disagreement about three youths who had broken into the Acapulco Mexican Restaurant and stolen beer. One of the young men had planned to join the Navy, and Stines worked a deal where the young man could pay restitution and avoid prosecution, but before the young man started Navy training, he was caught in another major theft. Again, the Navy recruiter and the youth's family wanted Stines to dismiss the charge, but this time Stines refused, telling the youth that he had blown his chance. Stines also accused the young man of lying when he had changed his story.

Miller chewed Stines out, telling Stines that he had "too much mouth" and that he should never call anyone a liar. Miller dismissed the charges against the youth.

By mid-October, the heat in the Bryan case got turned up several notches when Gail Zimmerman, a producer with the CBS news magazine show *48 Hours*, petitioned the Court to bring in her camera crew and film the second trial. The local story was going national.

By late October, Bright won a change of venue motion in the Bryan case: the new trial would be held in Thomasville. Also in late October, Miller called Stines to his office and told him that he was transferring him back to Valdosta to work in the child support office. Stines and some of the Colquitt County law enforcement officers were livid.

On November 1, 1999, Stines went back to Valdosta, but this time he would not be trying cases; he worked a desk job in the child support office, shuffling papers. He called it "a boring breeze" of a job.

By the end of November, Judge Frank Horkan had ruled on all the pre-trial motions in the Bryan case, and it was scheduled for trial on January 24, 2000.

It was not until late December that Miller approached Stines about retrying the Bryan case. Stines told Miller that staff in the child support office didn't try cases. The next day, Stines turned in his resignation letter to Miller.

"I didn't owe him any favors," Stines said.

Stines left Miller's employment on January 7, 2000, and took a job as Chief Assistant District Attorney in the South Georgia Judicial Circuit under District Attorney Brown Mosely, in Cairo.

Miller assigned the Bryan case to Brad Shealy, his right-hand man in Valdosta. Shealy would have two weeks to put together a case that Stines had worked on for four years.

A self-described "country lawyer," Shealy had tried about one hundred cases, two of them against Converse Bright – and he had lost both of them.

Shealy would be going into the courtroom battle facing several disadvantages, other than the short amount of time he had to put the case together. The major disadvantage was that his case no longer had a motive: all the insurance testimony was out. And there was little chance that Sheila would once again take the witness stand. Converse Bright would recognize that the first jury had not believed Sheila and he would not repeat that mistake. Shealy, among many others, believed that it was Sheila's own words on the stand that had convicted her in the first trial; she would be a total fool to take the stand again. With no motive, and without Sheila on the stand, Shealy would have to totally rely on Ralph Newell's testimony.

But there were other wrinkles. There is no rule of law that says the defense has to present the same evidence in a second trial. Since the first jury had obviously not believed the testimony about the fire starting from a short in the electric seat motor, the defense threw out that idea right away. Bright had another cause for the fire: the ignition switch.

If Brad Shealy had anything going for him in the second trial it was that Ralph Newell was *the* authority on ignition switch fires.

The weekend before the trial, Shealy went to Charlie Stines' home in Moultrie, and Stines tried to bring Shealy up to speed on the case. Shealy had a lot of catching up to do.

While Stines and Shealy reviewed the case, Sheila flew her new expert witness to south Georgia from Austin, Texas. His name was Gerald Hurst. Hurst was a scientist with a Ph.D. from Cambridge who had invented Wite-

Out and the Mylar balloon. Hurst had taken the case *pro bono*, meaning without being paid, because he believed that arson investigation was "junk science." Hurst had a web site called "Truth In Justice," in which he highlighted cases of people who had been wrongfully convicted in arson cases. He planned to add Sheila Bryan to his web page.

The second trial was going to be a whole new ball game: new attorneys, new location, new defense, and no motive.

CHAPTER FORTY-FOUR

Monday, January 24, 2000

Like the beginning of a bad novel, it was a dark and stormy night the eve of the re-trial of Sheila Bryan. Lightening flashed, thunder crashed, and winds howled. When dawn broke on the day of the trial, Mother Nature's mood had not much improved. In a cold, driving rain, all the parties gathered at the big, white-columned courthouse in downtown Thomasville. The aging courthouse, like the one in Moultrie, was scheduled for renovation, but that would come shortly after the Sheila Bryan trial.

Once again, Heinen took his seat at the prosecution table, only this time seated next to Brad Shealy. CBS's cameras and crew occupied the first two rows behind the prosecution table, but other than the national and local press, there were few spectators. Only about a dozen of the courtroom's one hundred seats were occupied by Sheila's supporters.

After the jury was selected and before the trial began, the attorneys tended to some pre-trial matters. The defense requested that Gerald Hurst be allowed to do some burn experiments during the trial, but the consensus was that the request was coming in a little late; there would be no experiments allowed. In fact, Hurst was coming into the case so late, he had not as yet looked at Sheila's burned Mercury Cougar. One photograph he had taken during an experiment was allowed into trial.

In opening statements, Shealy tried out a new motive in the case, saying Sheila was "worn down from the stress of caring for her mother." When Converse Bright rose to give his opening statement, Sheila started crying and cried during the entire recitation. Bright called Newell "the father of this prosecution."

When prosecution witnesses began taking the stand, it soon became apparent that Brad Shealy had pared down the case that Stines had put on at the first trial. Whereas Stines had called twenty witnesses, starting with

Anthony Clark, Shealy would call twelve, starting with Jamie Hinson.

Sheila had brought her youngest daughter, Karrie, to court to sit with Karlas behind the defense table. By the time Shealy called his second witness, Randy Stephens, the young child was sound asleep in her father's lap. It made a poignant picture for the cameras and the jury.

It was late in the afternoon, after wrecker drivers David Hickey and William Davis had testified, that Shealy called Chris Gay to the stand. Gay's testimony about Sheila handing over her drivers' license and insurance card brought a strong reaction from Sheila. *No, no, no,* she shook her head, leaving no doubt in anyone's mind that it was testimony that Sheila definitely disagreed with.

And it was during Gay's testimony that the air conditioner in the room turned on. Since it was barely forty degrees outside, the added coolness made a miserable day even more miserable. Strangers began to huddle together for warmth and to think about hot soup for supper.

Jamie Sullivan followed Gay to the stand, and then Rodney Bryan made his second appearance in the case. Bryan testified that on the visit to Sheila's home on August 27, 1996, Sheila had told him that she thought her mother had Alzheimer's. At the defense table, Sheila shook her head, *No, no, no.* Sheila had found a new way to testify without taking the stand. But Shealy made no objection.

Donald Davis was the prosecution's last witness for the day. While Davis testified, two of the jurors took notes. Converse Bright asked Davis if he had interviewed Danny Weeks the day of the accident. Davis said that he had not.

After court, like *déjà vu* from the first trial, a telephone call came in to the District Attorney's office. The tipster told Assistant District Attorney Jim Hardy that the investigators should talk to a woman in Worth County, who was a friend of Sheila's. According to the tipster, the Worth County woman and Sheila had hatched a murder plot to kill the woman's husband. Sheila had told the woman, "I know how to do it." The tipster also told Hardy that Sheila did not take care of Freda Weeks as well as everyone had thought.

Heinen sent two of his agents to Worth County to interview the woman.

Looking pretty spiffy in his gray suit and tie, Ronnie Dobbins took the stand to start day two for the prosecution. Dobbins told the jurors that "all fires are accidental until proven otherwise." Then he testified about the inspection of the car and how he had proved otherwise.

It was almost noon, during Bright's cross-examination of Dobbins, that

Bright asked Dobbins what an ignition switch looked like. Dobbins said it was wire and metal components. How big is it? What color is it? Bright wanted details and Dobbins tap-danced. Finally, in a stern voice, Bright asked, "Can you or can you not describe it?"

Dobbins saw the ignition switch spread out on the defense table. He considered his options. He knew that Newell, the expert on ignition switches, was following him to the stand, and he decided to let Newell handle that subject. "No," Dobbins said, "I can't describe it," thinking that would put an end to that area of cross-examination. Which it did, but not on a happy note.

It was a bad moment in the prosecution's case. Dobbins was saying he had eliminated the ignition switch as the cause of the fire, but then he had said he didn't know what one looked like. Unfortunately for Dobbins, Shealy did not have any re-direct, which would have given Dobbins the opportunity to explain his answer.

Bright was doing some damage to the prosecution's case. He had been able to bring out that the prosecution had no photographs of the tell-tale burn patterns in the driver's side carpeting. Using sarcasm, Bright would ask, "And we're supposed to take your word for it?" And Bright had made much of the fact that none of the investigators had interviewed Danny Weeks on the day of the accident.

After lunch, Brad Shealy lost his star witness: Ralph Newell was no where to be found. After some running around and huffing and puffing, Newell arrived, dressed in, of all things, a business suit. Well, the cameras were rolling. Through all of Newell's long and sometimes highly technical testimony, the jury appeared attentive.

It was late afternoon when Bright began cross-examination of Newell. Bright pointed out that of all the dozens of photographs Newell had made of the burned Mercury Cougar, he did not have one photograph of the ignition switch. "Didn't this at least earn one photograph?" he asked the state's star witness.

On re-direct, Shealy had Newell say that the Mercury Cougar had "none of the earmarks of an ignition switch fire." Newell testified that the ignition switch had not burned up, the copper components were still there, and only the mynlon casing was missing.

Dr. Anthony Clark, who had been Stines' first witness, was Shealy's last. During Clark's entire testimony, Sheila cried while the CBS camera zoomed in on her bowed head. Clark said it was his opinion that Freda Weeks was alive when the car "went down the hill." On cross-examination, Bright, of course, brought out that Freda Weeks could have been dead before the fire began.

Wednesday, day three, began with the scene view, as it had in the first trial. Strangely, when court reconvened around noon, very few people were to be found in the courtroom, including the defendant. Judge Horkan asked Shealy, "Does the state rest?" and Shealy said, "Yes." Other than the attorneys, one reporter, and Bright's wife, Jill, no one was present for the climactic moment.

Shealy had rested his case without bringing in his surprise witness.

The reason why the Worth County woman never got on the witness stand would depend on whom you asked. Ronnie Dobbins would say that the woman was so upset and crying so hard, and was so afraid to testify, that Shealy had decided to let her leave the courthouse. Heinen would say that the woman had so "watered down" her story by the time she got to the courthouse – writing the whole thing off as "just girl talk" – that Shealy had decided to let it go. As for Shealy, he would deny that the entire incident had ever happened.

Perhaps in celebration of the end of the state's case, Sheila came to court in a new hair do: a French twist.

The defense would call thirteen witnesses to the stand, some the same as the first trial: Peggy Dean, Mary Woodall, Kay Weeks, Mary Ann Bryan, Ernest Weeks and Karla Bryan. But, they would also add new witnesses and call some of the state's witnesses at the first trial: Danny Weeks and Brian Hargett. And, they would add a new character witness: Molly Cable Hooper, Freda Weeks' younger sister, whom the defense had flown in from Michigan.

When Chris Bloom, a new defense expert witness, took the stand, Sheila's supporters were all atwitter: "Is that him? Is that the one we flew in?"

Bloom testified that while ignition switch fires are not common, "They do happen." Shealy was able to bring out on cross-examination that Bloom had never seen the Mercury Cougar, had only become involved in the case three weeks before the trial, and had not even read Dobbins and Newell's report. He also brought out that of 23 million cars, only 8,000 had an ignition switch problem, and Bloom had only seen 30 of the 8,000.

It was on Thursday that the defense's star witness took the stand. When Hurst testified that he had invented the Mylar balloon and Wite-Out, one of the jurors responded with a big grin, as though she had just met a celebrity.

Hurst testified that burning plastic, not an accelerant, had caused the damage to the Mercury Cougar. He said that the burn patterns from dripping plastic could not be distinguished from an accelerant. Hurst said that the dripping plastic could "cause a holocaust" and was "hotter than gasoline." Hurst also said that if an accelerant had been used it would have been detectable. "You could wash that carpet for a month and you wouldn't get the gas out," he said.

Hurst went on to say that the melted goo on the driver's side threshold was caused from "flowing plastic, not an accelerant." Hurst said that the fire was probably caused by the ignition switch, which ignited the plastic, which went up the steering column, across the dash board, and dripped burning plastic on the carpet, causing it to catch fire. He said the damage could have been done in ten minutes.

On cross-examination, Shealy brought out that Hurst was a man on a mission: He only worked on cases where he thought someone had been falsely accused of arson, and he had made up his mind about what happened before he ever looked at the car or did his "experiments."

When pressed by Shealy to say if he knew *exactly* how the fire had started, Hurst said, "I can't definitely say it wasn't caused by a meteorite," and, "Maybe gypsies set it on fire with torches," and he added, "I can't be one hundred percent certain I am sitting in this chair. I might be dreaming."

Shealy also brought out that it was the first time Hurst had ever testified about a vehicle arson fire in a criminal case and that he believed that arson investigation was "junk science." Shealy also had Hurst admit that he had seen the ignition switch for the very first time that week.

After Hurst's testimony, the defense rested its case. It was 2:45 p.m. when Shealy said that he was calling a rebuttal witness. Everyone knew that Ralph Newell was about to take the stand to rebut Gerald Hurst's testimony when Walter Young took the stand to tell about finding Freda Weeks lying out beside the road.

Then both the state and defense rested their case. At the late afternoon break, before closing arguments began, on the courthouse steps, news reporters smoked and discussed the strange turn of events. No one could understand why Ralph Newell had not been called back on the stand to rebut what Gerald Hurst had said. Sinister and outrageous thoughts came to the reporters' minds. Although they were outrageous thoughts, the fact that Ralph Newell had not gone back on the stand was also pretty outrageous to those familiar with the case.

Nobody had been more shocked than Ralph Newell. When Shealy had told him he should go home, he did, shaking his head all the way back to Gainesville.

Later, Brad Shealy would take full responsibility, of course, for sending Ralph Newell home rather than putting him back on the witness stand. Shealy would say that he felt that Ralph Newell had lost credibility, and he did not want the trial to turn into a trial of Ford Motor Company.

The case went to the jury at 5:10 p.m., Thursday. By noon on Friday, the jury came in with their verdict: not guilty on all counts.

When the first "not guilty" was read by Horkan, Sheila threw her hands up in a "praise God" gesture. By the second "not guilty," the courtroom was in pandemonium. Tears, hugs, shouts of joy rang out.

Donald Davis sat in the back of the courtroom as morose as a human being is allowed to be without putting a gun to their head. When approached by a reporter who asked for a comment, Davis said, "Yeah, I got a comment. She just got away with murder. Write that down. Put that in your paper."

On the courthouse steps, Sheila, Karlas, and their supporters literally danced with joy.

"The Lord intervened and kept *that woman* from coming down here to hurt Sheila," one of the supporters said, attributing the turn of events to the Good Lord, rather than Brad Shealy.

"There's nothing that junk yard gang can do about this!" Karlas spat at a *Moultrie Observer* reporter. Sheila said that she didn't care what happened now. She was going home.

It was over. Or so everyone thought.

Having been convicted of arson and murder in her first trial and having been acquitted of arson and murder in her second trial, now everyone would cry, "Injustice!"

Sheila's supporters would claim that a real injustice had been done when she had been convicted and put in prison. Others would claim that a great injustice had been done when she had been acquitted and gotten away with murder. And both sides could point to a verdict that supported their view.

On the face of it, it did appear that one of the juries had been terribly, terribly wrong. But which one?

CHAPTER FORTY-FIVE

February 2000

Omega was something of a powder keg. After four long years, endless local debate, and two trials, the court system had resolved nothing for the residents of Omega, who were left, ironically, with a never-ending story and Sheila Bryan.

Some of the residents likened their situation to the people of Fall River, Massachusetts, a town left with a reputation – and legend – spawned more than one hundred years before when "Lizzie Borden took an ax and gave her mother forty whacks." Although the middle-aged spinster was eventually acquitted of the murder of her parents, the town never recovered from the crime, which officially remains on the books as unresolved.

After the trial, like Lizzie, Sheila was shunned by some of the local residents. "When she walks by, I turn my head. I don't even look at her," one resident said.

In a town where local gossip was supposed to remain local, the CBS film crew remained filming. In all, the crew would be in Omega for more than a month. By this juncture, many of the local residents had decided that Sheila liked all of the attention and that didn't sit well with them.

Police Chief Walter Young and Pastor John Spivey tried to hold things together, but it was not easy. "This is a very tense situation," Young said.

Young sat in his office at City Hall scratching his head and thinking that both juries had been wrong and everyone had been hoodwinked. He was one of those people who believed that there were two sides to every story, and then there was the truth. He didn't think Sheila was guilty of murder, but he did think she was guilty of arson. He believed that Freda Weeks was dead when she was put in the car. Then the car was burned to collect the insurance money. "She didn't do it alone," Young said. "It took more than one person to get that body in the car."

After the second trial, perhaps as a way to resolve the issue of Sheila's guilt or innocence, many people adopted the alternate theory of what had happened on Livingston Bridge Road voiced by Walter Young. The absence of carbon monoxide in Freda Weeks' body and the presence of the large beach towel in the car gave rise to this theory along with the fact that Freda Weeks had not been able to get out of the car when the fire began.

Heinen, who had been promoted to head the GBI's Kingsland office on the east coast, and was busy packing and moving, gave the second theory some thought. Heinen knew that the toxicology report had come back positive for the drug diazepam, known as Valium, and Heinen reasoned that between the Valium and Freda Weeks' befuddled mind, she might simply have been unable to get out in time. When some people wondered – assuming Sheila had committed arson and not murder – why she would not just have pled guilty to the arson charge, Heinen thought he knew the answer to that as well. In the state of Georgia, first-degree arson carries a one to twenty year sentence, and often enough, ninety percent of that sentence has to be served before a person is eligible for parole. Eighteen years was a long time in prison.

Around Valentine's day, a series of violent tornadoes ripped through four counties in south Georgia, leaving twenty-one people dead and $24 million in damages. It was a distraction. One tornado had torn through the outskirts of Omega, and local residents – including Sheila – busied themselves with the storm's aftermath.

Gerald Psalmond, who had not testified at the second trial, sat in his office at the Governmental Building in Moultrie thinking about the gas tank on the Mercury Cougar and the conclusions he had never been asked to testify about at the first trial. It was an observation he had made the day of the accident, which he had discussed with the firemen at the time – but with no one else. The burn pattern at the open gas tank went almost straight up. But the car, in the deep ditch, was sitting at a steep angle, nose down. If the gasoline fumes had burned during the fire, while the car was in the ditch, the burn pattern should have been slanted decidedly sideways, following the angle of the car.

Psalmond believed the car had been set on fire at the gas tank while the car was sitting on the shoulder of the road. The shoulder was more level, and it would account for the angle of the burn pattern at the gas tank.

Ralph Newell sat in his office in Gainesville, thinking the same thing. In fact, Newell would say that reading the burn pattern at the gas tank was the one mistake he had made in the case. Newell also believed that no one else was in the car when it was rolled down the hill – with Freda Weeks inside.

Newell thought that the hood had been raised while the car was sitting on the shoulder of the road, so anyone passing by would think Sheila was just having car trouble. Newell did not think that the open hood found after the fire had anything to do with Sheila trying to unhook the battery cables with her bare hands. Newell thought that Sheila, and whoever had helped her, after having been unsuccessful with setting the fire at the gas tank, had left the hood unlatched accidentally, because they were in a hurry when they rolled the car off the embankment.

Like Psalmond, who had not been invited to testify at the second trial, Newell, who had not been invited back on the stand to rebut Gerald Hurst, was mad. Newell thought Gerald Hurst's testimony was nonsense. "How does plastic flow uphill?" he asked.

Newell felt sure he had finally figured out what the accelerant was that Sheila had used. It was Zylene, which is found in paint thinner products. Once he had the accelerant figured out, Newell had gone to great lengths to test his theory. He went out and bought a 1987 Mercury Cougar identical to Sheila's. At his burn site, he re-created the crime scene (with identical angle of the car) and then re-created the Zylene being poured in the car as the arson investigators believed Sheila had done. He poured in the accelerant, slammed the car door shut, and then let it burn for some fifteen minutes before putting out the fire.

Bingo. Newell said that the results were exactly the same as what the investigators had found on August 28, 1996, the day of the initial investigation. Even the same gooey burn pattern had appeared on the driver's side door threshold. Newell had not one doubt in his mind about how the Mercury Cougar had been burned.

It was in April that whatever semblance of normalcy left in Omega was shattered: CBS aired the *48 Hours* show about Sheila Bryan. Then, all hell broke loose.

It was a story about this sweet, innocent housewife in Omega – who had not one skeleton in her closet – who was convicted and sent to prison because of this big, bad arson investigator named Ralph Newell. And then, along came Converse Bright and Gerald Hurst – like knights on white horses – to save the day. It made a great story. But how close it was to reality was a matter of heated debate.

After CBS put everyone on national television, Pastor John Spivey could no longer hold things together. He resigned. "It was simply a no win situation," Spivey said. Spivey could not resolve the split in the church and so, unable to save the church, he tried to save himself. He packed up and moved his family to Buford, South Carolina, leaving Omega Baptist Church with an interim pastor, and Sheila Bryan.

In May, Ralph Newell hired attorney Guy Burnette to sue Chris Bloom, one of the defense's expert witnesses at the second trial. According to Newell, in March 2000, Chris Bloom had posted comments about the case and Newell on the message board of the International Association of Arson Investigators (IAAI), implying that Newell did an incomplete, inadequate, biased investigation that was contrary to nationally recognized standards and guidelines. Newell also accused Bloom of telling five people that he had deliberately withheld evidence in the case and falsified his testimony. It was a suit for slander, libel, and defamation.

An ugly situation had just gotten uglier.

Donald Davis would never waver in his belief that Sheila Bryan was guilty of arson and murder. One of the most frequently asked questions by the people of Omega after the second trial was, "Did she get the money?" Davis knew the answer to that one: "NO!"

And Davis had a hypothetical question: "If she was really innocent, and if the fire had really been started by the ignition switch, does anyone doubt for one second that Sheila Bryan wouldn't sue Ford Motor Company? Any lawyer would take the case on a contingency basis, if she actually had a case."

Davis had cooked up another question: "How many couples do you know where the husband and wife both went on trial for murder, in separate cases, and both were acquitted?"

As for Sheila and Karlas, they were busy hatching another get-rich-quick scheme – one that did not involve suing Ford. Although they had sold their building lot at Lake Mary in Tifton and had given up their immediate plans of building their dream home, they hoped to recoup some of their financial losses from Sheila writing a book about her life.

"I know I can't wait to read that one," Davis said.